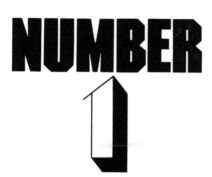

Books by Peter Golenbock

DYNASTY

THE BRONX ZOO with Sparky Lyle

GUIDRY

NUMBER 1 with Billy Martin

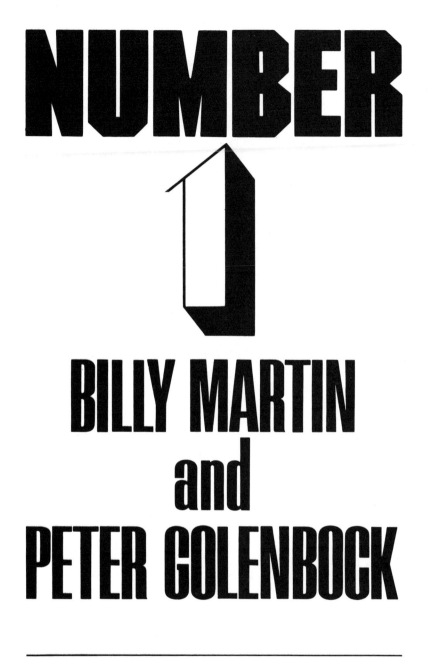

NUMBER 1

BILLY MARTIN
and
PETER GOLENBOCK

DELACORTE PRESS/NEW YORK

Published by
Delacorte Press
1 Dag Hammarskjold Plaza
New York, N.Y. 10017

Manufactured in the United States of America

First printing

Designed by Giorgetta Bell McRee

Library of Congress Cataloging in Publication Data

Martin, Alfred Manuel, 1928–
Number 1

1. Martin, Alfred Manuel, 1928–
2. Baseball Managers—United States—Biography
I. Golenbock, Peter, 1946–   joint author   II. Title.
GV865.M35A35   796B357′092′4[B]   80-23711

ISBN 0-440-06416-3

A man's character is his fate.

—HERACLITUS

There is no substitute for victory.

—GENERAL DOUGLAS MACARTHUR

Never take shit from nobody.

—JENNY DOWNEY

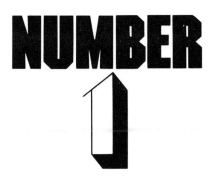

INTRODUCTION

For Billy Martin there could have been no other way. He was determined not to pull punches, to write an autobiography naming names, protecting no one, putting his heart, soul, and guts on paper for public appraisal. "This is the United States, not Iran, not Russia," Billy told me, "and it's about time someone stood up and told the truth for a change."

Here are the truths as Billy Martin sees them. Maybe others will have different versions of some of the events. That is bound to happen no matter who is doing the recounting. In these pages Billy has reconstructed the events exactly as he remembers them, even though some do not reflect favorably on Billy or on others. This is Billy's way, to be forthright, to be honest, not to hedge, not to cover up. "This is a book *I* want to be proud of," he said. "I want this book to be special." It is.

Billy Martin knows what it takes to produce a winner. When he was a player on the New York Yankees, he played five full seasons. Each of those teams won a pennant. He managed the Minnesota Twins and Detroit Tigers to division titles, and after leading the hapless Texas Rangers to a strong second-place finish, Billy returned to New York in 1975 to manage the Yankees. In his two full seasons he lead the team to a pennant and a World Championship, though he was fighting with owner George Steinbrenner every inch of the way. In his third season

Billy was pushed into exile only to return a year later in mid-season. A month after that season ended, Billy was involved in a fight with a marshmallow salesman in a Bloomington, Minnesota, hotel, and he was fired by the Yankees for good—or at least for now. His new team, the formerly inept Oakland A's, will be pennant contenders, Billy vows, and who would doubt him?

Billy Martin has become a legendary American figure. He has become a folk hero to the working man, a feisty battler unafraid to criticize anyone. He seems to go through life feeling—no, knowing—his way is the best way. Though his attitude gets him in trouble time and again, Billy never wavers, regardless of consequences, so strong is his belief in himself. He is the rare individual who is fearless. Here, without fear, are the memoirs of Billy Martin.

I would like to take this opportunity to thank those who helped in the publication of this book: Louise Caffin, for her voluminous files of material; Art Fowler; Mickey Moribito; Bob Short; Billy's parents, Jenny and Jack Downey; Billy's sisters, Joan and Pat; and Ron Fimrite, for sharing their time and information with me; Howard and Beulah Wong for their hospitality; Alexa Pierce for her dedication in transcribing the many hours of tape; Rhonda Sonnenberg for her editorial assistance and love; Tom Biracrea for putting me on the right track; Keith and Sandy Sohn, Roger and Wendy Kahn, Glenn Anders, and Herb and Roberta Ross for their support; Delacorte's fine editor Nick Ellison for his encouragement and assistance; Susan Flato, Nick's assistant, for her help; and to Doug Newton and Judge Eddie Sapir, who provided much important information and who helped guide the manuscript through its final stages.

PETER GOLENBOCK
Englewood, New Jersey

PREFACE

When Peter and I began this book, he said, "Billy, everything in here has to be the truth. We can't fudge, can't
be self-serving. We have to tell everything that happened in
your life, the bad as well as the good." I agreed to do that, and
have kept my word. Meanwhile, I had a meeting with baseball
commissioner Bowie Kuhn in his home, and during lengthy
discussions I made remarks to the commissioner regarding my
future, all of which he acknowledged as being sincere. I trust
that in no way will the publication of this book be seen as a
breach of those promises—this is my intention.

Much has been written about the fighting incidents in which
I have been involved. I deeply regret each and every one of
them, and sincerely hope there will never be another. After almost every incident, the other party and I met and talked it
over and mutually reached the conclusion that we wished it
never happened. I'm sure that if somewhere along the line Mr.
Joseph Cooper and I were to meet, we, too, would agree that
our altercation was most regrettable.

I have told the commissioner of my sincerity not to get involved in future brawls. I would hope that he would make it
clear to the public that it is most unfair for me to be a target to
any individual who would wish to throw things at me, badger

me, or, for whatever ulterior motive, to make headlines by starting a fight with me.

Conversations with ballplayers and coaches have been quoted exactly, but as you read them, please be aware that sometimes I say things for the purpose of motivating them or to smooth over a situation in the best interest of the ball club. The context of these conversations must always be taken into account.

Number 1 is *the* story of my life. I hope when you're finished, you will have a better understanding of me as a player, manager, and person.

BILLY MARTIN
Oakland, California

CHAPTER 1

I never should have agreed to manage the Yankees when I did in 1975. The contract George Steinbrenner and Gabe Paul wanted me to sign was an insult. The salary wasn't too bad—it was the same $72,000 I had been making with Texas when I was fired there—but there were special clauses in the Yankee contract that just didn't sit well with me. There was this one clause that said I was to "personally conduct yourself at all times so as to represent the best interest of the New York Yankees and to adhere to all club policies" whatever those policies were. Then there was that clause that forbade me from criticizing management in any way. Where was the clause that forbade them from criticizing me in any way? What kind of one-sided crap was this? And finally, there was a clause that I had to keep myself available to management to consult with them on unspecified matters. I didn't know what that was all about. During the season I'm at the ball park every single day. How available did I have to be? The kicker was the paragraph that came after the clauses. It said that if I didn't do the above three things to management's satisfaction, they could fire me and I'd lose my pay.

They hadn't even hired me, and here these people were talking about firing me! I had to be out of my mind to sign that contract. Furthermore, I had one more year left on my Texas contract. I could have sat out the rest of the year and all the next year and collected my money.

I was fishing with friends in Grand Junction, Colorado, when I got a message that my father-in-law was trying to reach me. I drove to a local gas station and called him from a pay phone, and he told me that Birdie Tebbetts, who scouts for the Yankees, wanted to meet me in Denver. Birdie hadn't said what the meeting was about, but, said my father-in-law, he said it would be "very lucrative" for me. I had been scheduled to be in Denver to give a talk at a banquet, so I had my father-in-law call Birdie and tell him I would meet him.

I met Birdie in Denver, and Birdie told me he had been sent by Gabe Paul and that the Yankees were interested in my managing the ball club. Birdie showed me the contract they were offering, and as I said, it was for the same $72,000 I would have gotten anyway, and there were those clauses in it that I didn't like. Also, I was still hurting inside from getting fired at Texas, because there had been no reason for it, and I had intended to sit out the rest of the year and let time heal my wounds. After looking over the contract, I told Birdie I was sorry, but I wasn't interested.

Birdie was patient with me. He asked me if I wouldn't mind waiting in the lounge of the hotel while he called Gabe in New York, and it turned out that Gabe wasn't in New York at all. He was actually in the room right next door to Birdie's room. He'd been listening to our conversation the whole time! When I returned to Birdie's room, he asked if I wouldn't come back the next day to talk to him, and I agreed.

The next day when my wife, Gretchen, and I met with Birdie, Gabe was there, too. I told Gabe the same thing I had told Birdie, that the money wasn't enough and that I didn't like the clauses. I didn't like the trap that I was being set into. I could have stayed out. Why should I put myself in a weak position? I just didn't like the whole thing. It smelled. I was putting myself in a position where this George Steinbrenner, the Yankee owner, could handcuff me, and I didn't know him very well. I had heard he was wild and erratic, but I had only met him one time in a restaurant for a quick hello, and I really didn't know anything about him. For a second time I refused the job. "No, Gabe, I don't want to do it," I told him. Gabe said, "Billy, don't be so hasty. Why don't you talk to George?" and he called George and put him on the phone.

George said, "Billy, I would like to have you as our manager."

I said, "I'd like to be the manager of the Yankees," but I told him I didn't like his offer.

George said, "If you don't take the offer now, you will never get it again. C'mon, Billy, be the manager." It was like a threat. He said, "Here's your big chance to manage the Yankees, something you've wanted to do." And he was right. It was something I had always wanted to do. I had started my playing career in 1950 with the Yankees, and in the five full seasons I played in New York the team won five pennants and four World Championships, and if Dodger outfielder Sandy Amoros hadn't been playing out of position in the final game of the 1955 Series, we would have won that one, too. Nevertheless, as I weighed George's offer, I couldn't see signing that contract with the clauses in it. I told him, "I'm not going to take it now." He said, "You go home and think about it."

Gretchen and I went back to our hotel, and the phone rang. It was Bob Short calling from Minneapolis. I have a lot of trust in Bob Short. I campaigned for him when he was running for governor of Minnesota, and later when he owned the Texas Rangers he hired me as manager. Short is the type of guy you meet very seldom during your lifetime. He cares about other people and he's a man of his word, and he always cared about me.

Short said, "Billy, you ought to take the job. It would be the best thing for you. You don't get an opportunity like this every day." I said, "Bob, I don't like it. I don't like the terms of it, telling me I'll be curtailed this way and that way. Also, I don't want to go back this year. I'd rather wait until next spring."

Bob said, "Don't worry, Billy, it'll work out. I'm sure it'll work out. If the man wants you that badly, it'll work out." Of course, I don't think Bob ever knew Steinbrenner as I found him to be, which is understandable because Bob never had to work for him. Everybody who's never worked for George always likes him. It's the people who work for him who can't stand him. I told Bob so.

Bob asked me if he could talk to Gretchen, and for about a half an hour they talked on the phone. Gretchen always had good sense, and after she hung up, I asked her what she thought of it. She advised me to take the job.

"You always wanted to go back to the Yankees," she said. Also, I think she was worried that I wouldn't get another job. She told me that Short had convinced her that it would be a good job for me to take, that my being in New York would be ideal. After all, it had been Gretchen who talked me into taking my first managerial job at Denver in 1968, and she was right then. Maybe she was right now. Still, those clauses really got to me.

When I went to bed that night, I was still undecided. I felt I could work with Gabe. I trusted Gabe. But Gabe wouldn't be there forever, and I had bad vibes about Steinbrenner, his clauses, the way he had threatened me, the way he had apparently called Bob Short to push me into this. My every instinct argued against signing this contract.

When I woke up the next morning, I was still saying no, but when I met with Birdie and Gabe that day, I caved in and agreed to it.

The next day Gretchen and I flew to New York, where George hid me in a hotel. The next day was the Yankees' annual Old Timers' Day game, and George had planned a surprise introduction. He wanted to introduce all the old Yankees, guys like Whitey Ford, Yogi Berra, Mickey Mantle, and Joe DiMaggio, and then he wanted to introduce me as the new Yankee manager.

George came over and told me he was going to do this, and I pleaded with him to let me come out earlier. Traditionally, the final introductions are reserved for the Yankee gods, Mantle and DiMaggio, not for a lifetime .250 hitter, and I was embarrassed at being sent out last. "Can't I go out in another spot?" I asked George. "No," he said, "you go out last." Waiting there I was uptight, nervous. I was coming back so many years after the Yankees expelled me, so to speak, in 1957, when they traded me to Kansas City after the Copacabana incident. It was eighteen years later, and here I was coming back as the leader. I thought back to Casey Stengel, and how he had given me my start in baseball, and here I was now in his shoes. I felt funny. I only wish it had been in Yankee Stadium instead of Shea Stadium, where the Yankees were playing temporarily until the stadium could be remodeled.

I was so light-headed it barely registered when I heard my name over the loudspeaker, and I ran out there and everyone was happy for me, and the applause was deafening, and in the stands I could hear some boos, which I could understand because Bill Virdon was well liked, but I said to myself, "They're booing right now, but before I'm through everyone will be cheering."

On the flight to New York I started thinking about what would be the best tactic for me to take when I took over the ball club, and I made up my mind that the best thing would be to do nothing, to just come in and soft-shoe it, to observe the players and let them reach their level. I also wanted to see who were the clubhouse lawyers, alibiers, and complainers, and get rid of them. You can't keep those types and still have a winning team. I'm a firm believer in the Peter Principle, the idea that people will tend to sink or rise to their level, and before the 1975 season several of the players ended up sinking.

No sooner had I arrived than the first thing I read in the paper was that one of the Yankee pitchers, Pat Dobson, told a reporter that if I thought I was going to tell the players what to do, I was crazy. Dobson was a nice person. I certainly had nothing against him, but comments like that don't win you personality contests. He was a mediocre pitcher, and he wasn't the type of pitcher I thought we'd win a pennant with, and I made a little note to myself that he'd be the first guy we'd get rid of at the end of the season.

Another pitcher we had, Doc Medich, one day was blaming his outfielders for his getting beat. He was telling reporters, "If we had better outfielders, blah, blah, blah, I'd have a better record," and I went over to him and said, "Doc, for a person who's going to be a doctor someday, you should learn to appreciate your teammates a lot better than you do. And even if you feel that way, you should be smart enough not to express your feelings in the papers." He sounded like a little baby saying, "If you don't play the game my way, I'm going to take my ball and glove and go home." I told him, "If you have anything to say, tell me, and I'll tell the other players." We got rid of Medich at the end of the year, too.

Another guy we got rid of was Bobby Bonds. It was the last week of the season, and Bonds was complaining that his leg was bothering him and he didn't want to play anymore. The team had been winning toward the end, and I felt it was important for the team to keep winning because a winning attitude carries over to the next season, and I wanted Bobby to play, because he was a solid bat. I put Bobby's name in the lineup, and he came over and said, "I ain't playing." I said, "Well, okay, you're not going to play," and out of the lineup he went. So when it came time to talk trades, I told Gabe, "No man's going to tell a manager whether he's going to play or not. If he's hurt real bad, that's one thing. But he wasn't hurt badly. He could have played." And I recommended that he be traded.

From the day I walked into the clubhouse Old Timers' Day, my mind was on the next spring. I was four months ahead making plans, thinking about what we had to do to improve ourselves. Aside from getting rid of the clubhouse lawyers and malcontents, which I do every time I take over a new ballclub, I also had to change the attitude of the players. When I arrived, players were bringing their friends into the clubhouse before the game, others were baby-sitting their own kids, and I noticed that in the bullpen during the game the pitchers were playing cards and eating sandwiches and acting like it was a country club. When I'm managing, you'd better take your job seriously, or you won't be around long. If you play for me, you play the game like you play life. You play it to be successful, you play it with dignity, you play it with pride, and you play it aggressively. Life is a very serious thing, and baseball has been my life. What else has my life been? That's why when I lose a ball game I can't eat after a game. Sometimes I can hardly sleep. If you're in love with the game, you can't turn it on and off like a light. It's something that runs so deep it takes you over. If I lose, I say to myself, "What if I'd have done this or that? What if so-and-so had done this?" You're second-guessing yourself, but in a positive way, trying to reach perfection to where if a similar situation arises in the future, you handle it better the next time. Or maybe you try something different. Maybe the batter screwed up a sacrifice bunt. Maybe the next time I should go to hit-and-run. Maybe I should go against the book and let him hit. These things go through my mind, and a lot of times after a ball game if a player makes a mistake, I'll think and think and think and think and I'll go over it four different ways, trying to figure out the right way to talk to the player to get my point across without hurting his feelings. As a manager I give one hundred percent of my effort, and I expect the same from my players.

When spring training rolled around I set down my rules, and this nonsense stopped cold. But when I got there, that wasn't the Yankee clubhouse the way I remembered it, with anyone who wanted running around the clubhouse. It wasn't a professional way of doing things, and this lack of professionalism was reflected in the way the team was playing. The execution was weak, the players were not doing the basic things on the field like hitting the cutoff man or advancing the runner, and too many of the players weren't being aggressive enough on the field. But because I had come so late in the year, I figured that it would be best for me to wait till spring training to teach my system. Though we played pretty well toward the end of the season, we were never in the race, and we ended up finishing in third place, twelve games behind the Red Sox.

My first order of business in preparing for the upcoming spring was to assemble a coaching staff. I wanted Dick Howser to stay on. He was an excellent third-base coach, and I liked him very much, and I wanted Elston Howard to stay on because I always admired and liked Ellie. Ellie would work with the pitching coach, and he would come and tell me what was going on with the pitchers. He'd say, "So-and-so is mad that he isn't pitching enough." I'd tell him, "You tell him the reason he isn't pitching is that some of the other guys have to get work," and Ellie would be my bumper with the pitchers. The first new coach I wanted was Yogi Berra. It was my idea to bring Yogi back to New York. He had managed the Yankees to a pennant in 1964, and then he was fired when the team didn't win the World Series. Then he went to the Mets, and he led them to a pennant, and they also fired him. I really didn't know whether Yogi would come back to the Yankees, but when I told Gabe that Yogi was one of the coaches I wanted, he agreed.

I called Yogi on the phone. I told him, "I know it's hard for you to come back to the Yankees, but I'd really like to have you with me. You'd be working closely with me, and I really think it would be great." Yogi asked me what his duties would be. I told him he'd be on the bench with me, and help me handle the substitutions, and I told him he'd be my ambassador to the guys on the bench. I said, "The guys will tell you when they're mad at me, and you'll tell me, and I'll take care of it." Yogi thought about it for a few seconds, and he said, "Yeah, I'd like to." Which really made me happy. Yogi's a rare breed. He's such a good guy. And he's a great bumper for me. Yogi has his own way of teasing guys and getting the best out of them, and when he wants to get your attention, he's got such strong fingers, he'll poke you in the chest and put a hole in it. The man has fingers of iron.

The other coach I wanted badly was Art Fowler. Art had been my pitching coach since I began managing Denver. Whenever I got a job, Art came, too, because in my opinion Art Fowler is the best pitching coach in the business. He's coached more 20-game winners than anyone, including Johnny Sain, who the media has made into a legend, and Art is excellent at working with me at molding pitchers into winners. I'd tell Art how I wanted a pitcher to pitch in a certain situation, and he'd talk to the pitcher and get it done. I wanted Art because he would have been a real help to me, and he would have helped the Yankee pitchers.

However, Gabe and George refused to let me have Art as my pitching coach. I asked Gabe why not, and he'd say, "George doesn't want him at all." And I'd ask George, and he'd say, "It's all right with me, Billy, but Gabe just doesn't want you to have him." I'd go back to Gabe, and he'd say, "Don't you believe that, Billy," and I never did know who to believe. Deep down, though, I think it was Gabe who really didn't want to hire Art. Art played for Gabe at Cincinnati about twenty years ago, and they didn't like each other then. For three years he was a starting pitcher and a good one, and the most he ever made was $11,000. In 1957 he was asked to go to the bullpen, and he did, and he was 3 and 0, and for his trouble Gabe tried to send him to the minors 'cause Gabe was having roster problems and he needed to send someone down. Art told him, "If I can't pitch on this team, it's a disgrace, and I might as well quit and go home," and Gabe said, "Well, why don't you just do that," and Art did. When I told Art I was going to be Yankee manager, I told him, "You're my pitching coach." Art said, "Billy, there's no way." And he was right. Anyway, Bob Lemon's name came up, and Gabe asked me if I would take Lem, and I said, "Heck, yes." I said to myself, "I'll bide my time, and maybe eventually I'll get Art." Which I did later.

The next order of business was to strengthen our team during the winter trading period. To be a contender we needed to shore up the infield and outfield defense, which I thought was weak, we had to add more power to the lineup, and we needed a couple more solid starting pitchers. In three trades Gabe got the job done. First he traded Dobson to the Indians for Oscar Gamble, who is quite a guy on a ball club. Not only is he a great hitter, but he did a fine job for me in the outfield. Wherever I go, I'd like to have Oscar Gamble on my ballclub. Gabe completed the other two trades on the same day. He sent Bonds to California for pitcher Ed Figueroa and center fielder Mickey Rivers, and he shipped Doc Medich to Pittsburgh for starting pitcher Dock Ellis and second baseman Willie Randolph. Gabe asked me about the Randolph deal. I said, "Gabe, I'll go along if you let me have Art Fowler for my pitching coach." But when he still wouldn't give in, I agreed to it, and he made the deal for Randolph. Everyone expected Randolph to be a great player, which he was, but for me the special bonus was the great work of Dock Ellis. Dock was super. I had heard a lot of stories about how he was a disruptive force on a club, but I never found him to be that way at all. I called him in and said, "Look, Dock, I'm going to treat you like a man, and I expect you to treat me like one, also. It's going to be a two-way street." Dock said, "You got it, Skip," and I never had one bit of trouble from him. In fact, we had such a good relationship, he was like a son to me.

The Bonds deal was kind of controversial when it was made, but time proved Gabe to be right. Figgy stepped right into the starting rotation and proved himself a consistent winner, and Mickey Rivers, who had a reputation for not always playing his hardest, gave me no trouble, and when he was at the top of his game, he would carry the club all by himself. After Gabe made those trades, I was very excited about the coming season. I felt we were going to win, and I couldn't wait to get to camp.

George Steinbrenner, on the other hand, didn't think we would win the pennant. In fact, he bet me a tugboat that we wouldn't. George had asked Yogi, Ellie, Whitey Ford, Mickey Mantle, and I to run a baseball clinic on the island of Curaçao, off the coast of Venezuela. It was late December, but it was still hotter than hell there. George had been trying to build a shipyard there or he was trying to get something else for his ships from the government, and I guess he figured the clinic would help him get it, and so he asked us all to do this for him, and we agreed.

It was night, and we were in the gambling casino, and George gave each of us five hundred dollars. Whitey busted, and I think Ellie busted, and of course Yogi used everyone else's chips, but I was winning and I ran my chips up to fifteen hundred. George came over and gave Whitey and Ellie another five hundred, and I said, "Where's mine?" He said, "You're winning." I said, "You mean to say that you're going to penalize me for winning?"

Later we were all sitting around a table having drinks and talking, and we started discussing the coming season. George said, "You know, we have a lot of holes." I said, "George, don't worry about it. We're going to win the pennant." He said, "You're going to win the pennant?" and he kind of chuckled. He said, "You are like heck." I said, "What do you want to bet?" He said, "Tell you what. I own some tugboats. If you win the pennant, I'll give you a tugboat." All the guys heard him. I said, "A tugboat is worth about three hundred thousand dollars, right?" He said, "You win, you got it." Well, we won the pennant just like I said we would, and we lost to the Reds in the World Series. After the season I remembered his promise about the tugboat and I asked him for it. He said, "I promised it to you if you won the *World Series*, not just the pennant," which wasn't true. So as far as I'm concerned, George still owes me a tugboat.

During the winter I had sent the players a letter telling them what I was going to be stressing in spring training, telling them about the more rigid discipline, the stricter rules for the clubhouse, and my dress code. I also let them know that baseball was going to be fun again, that we were going to have fun winning, that we were going to bring back the Yankee pride and tradition.

When camp opened, everyone was ready, and I ran it exactly as I said I would. I have my own system for running a spring training camp. We start about ten in the morning and only go until one, but during that time everything is so organized that everyone gets more work than most guys on other teams who work out twice a day. Under my system we use two fields, giving more players a chance to hit. Nobody stands around for a second. Every day the hitters practice their bunting on the machines, with instructors there to make sure they learn correctly. We work on relays, run-downs, pick-off plays, on both fields every day. I have my pitchers practice covering first base on grounders to the first baseman. In other words, I make sure that by the time the season starts, everyone has his fundamentals down.

I'll show you how organized it is. During batting practice the first pitch is a hit-and-run situation, where the batter has to try to go to right field. On the second pitch the batter tries to move a runner on second over to third. On the third pitch he tries to hit a sacrifice fly. The fourth pitch is a suicide squeeze, and on the fifth pitch the catcher calls for a pitchout to give the pitcher a chance to throw a pitchout properly and the catcher a chance to practice getting in the right position to catch it. After that the batter gets four swings, and then he becomes a runner. By one o'clock the pitchers would get their time practicing, and the hitters would get their hitting in, and we would still have enough time to cover everything else.

During practice one day George came over and asked me why I wasn't holding split sessions like some of the other teams were having. "They should be working three hours longer," he said. I told him that isn't the way I do it. "You burn them up down here in spring training, and by the end of the season they have nothing left," I told him. But George couldn't understand what I was doing, and neither could Gabe. I just don't think George knew what he was seeing when he was walking around out there. This was something I never understood. I managed in Minnesota, and I won the division there, and I managed in Detroit, and I won the division there. And then I took over the Texas Rangers, which at the time was one of the worst teams in baseball, and in one year I had them to within an eyelash of the pennant, and here I was managing the Yankees, and I was still being second-guessed. It's like they were saying, "Billy, are you sure you know what you're doing?" Still, compared to what I was going to have to go through in later years, my problems with management in 1976 were few and minor. Early in the season Gabe asked me if I would play one of George's tape recordings in the clubhouse, and I told him I wouldn't do that. Gabe said, "George wants to motivate the players," and I told him that I didn't need his tapes to motivate my players, that I could do my own motivating. Gabe was also insisting that I meet with him in his office around three in the afternoon before each game. He wanted me to come in every day and bullshit with him, just to sit there while he was on the phone, and we'd talk about personnel, and after a while I finally told him, "Gabe, lookit, I got a lot of things to be doing in the clubhouse. I can't be coming in here doing this all the time." He said, "This is the way we want it." I told him, "This has got to change. This time should be spent with my players, not with you."

Aside from those minor annoyances, during most of 1976 there was no interference from the front office. We were a very happy ball club. There was no animosity among the players, and when the season opened, we won 15 of our first 20 games and held the lead from beginning to end. It was the happiest ball club I think I ever managed. The guys were just having fun, playing hard, aggressive baseball.

On May twentieth Lou Piniella crashed into Boston catcher Carlton Fisk trying to score. It was a good play on Lou's part. Fisk was blocking the plate, and Lou tried to bowl him over. It was a good, clean, aggressive play. Graig Nettles had rushed over to make sure Lou was okay, and Bill Lee, the Boston pitcher, ran in and slapped some words on Graig, and Graig picked him up and threw him to the ground and Lee dislocated his shoulder. He shouldn't have messed with Graig, 'cause when he messes with Graig he's way out of his league. Lee is really a kook, a flake. He's great at shooting off his mouth in the papers, but if you stood close to him, he wouldn't say a word to you. He's got about as much guts as a pussycat. I really shouldn't use a pussycat as a means of comparison. Probably a lot of cats got more guts. Maybe he has, but I've never seen it.

The point is that Lee had no business being over there. It was Lou trying to barrel Fisk over, and Fisk had a right to get mad. It's his prerogative, just like when a runner bowls a second baseman over. It's between the runner and the second baseman. Piniella and Fisk went at it like men, and it wasn't a big deal. It was just good, hard baseball. But when Lee got into it, he was asking for it. He should learn to stop popping his super mouth of his.

One of the things I stress to my players is that you have to be aggressive. You can't lay back and wait to get beat. You have to go after the other guy, and if you have to knock somebody down to jar the ball out of his hand, then you knock him down. That's baseball. And you expect the other guy to do it to you, and when he does, you don't jump up and down and get mad, you just say to yourself, "Okay, I'll wait till I get my shot, and I'll get you back."

We had some great competitors on the team, guys like Graig and Lou and of course Thurman Munson, who I loved. He was good to me right off the bat. He enjoyed teasing and agitating me, and I'd pretend I would get mad, and he'd laugh. Oscar Gamble did a tremendous job for us in the outfield and hitting. He was funny on the bench, livened everything up. When he came to spring training the first day, he had an afro that was about four feet high. I couldn't believe it. He said, "Your new outfielder is here," and all the players looked at him knowing that George had instituted a dress code, and everyone's hair had to be neat, and they were waiting to see how I'd react. I couldn't get mad at Oscar, he's such a great guy. I said, "You've got to be shitting me!" He said, "Do I get a uniform?" I said, "I think you'd better get a haircut. The club will pay for it." It cost seventy-five dollars. But he was good about it, like he was good about everything. Rivers, of course, was in center. I loved Mickey. We had such a good group. Nettles, the agitator, played third. He's so witty. He could get on Thurman, anybody, it would make no difference. He could agitate anybody. During a game with Cleveland he came up with one of the funniest one-liners I ever heard. He said, "Skip, that's the first time I've ever seen that." I said, "What's that, Graig?" He said, "A player with his home address on his back." I said, "What do you mean?" He said, "Look at their first baseman." The Indian first baseman was a large black player by the name of Cage. When we finally figured out what Graig was saying, it cracked everyone up. I started laughing so hard I had to go down the runway.

Fred Stanley, who was our shortstop, was super all year. He played solid, steady baseball and did everything I asked. And of course people like Willie Randolph and Roy White and Chris Chambliss never give you a bit of trouble. They were all fine ballplayers, gentlemen, people I was proud to have on my team. Everyone on the club was happy and hustling, and there was no dissension or controversy at all. Oh, petty things would come up every once in a while. They do on every ball club. The bench guys would be complaining that they weren't playing enough, or a pitcher would get mad he wasn't getting enough work. Dick Tidrow was coming to my office all the time complaining he wanted to pitch more, and when I'd pitch him more, Sparky Lyle would be complaining he wasn't pitching enough. It's part of the game. You get to like these guys so much it's hard sometimes to make a decision to take a guy out. Sometimes you hear the fans chanting to put a player in, but you know he's struggling, and you know for the good of the team it's not the best thing to do because the guy's struggling, having a hard time. If you live with the guys every day, you travel with them every day, you become their father, their teacher, the baby-sitter, the policeman, the father confessor when they have problems. Yet when I'm managing, I must divorce myself from all those other things and just do what I think is best for the club even if it's going to get a player mad at me. I had one pitcher, Larry Gura, who complained that he wasn't pitching as much as he thought he should be pitching. One day he told me he was a better pitcher than Catfish Hunter. I said, "If you are, your record doesn't show it, and I haven't seen it." I told Gura that if I went to five starters, he might be the fifth starter, but until then he'd have to be satisfied with being a spot starter, which he didn't like, and I understood, because he's a control pitcher and he has to pitch a lot to be effective. But I told him he couldn't pitch as much as he wanted because I didn't think he was better than the guys who I had starting. It was nothing personal. He just wasn't my kind of pitcher. He had too many guys on base all the time, he was always in trouble, and if the defense wasn't good, you knew you were eventually going to lose the ball game. I told him, "As far as the coaches are concerned, you happen to be low man on the totem pole." In May we traded Larry to Kansas City for Fran Healy, who proved to be a valuable backup for Thurman.

Another good deal Gabe made was trading pitcher Kenny Brett and outfielder Rich Coggins to Chicago for Carlos May. May proved to be a valuable bat and really strengthened our bench, plus he was another great guy to have on a ball club. I had liked Brett. I really didn't like losing him, but sometimes you have to give up somebody to get somebody, and at the time we felt we needed May's bat more than Kenny's arm.

In June George made a trade that I couldn't believe. It was one of the most ridiculous trades I had ever seen or heard of. He came up to me and said, "This trade just won you a pennant. You now have the best team on paper, and now you're just a push-button manager." Well, we were about twelve games in front at the time, so it was good of him to acknowledge that we had a shot at the pennant, and I asked him, "Who'd we get?" He said, "We got Kenny Holtzman." I said,

"Who did you give up?" He said, "Tippy Martinez, Scott Mc-Gregor, Rudy May, Dave Pagan, and Rick Dempsey." I was in a state of shock. Martinez, McGregor, and May were most of our left-handers, who you need very badly in Yankee Stadium, and Dempsey was a great young catcher who I felt would be an all-star one day. Besides, even *with* Dempsey I didn't feel we had enough catching. You never have enough catching. I asked, "Who else did we get?" He told me: Doyle Alexander, a journeyman pitcher; Ellie Handricks, a catcher who wasn't nearly as talented as Dempsey; Jim Freeman, a young pitcher; and Grant Jackson, a relief pitcher who turned out to be the best of all those players we got from the Orioles. He was a super pitcher, and a super guy, one of those players that every ball club wished it had on it. But the very next year we lost him in the player draft. I was against putting his name on the list. I knew some club would grab him, but again I had no say in this, and Grant was the very first player drafted, and that really upset me because it hurt our club when we lost him. Later I heard that George's little boy, who was about twelve at the time, saw Holtzman pitch for Baltimore, and he told George, "Dad, get him, he'll win the pennant for you," and George went out and got him.

By July we were fifteen games in front and running away with it. I wasn't surprised in the least because I knew what we were capable of doing, but it sure surprised the hell out of George. Then in August we were nine games up and we lost six out of seven, and two things happened as George began to panic. I hadn't let him play a tape recording in the clubhouse during spring training, and he had stayed away. But during our short losing streak he asked me if he could come in the clubhouse before the game and talk to the pitching staff. I told him he could, and as I stood embarrassed with the pitchers in the clubhouse, with my head down, I listened while he chewed them out like he was talking to a high-school football team. He was giving them the rah-rah talk: "You guys don't want it bad enough. You're not giving a hundred percent. You guys are Yankees, and you have to play like Yankees." It went on like that. It was ridiculous, but it's his ball club and he's entitled to do what he wants. After he left, the pitchers were all making fun of him. They didn't pay any attention. He thought they did, but they didn't. I just couldn't make him understand that he was hurting the club doing things like that. In later years he'd call in a young pitcher like Kenny Clay or Jim Beattie, and he'd read him the riot act, and the pitcher would go out and he'd be so scared he could hardly throw the ball. He'd yell at them about Yankee pride. What does George know about Yankee pride? When did he ever play for the Yankees? When did he play in the major leagues? What does he know about major league players' feelings? He doesn't. He'd call me on the phone and yell at me to "chew this guy's ass out." Or he'd say, "Bat this guy lower in the order, that'll show him up." You don't do that. Children do things like that. If you want the players to run through walls for you and play hard for you, you don't treat them like that. If you have something to say to them, say it like a man. "Lookit, I don't think you're doing this right. I want you to start doing it like this." And you'd tell him what you want him to do. You have to get your point across without humiliating the player, without embarrassing him. That's the worst thing you can do to a player. One time in Detroit I had to embarrass Willie Horton, and later I did it to Reggie Jackson and Mickey Rivers with New York, but they had embarrassed me, and I felt they deserved it. But ordinarily, you never embarrass a player publicly. You don't show them up in front of the other players. You get them alone when you talk to them.

The other thing George was doing was: When a Yankee player did something on the field he didn't like, he'd make a funny face, and all the press would be watching him as he sat in his box, and they'd write it up. When I see a player do something I don't like, I mask my feelings. I don't let anyone see how I really feel. I don't go screaming and ranting and raving like a little kid who somebody just took his candy bar away from. You can't do that. When I first started managing I used to do it a little bit, and Harmon Killebrew, who was one of my star players in Minnesota, came over and said, "Skip, you know it kind of makes us look bad your kicking the water cooler like that." I hadn't realized it, but Harmon was right, and I quit doing it. You have to bite the bullet and mask your feelings because the camera is on you all the time, watching you. Now I show them the old stone face. I don't want anybody to know my feelings, especially the players. You don't want them to get down, and start dragging their heads. You have to keep going, keep pushing, especially when you're losing, because they look at you and see how you're handling the situation, and even if you feel deep inside that you have no chance of winning, you have to act like you still can. And sometimes, even when you're losing by five runs, the team can come back and surprise you.

Around this time something else happened that made me angry. We were in the middle of this losing streak, and at the time I was negotiating for a long-term contract to manage the Yankees, and I come out to give the lineup to the umpires, and who is sitting with George in his private box but manager Dick Williams. That was his way of trying to intimidate me, to let me know if I didn't do the job, someone else was waiting in the wings. It's the way he does business. It didn't intimidate me, but it sure made me madder than hell.

Despite that, George and I were getting along very well, and I wanted so badly for him to like me as a person that I bent over backward to show him I was with him. I was overtrying to get him to like me, and sometimes I'd go up to his office and he'd be so nice to me that I'd leave there just happy as heck. It was so important to me that he liked me, and everything was really great—until it began to look like the team *was* going to win the pennant, and at that point I began to feel that George was acting jealous of me. He seemed to resent that he didn't have a big enough hand in it, seemed to feel that he wasn't going to get enough of the credit, and it bothered him that I was getting so much publicity. Hell, everybody knew it was George who put the team out there, that it was his money, that it was George who remodeled Yankee Stadium, and it was George who did all those wonderful things to bring the Yankees back, and there was no reason for him to resent me or feel jealous of me, none whatsoever. Wherever I went it was the same thing: Minnesota, Detroit, Texas, and New York. It became Billy Martin's team, and whammo, I'd run into jealousy from the owner or the general manager for leading the team. I don't want publicity. I made my niche in baseball as a player, and that was enough publicity to last a lifetime. I always felt that the glory was in doing it, not in reading about it in the papers or sticking your chest out at a banquet during the winter. The Yankees were supreme again. That was the real glory, and he should have been happy and let it go at that. He can go to downtown New York and stick his chest out, and I would be very happy for him, and I would stay in my apartment in New Jersey and be very content with just having managed the team to victory. That's one reason I never could understand why we didn't become close. I never stepped on his toes, tried to horn in on his territory. He had no reason to feel jealous of me, and we should have been best of friends, because we were both working toward the same goal, and we both did what we had to do, and away from the game he had his world to hang out in and I had mine, so we never clashed. They asked me to do a job, and I did it. What more did the man want of me? But ego creeps in, unfortunately, and like other owners, the man likes to read his name in the papers, and he feels it necessary to tell people he was responsible for the success of the Yankees. Not the twenty-five players or the coaches or the manager, mind you. But him.

The play-off with Kansas City for the American League championship was one of the most exciting ever. It started off with Larry Gura and George Brett popping off before we even started. Brett told the reporters that I had lied to his brother, Kenny, and Gura said I had lied to him. I still don't understand why Brett said that about me and his brother. I liked his brother, but Chicago wanted him, and we had to give him up. I don't know why Brett came out of the blue and said that. There was no truth to it whatsoever. As far as Gura was concerned, he said I promised him a starting job, and I had told him straight to his face the other pitchers were better. Our guys really gave it to George Brett, and his error in the first inning handed us all the runs we needed to win the game. I personally got on Gura. I was yelling at him from the dugout, really getting on him, but for me it was a psychological thing.

Gura's a control pitcher, and I was trying to get him mad, to reach back and throw harder than usual. I was trying to force him to be a different pitcher, and when he did that, he played right into our hands. After the game the reporters asked me if I had anything to say about Gura, and I told them, "No. He lost. I don't talk about pitchers after they lose." And the funny thing was we beat Gura again the next year, but in the 1978 playoffs, when I wasn't there, he won and popped off about me. When he got beat, I never knocked him. Never said one word about him after a game. But after he beat the Yankees, I wasn't there, and he took cheap shots at me.

We lost the second game to Paul Splittorff, a left-handed pitcher who is always rough on us, and Dock Ellis came through in the third game, even though he gave up three runs in the first inning. Chris Chambliss hit a home run, and Sparky Lyle, who during the season won 7 games and saved 23 more, got the save. In the fourth game I took a chance and started Catfish with three days' rest. Holtzman was available, but I had the same situation with him that I had had with Gura. Holtzman's a control pitcher, and he needed a lot of work to stay sharp, but the coaches and I didn't feel he was as good as the other starters, and so he didn't get the chance to pitch he needed to be sharp. Cat, unfortunately, didn't have it that day, and we had to go to a fifth game. I saw in the papers that Kansas City manager Whitey Herzog was quoted as saying that "if I had a Holtzman, I sure would use him." Managers shouldn't comment about another manager's personnel. I've never second-guessed another manager in the press. I never tell another manager who they should be pitching or playing, and I don't think they should be telling me who to play. It didn't bother me, though. I just went out and beat him the next day in one of the most exciting games baseball has ever seen.

Figgy started and held a 6 to 3 lead going into the eighth, but George Brett hit a three-run home run to tie it, and the whole season came down to who could score one run first. We couldn't score in the bottom of the eighth, and Tidrow held them in the top of the ninth. In the bottom of the ninth a pitcher by the name of Mark Littell was on the mound for

Kansas City, and it was funny, but Chris Chambliss was the first batter and when he walked up to the plate I had a feeling that he was going to hit another one out. Chris is a guy who really gets geared up for the big game, and Littell threw it in there, and Chris lined it into the right-field stands, and the Yankees had their first pennant since 1964. It was a great feeling, and I was so excited, because when I came back to New York to manage the Yankees, all I was hearing was Mets, Mets, Mets, Mets. Even when I was playing with the Yankees, there wasn't the enthusiasm for the Dodgers and the Giants the way there was years later for the Mets. Before we won that pennant, people had forgotten what it meant to root for the Yankees, what it meant for the Yankees to win the pennant year after year after year.

One night I was watching a quiz show on TV, and the question was, "Name a baseball team synonymous with winning." One girl said, "Dodgers." The other girl said, "Giants." That made me madder'n hell. I kept saying, "Yankees, you dummies." And of course the answer was "Yankees."

It was a struggle to beat Kansas City, and because we were forced to start the World Series the very next day, our pitching staff was all screwed up against the Reds. It was unfair, really. The Series opened in Cincinnati, and it rained and they covered the field on us, and so we didn't get a chance to work out, and though that put us at a disadvantage, it was our pitching that hurt us the most. I had to start off the Series with our number five pitcher, Doyle Alexander, and though he pitched pretty well, we couldn't do a thing with Don Gullett. In the second game I went with Catfish, and he pitched a beautiful game, only to lose it in the bottom of the ninth on an error by Fred Stanley. Incidentally, the next spring George came up to me and told me that if I played Stanley at shortstop, he'd trade him away. "I'll get rid of him, Billy, if you play him," he told me. That's how angry he was about Stanley's error in the Series. I finally convinced George that if I couldn't play him at shortstop, the least he could let me do is keep Stanley as a utility infielder. George agreed to that. But he had made up his mind: no way Fred was going to start in 1977. One of the toughest things I ever had to do as a manager was tell Fred he wouldn't be playing, especially after he had such a fine year and helped us to the pennant. He just couldn't understand it. I couldn't tell him the truth, that George had threatened to trade him if I played him. I just told him we were going to play Mickey Kluttz and that George wanted him to play short. I was lucky I was able to convince George to let me keep Fred as a utility player.

In the third game Dock got knocked out early, and we lost, and we weren't much better in game four, when Bench hit a two-run homer off Figgy and a three-run homer off Dick Tidrow.

What also hurt us was that Mickey Rivers, who had been hitting about .330 with about three weeks left in the season, suddenly started dogging it, and in the Series he didn't hit much and didn't get on base. If Mickey hadn't quit down the stretch, he would have won the American League's Most Valuable Player Award for certain. Meanwhile, Thurman was also having an exceptional year, and Thurman wanted to win the award very badly. Thurman told me, "Geez, I'd really like to win that award," and being that it was obvious Mickey was dogging it, I started talking Thurman up with all the writers. It made me very happy when he won it. He came in and hugged me. Thurman, in fact, was the only bright spot we had in the whole Series. He hit over .400, and when Sparky Anderson started bragging to reporters that even though Thurman played so well, he'd still take Bench over him any day, it really ticked me off. Thurman was such a great player. Sparky shouldn't have been running off his mouth like that.

After the final game I was really down. I was sitting on the floor of the trainer's room, and George came in, and he looked at me, and if daggers could have come out of the man's eyes, they would have. He was looking at me like "How can you do this to me?" as if I had lost the Series in four straight on purpose, like he was embarrassed. Who the hell wasn't embarrassed? The Reds outplayed us. It was then that George decided he was going to make some changes, that he was really going to get into things, because he wasn't going to be embarrassed like that again.

CHAPTER 2

The only person who ever stuck up for me was my mother. When I was in the sixth grade, I had a teacher named Mr. Cuttyback. I remember him because he didn't like me at all. I don't know why, but he did everything he could to make things hard for me. He even got me kicked off the safety patrol, picked on me all the time. If I was playing on the school playground, and I started fooling around, getting rough, or if I did something he didn't like, he'd haul me into his office and take a ruler to me.

I'd never tell my mother. I never did believe in squealing. But one time after I came home from school I was all welted up from where Mr. Cuttyback had hit me, and my mother saw the welts and asked me about them, so I had to tell her.

My mother's name is Joan, but everyone calls her Jenny. She's four feet eleven, maybe ninety-five pounds. The next day she showed up at school, and when she got to Mr. Cuttyback's office, she charged at him with both fists, and it took three other teachers to restrain her. Cuttyback was about six foot four, but she was itching to get into it with him. She screamed, "If you ever lay your hands on my son again, I'll come up here and break every bone in your body." And she would have, too.

She was the same way with the cops. I rarely missed school, except when I was sick. My sophomore year I had gotten poison oak real bad. I'd get it so bad I could barely see, and a couple of times I had to go to the hospital for intravenous treatments. I had to be fed through my arms.

This one time they had been burning grass in Beverly Hills, and the poison oak drifted down, and I got it all the way in West Berkeley. I couldn't go to school because of the poison oak, so I asked my mother if I could go over to my friend Howard Noble's house. Howard was one of my close friends. He lived about four blocks away, and even though we didn't have a phone, I figured he'd be home, because he cut school more often than not. Mom didn't see any reason why I couldn't go, so I went over to Howard's.

Howard and I were sitting on his front porch talking when the truant officer drove by. He stopped his car and got out and came over to us. "Why aren't you in school?" he asked me. I said, "I have my mother's permission to be here. I live at 1632 Seventh Street. I have poison oak, and I . . ." He grabbed me by the scruff of my neck before I could finish the sentence.

He was embarrassing me in front of Howard, and that's the worst thing you can do to a kid. I screamed at him, "Turn me loose," but he had me and he was pulling me toward his car to take me away. "You little punk," he said, and he shoved me against the car. I braced myself with my hands when I hit the car, and when I bounced back I turned and nailed the hooky cop with a right hand, knocking him colder than a cucumber. I stood there thinking to myself, "Holy shit. I've just punched out the hooky cop!"

I said to Howard, "I think I better get home," and though I didn't run because I didn't want the poison oak to spread any worse than it was, I was hoofing it pretty good.

When I got home I told my mother what had happened. She said, "Don't worry about it, Billy. I'll take care of him," and a few minutes later, when the cop came to the door, my mom was ready to take him on. She said, "I raised my boy to tell the truth, and if he tells you he has permission to be there, he has permission to be there. If you ever put your hands on him again, I'll beat the living shit out of you." I never had trouble with him again.

Even when I got older, my mom was always there when I

needed her. When I was in the Army, I sent home almost my entire paycheck. I had sold two of my cars because I needed money, but I was still broke because of all the people I was supporting. One weekend I went home on a three-day pass, hadn't been home for quite a while, and the first night I stayed home, didn't go out. My mother said, "What's the matter with you?" I said, "Nothing, why?" She said, "You sick?" I said, "No, I'm not sick." I didn't want to tell her I didn't have any money. I didn't want to go out with my friends and not be able to pay like everyone else, didn't want to be a freeloader, so I stayed home.

The next day my mother went out, and when she came back she came up to my room, where I was, and she opened up her apron, and three thousand dollars fell out of it onto my bed. I said, "Where did you get that?" She said, "I put another mortgage on the house. It isn't right you being here. Get out of the house and go have a good time." I took some of it. I said, "Don't worry, Mama, when I get out of this I'll pay this house off, I'll buy you a Frigidaire, I'll buy you a car." I think I bought her four cars, and she doesn't even know how to drive. But I kept my word to her.

I'm fifty-two years old, and she's still looking out for me. George had just fired me, and I was visiting my mom and dad, it was their fiftieth wedding anniversary, and Mom and I were dancing. She said, "Billy, Dad and I are getting social security, we have plenty to eat, and anytime you want your old room back, you can always live with us."

All her life she stood up for her children. I have an older half brother we call Tudo, and out our window Mom saw a neighbor picking on him, and she came running out of the house to fight him. She had kicked Tudo's father out of the house, and she was raising him by herself, and she told him, "I'm his mother, I'm his father, and now you're going to have to fight me." The man had been a soldier during the First World War, and when she came toward him, a group of guys putting in the sewers on the street moved to come to her aid. Mom told them, "Don't anybody move. I don't want nobody to help me," and she went after the neighbor with both fists. To stop her, the man threw dirt at her, but it only made her madder. She beat the hell out of him, and Mom didn't get a scratch.

The next day Mom learned that the man had suffered from shell shock during the war and that he was poor and his family didn't have much to eat. When she found that out, she started bringing them groceries and firewood to make sure they were warm, and they ended up becoming friends. Later the man told my mom, "I was in the war, and I never had anybody beat me like you did."

Mom never took shit from nobody. It was her motto, something her mother had taught her. She told me how when she was a student in school, there was once a teacher who gave her a hard time. One day Mom had enough. She went up to her and ripped her dress to shreds.

She told me that Berkeley had been a very cliquish place when she first moved there around the turn of the century. People gossiped a lot, and she was one person who could never stand to have people saying things about her. Didn't matter who it was, if my mom found out someone had said something she didn't like, she'd get on the trolley and confront the person who was supposed to have said it. She'd ask, "Did you say that about me?" and if the person hesitated one second, she hauled off and slugged 'em. My grandma Nona was the same way. If you said something she didn't like, she'd grab you by the hand and start biting you.

Whenever my mother felt she was being wronged, she'd stand up for herself, and that's the way I was brought up, too. When I was very young, my stepfather was suffering from asthma, and for a couple months he couldn't work, so Mom had to go on welfare. It didn't last long, though, because Mom refused to be treated like dirt by the welfare people. She fought them tooth and nail until she vowed never to have anything to do with them again. The third week she went, she got her money for groceries, and she asked the welfare lady for a cigarette. The lady, who was puffing on a cigarette, said, "You're not supposed to get cigarettes when you're on welfare." My mom said, "You're smoking," and she got hot and told the woman off. She told her, "The hell with welfare. I don't want it anymore. I'll starve to death first."

When I was about eleven, she and I were walking down the street, and a group of men started whistling at her. My blood started to boil, and I was going to go after this one guy when my mother grabbed me by the neck. She said, "Billy, what are you doing?" I said, "Mom, I don't like men whistling at you that way. It ain't nice. It's no respect."

"Do you know why they're whistling at me?" she asked. I said, "No, Mom, why?" She said, "Because I have the best-looking ass in town, and don't you forget it." At her fiftieth anniversary party she told me, "My breasts are gone, but I still have a nice-looking ass." She's hot stuff.

She's been married three times. Her mother ran a boarding-house, and when she was seventeen, my grandmother arranged for her to marry one of her boarders by the name of Pesano. Mom didn't like Pesano. She liked this guy Vittorio who lived in San Francisco. However, the old Italian tradition allowed for the parent to arrange a marriage for the child, and that's who you had to marry.

One day my mom came home from high school, and Grandma was sitting at a table sewing sheets. Mom said, "Gee, those are nice. Who are you sewing them for?" Grandma said, "For you. You're getting married." Mom said, "You're going to let me marry Vittorio?" Grandma said, "No, you're marrying Pesano." Mom said, "I don't like him. Please don't make me marry him." Grandma said, "That's who you're marrying." Ma said, "Okay, I'll marry him, but as soon as I find another guy, I'm going to leave him."

They were married about three years, and she bore a son, Tudo, my older brother. Then she met Alfred Manuel Martin, my father, and she left Pesano. She told him she didn't love him anymore and he was to get out. Pesano went back to Italy, remarried, and when he came back to the United States he was found murdered in the snow in Little Rock, Arkansas. Mom said Pesano had a habit of jingling the coins in his pockets. Apparently he shook them once too many, and someone robbed him and left him dead.

Alfred Manuel Martin was a Portugese musician from the island of Kauai, Hawaii. He was about six foot one, a handsome guy. I haven't seen him in years, but the last time I saw him if you'd have seen us together you'd have said we look alike. I've been told he was one of the toughest guys on the islands. He was not, however, as tough as my mother.

Mom had a girl friend who was Hawaiian who used to give her hula lessons, and Mom met Alfred Martin through her. They weren't married a year. She was deeply in love with him, and was three months pregnant with me when she kicked him out of the house.

My mom says that my dad stayed out till two, three in the morning playing his music in various clubs around Berkeley, and it bothered her that he'd come home so late. Later he was out of work, and Mom got him a job driving a truck for the department of sanitation.

Apparently Dad was doing more during the day than just hauling garbage. One of the first gifts my mom gave him was a beautiful, expensive wristwatch. One day he came home without it, and when she asked him what had happened to it, he told her he didn't know. A few days later one of Mom's many friends told her that she had seen one of the students at the local high school wearing it. The girl was about fifteen years old, the woman said.

After she left, my mom went into the closets, pulled out all Dad's clothes, stepped all over them to get them dirty, threw them in a suitcase, and threw the suitcase outside the front door. Dad came home and wanted to know what was the matter. Mom said, "You're not chipping on me, you bastard. Out you go. And you stay out." She grabbed a hand mirror, went outside, and she broke every single window of his new car with the mirror. She had paid the five-hundred-dollar down payment on the car, and she wasn't about to let him get away scot-free. My mom only had to find out he was cheating on her once. That was it.

After they separated, another of her friends told her that Dad had a girl in the room he was living in. Mom said, "Oh yeah?" and she put her coat on and went to confront him. She beat on his door, forced it open, and when she found him in bed with this girl, Mom started punching and hitting them both. She made such a racket, the neighbors called the police. She yelled at him, "I'm still married to you, you son of a bitch.

We're not divorced yet." She felt better after she beat them up, Mom says.

Dad hurt my mom terribly. I know he did, because even though she divorced him, she never threw out the picture she has of him. Ever since I can remember, she has referred to him as the jackass. Whenever she'd get mad at me, she'd say, "Billy, you're just like the jackass." To this day, and she's older than eighty, she hasn't forgiven him. She told me, "I'm going to outlive that son of a bitch, and when they bury him, I'm going to go to the funeral, and in front of all his friends and relatives, I'm going to pull up my dress and piss on his grave."

After the divorce my dad was ordered to pay Mom sixty dollars a month. By that time I had been born. She had carried me for ten months when one day she was outside hanging clothes on the line, the line broke, and she fell backward into the bin. The next day I was born. Even though she had kicked him out, she named me Alfred Manuel Martin, Jr., after my father. Later my mom went back to court, and she got the support raised to sixty-five dollars a month. When she told Dad about the raise in support money, he disappeared, went back to the Hawaiian Islands, and we didn't hear from him for fifteen years, during which time he didn't send Mom a nickel.

I didn't know my real name was Alfred until junior high school. When I was a baby, my grandmother, who spoke Italian, called me Bellitz, which means beautiful. The other kids heard her call me Bellitz, and they thought she was saying Billy, and that's what everyone called me.

One day when I was in the seventh grade, I was standing in a classroom waiting to be assigned a homeroom class. The teacher called out "Alfred Manuel Martin," and I looked around the room to see who the other kid named Martin was. I thought it was funny that no one came forward. The teacher finished calling the names, and I was the only kid left standing there. I said, "Teacher, I don't believe you called my name." She said, "Who are you?" I said, "Billy Martin." She asked me my street address, and when I told her, she said, "Your name is Alfred." I said, "No, ma'am, there ain't no way my name is Alfred. I'll telling you it's Billy. I should know what my name is." She said, "You better go home and talk to your mother about it." And I did. I said, "Mom, you're not going to believe what happened. The teacher said my real name is Alfred." Mom said, "It is." I said, "How come you didn't tell me?" She said, "Because I didn't want you to know you had the same name as that jackass."

It always bothered me what my dad had done to my mom. It also bothered me that I never knew my real father like a son should know his father. When I was a kid, I'd ask my mom about him, who he was, where he was, and she'd never say anything. But it really didn't start to bother me until junior high school, when the other kids used to tease me about my not having a father, trying to say I was a bastard. Two things got me especially mad, somebody calling me a dago, or wop, or somebody saying I didn't have a father. Those were two things I heard all the time.

When I was fifteen, my dad came back. One day he showed up at the house. He wanted to take me to buy some corduroys, and while we were together I treated him coolly. It was very difficult for me, because seeing him made my mother furious, and I didn't want to dishonor her by being friends with him. I saw him a couple more times, once when I was in high school, once in the minors, and once when I was with the Yankees. That last time I told him, "This is a terrible thing for a son to say to a father, but you're nothing to me. You're a stranger. I hardly know you."

It was very unfair to him, but because of my mother I really didn't have a choice. I never did dislike him, in my heart I have never faulted him, but I had to do what was right by my mother. She had raised me, and I had to do what she thought was right. Maybe when Dad reads this book, he'll understand.

After my mom kicked my dad out, she got real lucky. She found a great guy by the name of Jack Downey. I was eight months old when she met him. A friend of my mother's told her she wanted her to meet an awfully nice guy, and they arranged to meet him in Sausalito, where he lived. To get there, they took the San Francisco-to-Sausalito ferryboat, and all during the trip as my mom sat on the ferryboat, one of the cooks was making eyes at her. Mom thought, "Gee, I wish he was taller," but she thought he was rather nice looking, and when he'd smile at her, she'd smile back at him.

They got off in Sausalito, and my mom and her girl friend were sitting in her friend's car waiting for the guy who was supposed to meet them there. Who should come over to the car but the cook who'd been flirting with her. My mom said to her girl friend, "That's the guy who was flirting with me." Her friend said, "That's the guy you're supposed to be going out with."

The man got in the car, looked at my mother, and in an Irish tenor started singing to her, and right then and there she fell in love. The man, Jack Downey, had been a professional singer with station WBBM in Chicago.

Riding on that ferryboat was one of my first childhood memories. I was very young, and I didn't know who he was. I don't even remember him. I do remember that I carried a little blanket with me wherever I went. I was a blanket baby like Linus in the Peanuts cartoon. Mom and I would ride back and forth on that ferryboat while Jack was cooking for the passengers.

Because of Jack we always had a roof over our head and plenty of food, even in the middle of the Depression. Except for the month when Jack suffered from asthma and couldn't work, he always did something, whether it was shoveling prunes in a factory, or lumping, or driving a truck, he was always able to find work. Jack weighed about 120 pounds, and when he worked as a lumper he'd pick up hundred-pound sacks and heave them into the truck like it was nothing. The boss would go there and watch him, and he saw how Jack worked hard, did his job, and never gave anyone trouble, and he then hired him as a truck driver. He was making nine dollars a day driving a truck. During the Depression Jack worked for the WPA. He did carpentry work, was very handy. In fact, he started at sixty-five dollars a month, and he was such a good worker they gave him a raise to eighty-five a month in no time. At the same time he took his Model T Ford, stripped it down, and converted it into a saw. He'd go down to the beach, collect driftwood, cut it up, and he'd sell it to people for firewood. He'd cut wood all day long. He was a hardworking little man. He was always working, always doing something. After the Depression my brother Tudo was working for a cider company, and he went to his boss to try to get Jack a job. The boss asked him how old Jack was. Tudo told him he was thirty-five. The boss said, "He's too old." It was a strenuous job that required a lot of lifting. Tudo said, "Come on, try him." The boss said okay. The next day Jack went, and after a day's work the boss said to Jack, "I'm going to give you forty cents an hour, but don't tell Tudo." Tudo was only making thirty cents an hour. That's how good a worker Jack was.

My mom had one dress, and she couldn't afford a coat, but she always made sure their kids, Joanie, Pat, Jackie, and I, had allowance money and money for lunch. I used to drive my mom crazy because I was always playing tackle football and coming home with a torn shirt. One day I was playing with my buddy, playing on a makeshift raft at a local pond, and while we were on the raft I took my shoes off, and accidentally I kicked one shoe into the water. It was the only pair of shoes I owned. That evening my mom and I had planned on going to the Rivoli Theater to see the latest movie. They used to have a drawing once a week. You'd buy a ticket, they put the stubs in a big box, and they'd draw numbers. The winner got five or ten dollars. It was getting late, and my mom was out looking for me, and when she saw I only had one shoe, I had to tell her what had happened. She said, "We're going to the movies even if you have to go barefoot." We bought our tickets, they held the drawing, and we won. With our winnings Mom went out the next day and bought me a new pair of shoes.

My mother tried so hard all the time to do things for us. She did her utmost to clothe us, and we always ate well. She cooked Italian style. She made macaroni on Thursday and Sunday, and she'd make soup and a roast during the week, and she would bake her own cakes, upside-down cake, banana cream cake. She didn't like to go to restaurants. Not that we could afford restaurants. She had once been a waitress, and after she saw what went on in the kitchen, she swore she'd never eat in another restaurant.

We used to make wine in the backyard. My grandma Nona

had a press that looked like a big tub, like a water tower on top of an old hotel. We'd fill the tub with grapes, climb in wearing our shorts, and we'd mash the grapes with our bare feet like you see in the movies. Every year Grandma would make a hundred barrels of wine, and she'd test every barrel. She made very, very good wine, and she would trade for the things we needed. She was a great trader. A man would come with the old horse and wagon filled with fruits and vegetables, and she'd trade him wine for his goods. The baker would trade her bread for wine. We always had food on the table, even when the Depression was at the worst.

My mom's mom, my grandmother, was named Raphaella, but we called her Nona, which in Italian means grandmother. Nona also had an arranged marriage. She was very young at the time she came to America to meet her husband. He was about thirty years older than she was, and she took one look at him and told her mother that he was too old, that she wouldn't marry him. Her mother said, "You've come all the way from Italy to marry him, and you're going to marry him." And she did, and they had a very happy marriage. He turned out to be a wonderful man. He died in 1924. He was very good to my grandmother. A quiet man, I'm told. Mom says he never said two words, he was so quiet. My grandfather used to work on a fishing boat. He'd go to Anchorage, Alaska, for six months at a time, and when he came home, he never had less than two hundred dollars, and it was like Christmas for the family.

Nona, meanwhile, worked for the rich people in the hill section of Berkeley. She'd cook for them, make ravioli, and she'd clean their houses. Nona, who was from San Francisco, bought her house in Berkeley the year before the big earthquake in '06, and three months before the quake she moved into it. She still lives in that house today. When the quake hit, it destroyed the house my mother was born in. It collapsed right to the ground, and Mom says that after San Francisco was destroyed, dozens of her San Francisco relatives came to Berkeley to stay with her. They slept under tables, in the bathtub, anyplace they could find.

Until I was ten, my parents lived about a block from where they do now. My grandmother lived on Seventh Street, and

Nona gave Mom the plot next door, and she moved our house there so we could be near her. After we moved, I'd live at both houses. Until I was fifteen, I slept in my Nona's bed. By then I was kicking too much in my sleep, and Nona had to put a cot at the end of the bed for me. Though I slept at my grandmother's, I'd still be with my mother all the time. I had a heck of an appetite when I was a kid, and sometimes I'd eat at Mom's, run out the house, and eat at Nona's, too.

When my grandfather died, Nona had to support ten children, plus two kids of one of her daughters who had died young. Of a broken heart, my mother says.

The daughter's name was Antoinette, and she had married a man she loved deeply, and they had two young children. One day one of Antoinette's neighbors called to her from a second-floor window, "Antoinette, Antoinette, did you hear? Your husband drowned last night."

A boat called the *State of California* had crashed into another boat, and her husband, who was on it, had died. When Antoinette heard the news, she fainted, and rolled all the way down the stairs to the first floor. With her husband's death, Antoinette lost her will to live. My mother says she did everything she could to help Antoinette, even slept in the same bed with her to keep her company.

Several days after the accident the captain of the *State of California,* who had survived the crash, paid a visit to Antoinette to tell her how sorry he was. When Antoinette found out who he was, she went crazy. She started screaming and yelling for him to get out. "You drowned my husband," she was crying. According to my mom, the captain was so taken with Antoinette that he proposed marriage to her on the spot. Antoinette, however, wouldn't forgive the captain, and she ordered him out of the house.

My mother was going to school at the time, and when she'd go off for the day, Antoinette would tell her, "Jenny, when you come home I'm going to be dead." Mom would tell her, "Netta, you're not going to die," but one day she came home and Antoinette was dead. She had died of a broken heart, Mom says.

Nona raised Antoinette's kids after fighting the welfare people for their custody for over a year. As I said, she also raised ten children, and I remember when I was growing up, every Sunday evening all the relatives would come over to Nona's for chicken dinner. The grown-ups sat at one table and the children sat at another, and while dinner was going on, Nona had one rule: no talking at the table. Mom told me that the tradition of no talking came down from my grandfather. She said that one time when he was alive, her brother Joe was talking during the meal, and grandpa picked up a plate and hit him right over the head with it and broke the plate in half.

At Sunday dinner the kids would be fed first, and we'd get out of there early, and the adults would sit all afternoon eating and drinking. It was the same every Sunday: everyone would come, and they'd be so happy to see each other, and they'd be hugging, and before long they'd start drinking Nona's wine, and then they'd start arguing, and swear words would be flying around the room, and someone would remember something nasty someone said the week before, and by the end of the evening everyone would leave mad as hell. The next Sunday they'd come again, hugging each other, and they'd start all over again.

Mom had a sister Theresa, who was the only one smart enough not to get involved in the fighting. Theresa had a speakeasy, and she was making a thousand dollars a week during the Depression, and she'd arrive in her chauffeur-driven limousine, and she'd come in and give each of us kids a quarter. She'd stay for the meal, and always before everyone had too much to drink, she'd leave, because she knew what was going to happen.

Mom would take me down to Theresa's place, and we'd sit on a chesterfield with my aunt, and Mom and Theresa would talk. I kept my mouth shut, because Mom always told me, "When I'm talking, don't butt in." One time my little brother Jackie went with us, and he interrupted, and Mom punched him on the mouth so hard she made his teeth bleed. He never interrupted again. We sat there, and during the day I would watch different men coming in and out, and I'd always wonder what those men were doing. The men would chat with my mom and buy me a Coke, and for several years Mom and I spent pleasant afternoons at Theresa's. The whole time I watched the men and wondered about them.

I was about sixteen, and it was during the war, and a couple of my buddies and I went to a local cathouse. I didn't have the guts, and I certainly didn't have the money, to go upstairs with one of the girls, but I enjoyed watching the ritual of the guy sitting there waiting for a girl to come, watching her take him away. It was very exciting for me.

A few days after I went to the cathouse, I was sitting down for breakfast, and I got to thinking about Aunt Theresa, and suddenly it dawned on me. "Mom," I called, "does Aunt Theresa run a cathouse?" She said, "Who told you?" No one had told me. I had finally figured out why all those men were coming in and out while I was sitting and talking with Mom and Aunt Theresa on her chesterfield.

Aunt Theresa was such a wonderful woman. I really loved her. She had once been married to the first violinist of the San Francisco orchestra. She was a classy lady.

After school one afternoon Mom came to get me, which was unusual. School was close to home, within walking distance. Mom said, "Billy, your Aunt Theresa is dead." Theresa had had a boyfriend who was insanely jealous, and one morning in her house he couldn't stand it any longer, and he blew her brains out with a gun and then turned it on himself. I was so sad. When I heard she was dead, I cried and cried.

Mom had another sister, Mary, who was always wonderful to me as a kid. One day Mary came over to visit Mom. Nona was getting old, and Mary said to Mom, "Why don't we put Nona in a home?" Mom became furious. She said, "Why you son of a bitch," and she grabbed Mary by the scruff of the neck and threw her out of the house. Since that day Mom hasn't spoken to her. I would go over to Aunt Mary's house, and she'd ask me, "How's that son-of-a-bitching mother of yours?" And when Mary's sons Nicki and Mario would come over, Mom would ask them, "How's that crooked-legged bitch of a mother of yours?" They hated each other. Refused to talk. But we grew up with it, and we didn't pay it any attention. We understood it, that that was the way it was.

I had four brothers and sisters in all. Mom had Tudo by

Pesano, her first husband, and I was next, and then there were Patsy, Jackie, and Joannie. When I was growing up I wasn't very close with my brothers, because Tudo was ten years older than I was and Jackie was seven years younger. Jackie and I played around some. He liked to agitate me, but we didn't really hang out much. I'd be playing horseshoes, and Jackie would come running into the pit, bothering me when I was about to throw. One day I was playing horseshoes, and I was staring at the post, ready to throw, and he came running into the pit, and trying to scare him I threw the horseshoe at him, and accidently I hit him and split his head wide open. He had to go to the hospital for stitches. Scared me to death.

I came home that night, and with Jackie sitting across the dinner table from me, my mother was saying, "If I ever get the guy who hit him with the horseshoe, I'll kill him." I was staring at Jackie, thinking, "If you say one word, I'll tip this table on top of you." I was sweating it out, because I knew my mother would hit me over the head with a pan if she found out I had done it. But Jackie didn't squeal on me. We weren't brought up to be squealers. Instead, he went up to my room with his BB gun. On the wall in my bedroom was a picture of me in a baseball uniform. Jackie sighted his gun, and he shot a BB right between my eyes in the picture.

Tudo hung around with older guys, and he didn't spend much time with me like brothers sometimes do. I remember one time when I was fifteen. Everyone was sitting around the dinner table. Tudo was in the Navy, and he was gung-ho Navy, had his hair cut real short in a crew cut, and while we were eating he started to get on me about my hair. I had a duck's-ass haircut, it came back in a long, greasy wave, and Tudo started hoorahing me about it. I told him he better leave me alone, but he kept at it, and finally I said, "For Christ's sake, Tudo, get off my back. I'm tired of listening to you." My brother is only five foot nine, but he wears a size twenty-two ring and he has the arms of a truck driver. He hit me, boom, knocked me out of my chair, and when I hit the floor he hit me again. I was seeing stars, but I have an instinct—I don't know where I got it—I held on until my head could clear, and then I started punching back. I landed one to his face, and I broke his jaw.

When I saw him lying there, his face all bloodied, I ran out into the backyard and started crying like a baby. My brother came out, and he started apologizing, and we were both crying, and we hugged each other for a long time. The worst part was for six weeks I had to sit across from him at the dinner table and watch him eat through a straw. Tudo had always been hoorahing me, putting me down all the time before that happened. Afterwards he came to appreciate me more.

From the time my mother let me out of the house until I went away to play pro ball, I spent a large part of my free time at James Kenney Park, which was about two blocks from my home. When I was little, I'd go every single day. We played baseball, basketball, football, volleyball, and we'd play a game called elephant. Ten guys would line up and lock arms, and the ten guys on the other team would line up about twenty feet away, and they'd run at you and jump as hard as they could on your back. If anyone broke the line by falling down, the other team got to jump on you again.

None of us had much money, we couldn't afford football equipment or baseball gloves, but when we played football, we'd play tackle even though we didn't have helmets or pads. We'd get bloody noses and get all banged up, and then we'd go home for dinner and a little rest, and in the evening we'd meet back in the park for capture the flag or boxing.

On Saturday afternoons the older kids and the adults played baseball. My brother Tudo had once tried out for professional baseball, but after a few weeks in Ft. Smith, Arkansas, he got homesick and came home, and then the war came and he got drafted, and when it was over he tried to come back but his arm was gone. Even so, he had a pretty good fastball, and in the park he managed and pitched for one of the teams and my Uncle Slits used to manage the other team, and he and Tudo used to have great pitchers' duels. Augie Galan, who was a star outfielder for the Cubs, was another guy who used to play. Augie and Tudo were great friends, and they'd play on the same team, and Joe Hatten, who played with the Dodgers, also would play sometimes. As I got older, every Saturday I'd go to the game hoping that not enough guys would show up and I could play, and every once in a while I did get to play. Later, of course, I got to play regularly. I always appreciated that when I was a kid they let me play.

When I was little, the park directors looked after us closely. They cared about the kids, knowing we didn't have much. A man by the name of Joe Haynes was in charge of keeping the park clean. He cut the bushes, planted flowers, kept it nice. Joe once tried to adopt me. He and his wife were alone, and they wanted a child, and he took a liking to me. I'd go over to the park, and he and I'd play what we called the penny game. He'd take me over to one of the shrubs, and he'd say, "Shake this tree," and I would, and out would fall a couple of pennies. Joe would put his palms up like, "Where did they come from?" He was such a nice man.

As I got older, the park continued to be the center of our social life. At night we'd have what we called Staley Night. The directors would warm up the oven, and we'd sit around drinking coffee and stale bread. Sometimes they'd organize a watermelon feast. Once I was the Watermelon King. I could eat a piece of watermelon faster than anybody. They crowned me by putting the rind on top of my head.

During the war Berkeley changed. Mexicans and blacks and new kids from other parts of the country came as their parents found war work. The neighborhood got very tough, and you had to be tough to get along. From the time I was about twelve years old until I was maybe fifteen, I awoke every morning knowing that there was a good chance I was going to have to get into a fight with somebody. A kid growing up in West Berkeley didn't have a choice in the matter. I have always said that I never started a fight in my whole life, and that was true even when I was a kid. But it was true then, as it is now, that I was taught never to back down if I found myself in a situation where I had to fight.

It was either fight or stay away from the park. That was the choice, and I loved the park too much to stay away. When I walked home from school, the most direct way home was to walk across the park, and waiting for me would be forty or fifty kids sitting there, agitating you, guys who wanted nothing better than to get you into a fight. These were below-middle-class kids, kids who grew up with nothing, kids who had nothing to do but fight. It was their entertainment. I'd be walking across the park, and a kid would come over and say, "I heard you said I was a . . . ." It didn't matter what it was, it was just an excuse to get into it with you. Or he'd call me a dago, anything to get me to fight him. He wanted to fight, and it was impossible to back down, because if you did everyone would see you were afraid, and that would lead to more harassment. To be respected by the other kids, you didn't have a choice, you had to fight. Fortunately I could take pretty good care of myself. I could hit like a truck, and after I beat everyone who challenged me at least once, fewer and fewer kids wanted to fight me.

I never lost a fight, but I remember one fight that seemed like it must have lasted an hour. The other kids stood around us in a circle, and we stood in there and punched and punched. Neither of us won that one. I was made what we called a Prussian general, a guy who could whip all the other guys. I was left alone, and I was able to concentrate on playing sports.

Why did the kids want to fight so much? I don't know. Maybe they had no other way to prove themselves. We didn't have roller skates or bicycles. My grandmother once bought me a bike. She scraped up the money and bought it for me, and I had it about a week when I went to visit a friend. I parked it outside his house, and when I came out it was gone. I never had a bicycle again.

What everyone did have was fists, and the kids in the park were not afraid to use them.

After a while our gang started fighting gangs of other towns. We had what we called the Prussian Army, about four hundred kids, and when we needed it we could call out what we called the Chinese Army, which was about eight hundred kids, all kids with no money, nothing to do. They'd go fight kids from neighboring towns. It was before knives and chains. It was just fighting. I didn't want to get involved in gang fighting. I only went to one. One time a group of kids from East Berkeley, where the rich kids lived, came down to our park to fight us. They thought they were a bunch of toughies, but they didn't know what they were getting into. We beat them bad. When we went back to East Berkeley, instead of our having a gang fight, I took on their leader. I stood out in front of my Chinese Army, and he stood out in front of his army, and we went at it. After I beat him up, the fighting stopped. There were no more fights, and the East Berkeley kids didn't bother us anymore.

During the war zoot-suiters used to hang around the park. They were called pachucos, tough Mexicans in their mid-twenties who carried switchblades. They wore peg pants with an extremely long coat with padded shoulders, and they always seemed to have a cigarette dangling from their lips, like in the movies. These guys, we felt, were guys not to mess with. There was one pachuco who hung out at the park. He had a car, and he'd drive us around in it, and we'd feel like big shots, and a couple times he made my friend Howard Noble and I steal him some gasoline for his car. We didn't want to do it, but he had been nice to us, and we thought it best that we do it. There was a big steel plant in Berkeley, and Howard and I snuck into the plant, crawled next to one of the company's jitney's, and siphoned a couple gallons out. We'd wait for the guard to pass, and then we'd run out of there with the gas can. We only did it twice. The second time we came home afterwards. We reeked of gasoline. Howard took out a cigarette. I told him, "Don't light it. You're going to blow both of us up."

When the kids weren't hanging out at the park, they were hanging out on street corners. Much later the police were smart enough to build a little center for the kids where they could play Ping-Pong and stay off the streets. During the war, though, it was the park and at night the streets. Our end of town was near the University of California, which had a lot of bars, so the Navy guys would come down to our part of town and hang out, too. The Navy guys would come up to one of our kids and hoorah him because he had long hair, and at first it would be five Navy guys hoorahing one kid, but all of a sudden there'd be twenty kids surrounding the Navy guys, and it could get ugly. It got so bad, in fact, that the Navy made West Berkeley out of bounds.

Despite all this I wasn't a bad kid. The one time I got in real trouble it wasn't even my fault. I was about eleven, and I was riding with a friend on the back of his bike to the movies. He was several years older than I was, and on the ride back he said, "I want to stop in my dad's car and get some stuff." We stopped, he went into a car, and he took some Christmas presents and put them in the basket of his bike. At the time I thought nothing of it, but the next day the police came to my house. They asked me whether I had been with my friend the night before. I told them the truth, that I had.

The cops told my mother, "We're going to have to take him in. He stole some packages out of a car yesterday." Mom asked me, "Did you steal anything?" I told her, "I didn't know Ronald was stealing those things. He said they belonged to his father."

Mom told the cops, "Search the house. Look in every room. You won't find a thing, because if he had stolen anything, I would have beaten the hell out of him." Mom said, "My son didn't steal nothing, and you ain't taking him anywhere." But they did. They took me to the detention home, and I had to stay there for two days until Ronald finally told the police the truth. I felt real funny being in there. I felt bad, and I was scared, and yet I knew I hadn't done anything wrong.

The police were very tough on us because we came from West Berkeley. They thought we were tough kids, and they never showed us any respect. One time I went bowling in Albany, a nearby town, and after we finished, this cop stopped me and asked me where I was from. When I told him West Berkeley, he shoved me against the wall, and when he shoved me, I slugged him. They took me down to the police station. The police called my mom and told her to come and get me. She said, "What do you have him for?" and they really couldn't tell her, and so she told them, "You took him. You bring him back." Boy, did she tell those cops off. They put me in the squad car, but they wouldn't drive me to the door. They left me off about a block away from our house. They didn't want to face my mother. The next day they called her to apologize.

Like most kids, we got into some mischief, but nothing very serious. We used to sneak behind Spanger's Seafood Restaurant where they'd pile up the crabs to cool, and we'd steal a crab or two and bring them home. Also, we had a favorite baker Mom bought all her bread from, and he'd always leave a couple loaves of bread out in front of his shop, and at night we'd sneak over there and swipe them. There were about eight of us who would split it up. The next day I'd go into his store to buy my mom's bread, and the baker would ask me, "How was the bread last night?" I'd tell him it was delicious, and he'd laugh. He knew who was taking it. It got so he'd put it out for us.

Another thing we liked to do was raid the neighbors' fruit orchards. At night we'd sneak into a yard, climb the trees, and grab the apples or plums or apricots. We'd jump down and hightail it. Sometimes the owner would see us in the dark, and he'd throw rocks at us, and we'd run like hell, which made it even more exciting.

One night we decided to hit my own yard. We had a deep backyard with plum trees, and very quietly we crawled under the cover of darkness into the orchard, sneaking from tree to tree picking plums.

My Uncle George, who was a hunter, somehow saw us, and he came running out with his shotgun. Fortunately George had salt in that gun and not buckshot, because he fired and hit me right in the ass, stung me good. Because it was dark and I was a distance away, he hadn't realized it was me he hit.

Later I came home for dinner, and I didn't say anything. We were sitting around the table, and Uncle George said, "Those sons-a-bitch friends of yours were up in our trees." I said, "No kidding." He said, "But I got one of them little bastards." I thought to myself, "You got one, all right. You got me."

When I got older, I had a job every summer and every winter until I went to play minor league ball. One summer I worked in the Heinz pickle factory. I was a laborer working with the winos on the conveyor belts. The bottles of pickles would be placed in boxes, and the boxes would come down the conveyor belt, and I stood with the winos at the end of the belt, picked up the boxes, and stacked them where a forklift would come and pick them up. The winos didn't move very quickly, so I had to work like a son of a gun so they wouldn't have to slow down the conveyor belt. I worked so hard I got tendonitis. And I'd go home with my check, and my mom would take it and give me five or ten dollars, and she'd use the rest for clothes and food for the family.

I had one job working as a laborer for Cutter's Laboratory. Penicillin had just come out, and they had me moving the stuff, and I don't care how many showers you take, that stuff sticks to you and smells moldy, and you can't get rid of that smell. One time I went to the movies, and I couldn't figure out why nobody wanted to sit next to me. Finally one of my buddies told me how bad I smelled. I couldn't smell it myself. I was immune to it.

Another job I had was working in James Kinney Park as a supply boy. All my uncles would come over, and I'd give them free towels. Towels were only a nickel then, but a nickel was a nickel, and I'd give them towels. I'd give my buddies free towels, too. I'd have the keys, and at night we'd break into the rec hall, and we'd put blankets over the windows so the lights wouldn't show, and we'd play pinochle until one in the morning.

It wasn't fashionable for a West Berkeley kid to be a good student. I didn't dare bring my books home from school, because the older kids would hoorah you so much, call you a sissy or a fag. Also junior high school was a tough period of learning for me. All of a sudden I was taking courses like algebra, and I wasn't picking it up, and it made me feel very bad. I also felt bad because I was being lazy not doing my homework. On the one hand, I did want to do it. But on the other, it was important at that age to try to be cool by not taking books home. There was so much pressure from the other West Berkeley kids not to. Most of them were not able to make it in an academic school, and ultimately they ended up dropping out of school and getting a job. Maybe they disliked kids with books because it made them feel inferior. I don't know. All the kids did know that any kid who walked across the park with a book under his arm was going to get a beating.

At Berkeley High I still didn't bring books home. There was no drive for me to go to college. There was no way I could go to college, and I knew it. If college had been something important to me, if I had understood the importance of college, maybe things would have been different, but for a West Berkeley kid to go to college, well, there was no way. We didn't have the money.

I could have been a good student if I had wanted to, however. I know it because one year in English I got a B the first semester, and then the next semester I didn't do a thing and almost flunked the course, and I had to study like heck to get back up to a C-plus. In history I got straight A's because I liked it. That was true of all the subjects I liked. I loved botany, and I got good grades in it. Whatever I liked and worked at, I got good grades. But if I didn't like the subject . . .

As it was, I could have gone to Santa Clara University on an athletic scholarship. They were going to take Babe Van Huitt, who was the school's only three-letter man, and me as a package. But Babe decided to go into professional ball, and when he decided that, I did, too, and so neither of us went.

Because I was from West Berkeley, I wasn't comfortable socially at Berkeley High. It was a very cliquish school run by the rich kids from East Berkeley, who we called the goats, because East Berkeley was up in the hills. The goats ran the school, really. They were on the student council, were elected the class officers, and they got the good grades and went to college. They were in the social mainstream, and we weren't. The goats also dressed sharp. Everyone wore jeans, but they always had the expensive jeans, and they'd have several pairs of them. I had one pair, and mine were so stiff you could have stood them up in a corner by themselves. They wore work shirts, like we did, but they'd wear cashmere sweaters on top or expensive Navy flight jackets made out of leather. We wore T-shirts and the cheaper Navy pea jackets.

I was embarrassed about my clothes. The jeans I wore stood out because you could see the white seams, and as soon as we brought them home, we'd take dirt and try to run out the white lines. On Fridays I would wear my letter sweater and my one pair of slacks which got so shiny from ironing you could see your face in them, they would glisten so. In my own neighborhood it wasn't bad, because everyone wore the same thing. But going to school, it was tough, because you saw the difference, you wanted to wear what they were wearing, but you couldn't afford it. When I was a junior, I was made president of the Block B society, the Circle B, but I turned it down because of my clothes. It was quite an honor for a kid from West Berkeley to be head of all the junior varsity athletes, but I just didn't feel I had the proper clothes to be president.

My clothes was one of the reasons I didn't date much. Another reason, and no one will believe this, is that I was bashful when I was growing up. I remember one school dance we had in the junior high school gymnasium. All the girls stood on one side of the gym, and all the boys on the other. It had been quite a while before I got up the courage to ask this one girl, who I had been eyeing for a long time, to dance. I walked up to her, asked her for a dance, and she said no. Then a little later another guy went over and asked her, and she said yes to him. I said to myself, "That's the last time I'll ever ask a girl to dance." I'll never forget it because it made such a great impression on me. It was such a blow to my ego, and it was embarrassing because when I came back the guys hoorahed me. I said to myself, "That's it," and so I went through high school and didn't date one girl from there.

There was one girl, Mary Allan, who lived in our neighborhood, but we looked at her like she was one of the guys. She'd play horseshoes, capture the flag, jacks, touch tackle with us. She was a very good athlete, but I don't think anybody gave a thought about trying to mess around with her. There was one girl I *was* crazy about, but I never told her. She lived down the street from us in a large house. It looked like her family had money. I used to make a point always to walk down the street just at the time when she would be coming out of her house to go to school. I'd walk with her, or usually behind her, and I never said a word to her, except to say good morning. I was just crazy about her. She was beautiful, a brunette, well built, a beautiful face. She was very polite. Once in a while when she saw me, she'd say hello. But I never did ask her out. I was afraid to, afraid she'd say no and I'd be embarrassed.

I remember the first time I made love with a girl. I was the assistant playground director at the park, actually the supply boy—I gave out towels, and gloves, and balls—and there was this one girl who Howard Noble and I were always trying to mess around with, and finally we got her. I was so naive, I didn't even know where to put my peter. I thought the place was higher up. I was trying to put it in her belly button. After we finally did it, I felt so bad that I had sinned that I cried. I went to the Father and confessed. I told him, "Father, I have had relations with a woman who was not my wife." He said, "My son, that's why we have confession. The Lord knew that people were going to sin, and he understands." That made me feel better. I didn't touch her again for a long time.

In high school everything, including girls, took a back seat to sports. If I hadn't had that great love for sports, I would have been like most of my other buddies, I would have said the hell with school and quit and got a job. But I went to school every day, because we had games on Tuesdays and Thursdays, and to play you had to have attended the day before. I went on Friday because that was the day all the lettermen wore their letter sweaters and got dressed up. I remember during baseball season I'd ask my teacher if I could have a window seat, and during class I'd spend the time staring out onto the field. I'd watch it, imagining there was a game, and I'd look out hoping it wouldn't rain.

During the winter I played basketball. I didn't get to play football in the fall because Mom wouldn't sign the insurance forms. A kid in the neighborhood hurt his back playing football, so she wouldn't let me play, which was too bad because I always felt that football was my best sport. I could run, I could tackle, and I could hit hard. In basketball I wasn't very big, but I was very aggressive. When I was younger I had played for the St. Ambrose Church team. The coach of the team was Father Moore, the priest, a wonderful man who during the three weeks my father was on welfare had brought us groceries. We were playing St. Elizabeth's, and they were really roughing us up. We were playing on their court in Oakland, and they were giving us elbows and shoving us around, and here we were, West Berkeley kids, we weren't giving it to them back because we didn't want Father Moore to get upset by our rough play. Father Moore called time out. He said, "I thought you guys were from a rough town. How come you're letting them bounce you around like that?" I said, "We didn't want to hit them back in front of you. You know, turn the other cheek." He said, "Not in sports. You have to be just as aggressive as they are. When they give it to you, give it right back to them." The whistle blew, and we started playing, and we beat the living hell out of them. We lost the ball game, but they got a physical beating they never forgot. Boy, that made an impression on me.

My first two years of high school I played junior varsity basketball. My senior year I finally made the varsity, was all-county in fact, though in the middle of the season I got thrown off the team for getting into a fight.

Piedmont High School was another school where the wealthy kids went. We were playing them in their gym, and they had a kid named Tom Witter, a kid a lot bigger than I was, who kept agitating me, calling me "little Greek."

As the game went on, Witter kept saying, "After the game I'm going to get you, you little Greek." Why, I don't know. I guess my aggressiveness got in his hair. I was always all over the court. When there was a jump ball, I'd punch the ball as hard as I could. I wouldn't give any ground. Not an inch. In baseball I was the same way. I'd slide in hard and knock the infielders clear into left field.

We lost the game 27 to 25, and as we walked into the dressing room, I was doing a slow burn because we had lost. They made the mistake of putting both teams in the same locker room, and when Witter came in, he came over to my locker. "Hey, little Greek, I'm looking for you," he said. He swung, I hit him two or three times, and he went down in a pool of blood. That was the last high-school basketball game I ever played. They kicked me off the team.

I don't know what it is about me. I never went looking for fights. Believe me, if I could give a speech to every kid in the country on staying out of fights, I would. Fighting is nothing to be proud of. When you win, you lose, you've got nothing to gain, and right after it happens, you feel sorry about it. It's not something to be proud of. It's just something that has followed me, and I'd be a very happy man if I could shake it. But it just followed me, from childhood. I honestly believe if I had been six foot five, I'd have never been in a fight in my whole life. Who's going to pick on a guy six foot five? Have you ever seen anybody pick on a great big guy? That's why they say big guys are easygoing. Hell yes, if I was six five, I'd be easygoing too. But I was small, and they couldn't take a small guy bouncing them off the wall. They couldn't stand a little guy who didn't show any fear, because I showed no fear of anybody. And it would make them mad. Like I was making fun of them or something by beating them. I always felt, "Why should I fear anyone so long as I don't go out and start anything?" Everyone says it's a coincidence that I've been in so many fights and never started any of them. It isn't a coincidence. There's something about me that gets people's backs up. It was always that way. I think it comes from not having much as a kid, from struggling all your life. You feel that people are going to try to cheat you out of things, and you have to battle them for it. You get nothing for nothing. It's a constant struggle, and the funny part is that even when I'm on top, I feel it's still a struggle, because somebody's always trying to knock me off the top. Why, I don't know. You'll see that all through my baseball career, there was somebody trying to undermine me.

My high-school baseball career ended the same way as my high-school basketball career. My senior year we were playing Hayward High. Hayward was an archrival, and whether we were playing them in basketball or baseball, their fans always gave me a hard time. They taunted me about my big nose, called me Pinocchio, banana nose, tried to agitate me, but we beat them every time. One of the Hayward players, a kid by the name of Pete Hernandez, had told everyone at Hayward that he was going to whip my ass after the game. The kids from West Berkeley got wind of his threats, and we must have had a crowd of about four hundred of our kids at the game, the biggest crowd we ever had for a baseball game, because everyone wanted to see me and Hernandez go at it. During the game I singled. Hernandez was the first baseman, and a couple times the pitcher threw over, and I dived back into the bag, and Hernandez slammed his glove into me. He said, "I'm going to get you after the game." Scare tactics. "I'm going to whip your ass." I said, "I'll be right there, pal."

Everyone knew there was going to be a fight. I even told our coach about it. He said, "Don't go after him, but if he comes after you, take care of him." The game ended, I was the short-stop, and Hernandez came running my way. He took a swing at me, but I hit him three times hard to the face, knocked him cold. I tried to pick him up to hit him again, but the coach grabbed me and said, "Billy, he's had it. He's already out. Go to the locker room."

As we ran to the locker room, the Hayward fans threw rocks at me. My coach didn't want me to turn around or do anything. He rushed me into the clubhouse. Fights broke out all over the field. Our guys cleaned up on them, kicked hell out of their guys.

The school principal called me into his office the next day to tell me I was kicked off the team. He said, "You should have turned the other cheek." I said, "That's ridiculous. Turn the other cheek when he comes after you after he's told everybody he's going to beat you up?" When he told me I was off the team, I cried. How could I have turned the other cheek? The guy had come after me. It was cruel. I couldn't believe anyone could be so unfair.

CHAPTER
3

After the Yankees won the 1976 pennant, the off season should have been a time for rest, relaxation, enjoyment, and celebration. Instead, it ended up being a sad, depressing period of my life. After the series ended, I returned to Arlington, where my wife Gretchen and I shared a home with our son, Billy Joe, but before the end of the month, I saw I had to leave. Gretchen and I hadn't been compatible for about five years. We had married in 1959, and we set up house when I was playing for Minnesota. I loved it there, and we were so in love. Gretchen's from Nebraska, and she didn't like it much in Minnesota. She was away from her friends, and then we started moving, to Denver, back to Minnesota, then to Detroit, and just about the time I began managing in Detroit, our relationship began to change. She started spending a lot of time with her girl friends, and I'd come home from the ball park, and there wouldn't be any food on the table and she wouldn't be home, and so I started staying away. It wasn't completely her fault. You spend so many hours at the park, and for night games I'd come home maybe two-thirty in the morning, and it would be time to go to sleep, and I'd get up at eleven, and it would be time to go back to the park. I feel sorry for women who are married to baseball managers. It's tough enough to be married to a player. A manager has to be at the park earlier and go home later, and the owner can call you on the phone at any hour, and they sometimes forget you're a human being and that you'd like to have a life of your own. And then in the off season, I'd be going to banquets, and I'd want to go duck hunting and relax, and there was so little time. We'd argue all the time, about little silly things. If I put wood in the fireplace, she'd tell me I put too much wood in. Whatever I did, it wasn't good, I was wrong, and I was finding it more and more difficult to take. And the only reason I kept staying all those years, through all those arguments, was that my dad had left my mom before I was born, and I grew up not knowing my dad, and I didn't want that to happen to Billy Joe, who was about eight when we first started fighting. Billy Joe's quite a boy. I'd like to see him go to college, something I never did. He's a good enough baseball player to make a college team. He's small, but he's aggressive, likes to play. He's a hell of a kid in many ways, and I'm not saying that just because he's mine.

When I got home after the World Series the quarreling continued. We weren't communicating at all, but before, whenever we had a disagreement, we had it out in private so Billy Joe couldn't hear. We had made an agreement that we wouldn't talk around him. One afternoon we were talking, having an argument, and Gretchen said, "See, Billy Joe. See, Billy Joe, see what type of man your father is. See what he said." I don't even remember what it was we were arguing about, but when she said that I knew I had to leave. Billy Joe was thirteen, and he had his own friends, and he was spending a lot of time away from home playing sports, and so I knew he'd be all right, and I packed up and left. Gretchen and I are both very stubborn individuals, both very hard headed, and she wasn't about to call me, and I wasn't about to call her. So instead of going home for Christmas, I spent the winter living in the Hasbrouck Heights Sheraton in a hotel room, and I got very depressed. It bothered me all through 1977 and all through the next year, too. Every time we'd come home from a road trip, the players' wives would be waiting for them, and they'd go to their homes and their kids, and I'd be going back to another hotel.

Added to that, not two weeks later I got a call from my first wife, Lois. Our daughter Kelly was in trouble, she said. Lois and I had married in 1950 when we were just kids, and we had had a daughter, Kelly Ann, before we split up a couple years later. When Kelly was five years old, she used to get on a plane and come visit me, and while we were playing at home, she'd stay with me, and then when the team had to go on the road, I'd send her back home. It was very difficult because I really didn't get to see her much, and then Lois married a high-school friend of mine, and he's been a great father to Kelly, and I saw Kelly even less.

Kelly grew up with a chip on her shoulder that her mother and father had gotten divorced, and she started hanging around with the wrong crowd, and she got in trouble.

Lois told me Kelly Ann had been arrested in Colombia in South America trying to smuggle cocaine out of the country in her pantyhose. From what I got from the CIA and the FBI, a so-called friend had asked her to do this, and then when they got to customs, he turned her in to take the heat off him. He was taking a bigger amount out of the country, and when he squealed on her, he went free.

Immediately I contacted a Mexican coach who had South American contacts. He called Colombia, contacted people he knew, and he told me they were working to get her out. They almost succeeded. Colombia is a rip-off country, it's as corrupt a country as they come, a cocaine and marijuana heaven. Why the United States even recognizes it, I don't know. Anyway, we were about to get her out, but the day before, they found out that she was Billy Martin's daughter, and just as soon as they found that out, they put the clamps on her, and the police started acting real rough with her, and they really scared her. She was allowed to call me collect, and when she was telling me this, I felt so helpless, it was a terrible feeling. The police interrogated her, just harassed her. Meanwhile I hired some people in Texas who promised they could get her out. They said they needed $6,500, and so I sent it to them, and they gave it to some Colombian lawyers, and I never saw that money again. They just gobbled it up. Split it up among themselves. I sent more money through some other people, and that money went to lawyers, and that money was gone, too. It was graft on graft. Finally I went to a Colombian company, and I won't mention their name because they'd get in trouble, and through a friend in New York they got some more money, and this time they were able to get Kelly Ann out. She was down there almost two years. Altogether it cost me $32,000. They wanted more, but they finally settled for that. Throughout all this, I was talking to Kelly's mother and her husband, and it was the friendliest her mother and I had been in years. When your child gets in trouble, people come together. Kelly is very happy now. She's married, and she had a little daughter, and I'm very happy for her, happy as heck that she has a nice home and family, and that everything has turned out all right. During the winter after the Yankees won the 1976 pennant, I wasn't at all sure of what was going to happen to her.

There were times during that next season when I would think about Kelly, and I'd think about Gretchen, and I would become very sad. One night in Baltimore I came out onto the field, and two guys in the stands started yelling at me, "How's your daughter doing in jail, Billy?" Oh, man, I'm telling you, if I could have gotten up into the stands I would have wrung their necks. They were laughing. They thought it was funny. "How's your daughter doing? The police making love to her?" I'll tell you, these weren't baseball fans, these were no-good rats, yelling something like that at me from the stands. These types never get close enough where you can grab them. And I've got news for you, if I could have gotten ahold of these two guys, I would have pulled them right out of the stands, because that's one thing I won't tolerate, anyone badmouthing my family. And they could have thrown me out of baseball for all I cared. As far as I'm concerned, you're a man first and a manager second.

In December of 1977 was the first free-agent player draft. One thing I have to say about George Steinbrenner: After our four-in-a-row loss to the Reds he swore to me that he would go out and get me more pitching and another home-run hitter, and he promised he would put the Yankees back on top, meaning give us the personnel to win the World Series, and on this score he was a man of his word. First he signed Reds pitcher Don Gullett, as good a pitcher as they come when he's healthy, and not only did this help us, at the same time it significantly weakened the Reds, who had beaten us. George told me he was going after Gullett, and I told him great, we could use him. I was sitting with Gabe and George, and I suggested that we go after Joe Rudi, because our lineup included a bunch of lefties like Rivers, Chambliss, Nettles, and Oscar Gamble, and I felt our biggest need was another top-rate right-handed hitter to go with Thurman. George said, "No, we're going to get Reggie Jackson. I want Reggie Jackson." That was all there was to it. When George makes up his mind like that, it's rare when you can make him change it. Still, I was very happy when George signed Reggie, because we had added another big bat to our lineup. Whenever I had played against him, I always evaluated him with a great deal of respect. Reggie always hit well against my clubs, and now he was going to be on my side.

The only thing I didn't like were the comments I read in the newspaper when we first got Reggie. George was taking Reggie to the 21 Club for lunch all the time, and I was sitting across the river in my hotel room the entire winter, and George hadn't taken me out to lunch even once. Reggie told a reporter, "It's going to be great with the Yankees because George and I are going to get along real good, and that's very important." I said to myself, "You're going to find out that George isn't the manager."

When spring training opened, Reggie was, well, Reggie. Every day he had the newspaper guys around him, and he would be doing everything he could to get his name in the papers. He was out to let everybody know he was going to be the leader, that the other guys better move over because Reggie was here.

About the third day of spring training I called Reggie into my office for a chat. I tried to tell him that a real leader does his leading on the field, not in the clubhouse. I told him, "You just feel at home here and do your own thing. If you do your job nobody will bother you." And I told him I hoped there wouldn't be dissension between him and Thurman Munson, who was getting bad vibes from the way Reggie was talking to the press all the time, telling them how he was going to be the big man. Thurman had been the Most Valuable Player of the league the year before, and he just didn't like the way Reggie was always talking about himself. Thurman was the Yankee captain, but he hadn't really wanted it. I had asked him to take it, had to talk him into it. But Thurman was very quiet, kind of kept to himself, and wasn't a very good speaker. With Reggie, on the other hand, the press would walk in the clubhouse door, and in seconds everyone would be standing around Reggie, and Thurman just didn't understand where Reggie was coming from.

When Reggie first came to the Yankees he was no problem. He came to camp a little overweight, but that bothered George, not me. George has this thing about weight. If a guy shows up five pounds overweight, he threatens to fine him if he doesn't lose the weight in ten days. He did that to a lot of them. He has the players going through weight training during the winter. If he had his way, George would have track meets in spring training camp, and everybody would pull leg muscles. During the spring, though, Reggie did everything I asked him to do, and when he had a problem, he'd come in and talk, and I would try to help him with his problems as best I could. In the exhibition games I would bat Reggie all up and down the batting order, anywhere from second in the order to seventh, depending on what I was trying to accomplish that day. Reggie always wanted to bat fourth, which is the traditional spot for the big hitter on the team, and when he saw he wasn't going to bat fourth every game, Reggie became upset, though he didn't say anything about it to me. He didn't like it, though, and neither did George, but I really didn't care. I was the manager, and I have always picked a batting order that was best for the team, and I wasn't about to change now. Besides, spring-training lineups don't mean a thing. You're simply trying to get guys in there to swing the bat, to get into shape for the season.

Though there were no problems between Reggie and me, I could see that the fact that George had given him a three-million-dollar contract was going to cause a lot of trouble. No one had complained when George gave Catfish Hunter more than two million dollars to sign, and no one who I know of was bitter about Don Gullett getting two million, because both those guys keep their mouth shut and do their job and try not to make waves, and nobody resented them. Reggie, on the other hand, was another story, and I'm not sure why, except that he liked to act like he was superior to the other guys, and he'd always be talking about his money, and just by his being Reggie he was pissing the other guys off.

From the start of spring training I was having trouble with Mickey Rivers, and this usually happens when Mickey is having money troubles. I loved Mickey like a son, but sometimes he'd decide he wasn't going to play, and there wasn't anything anyone could do to make him if he didn't want to. I wanted Phil Rizzuto, who was the best bunter ever to play baseball, to teach Mickey how to drag bunt, but Mickey wouldn't do it. "I know how to bunt, and I don't want anybody teaching me nothing and messing me up." I said, "Mickey, we're just trying to help you better yourself." He said, "I won't do it." And that was that. When he was upset about money, he'd become moody, and he wouldn't run out ground balls and wouldn't play well in the field, and sometimes I'd have to lend him some money just so he'd feel better about things.

At the start of spring training I held a meeting and told the team that if anyone didn't hustle, I wouldn't fine him, I'd embarrass him by yanking him right off the field. "I'm going to take you right out, in front of all those people and I'm going to embarrass you just like you embarrass me," I said. Before March was over I yanked Mickey out of one game because he didn't run out a ground ball, and he was the leadoff batter in the game. The pitcher threw one pitch, Mickey hit a ground ball and sort of half-assed it down the line, and I pulled him right out and made him sit with me on the bench the rest of the game. Three days later Mickey loafed after a couple fly balls he should have caught, and I yanked him again.

Though Mickey never mentioned Reggie's money, I know that Reggie's contract didn't sit well with Thurman. George had promised Thurman that he would always be the highest-paid Yankee, and on straight salary Thurman was making more than Reggie. But Thurman found out Reggie was making several hundred thousand in deferred payments, and he became really angry with George. Called him names, really felt George had lied to him. Graig Nettles was another guy who was complaining about his contract. He had signed a contract, and in it George had suggested that he defer some of his money and George told him how to do it, and Graig agreed to it, but after he signed it he seemed to think George's advice was the worst advice possible and would cost him a ton of dough, and so he wanted George to rewrite his contract, which George wouldn't do. I felt like I was back in Texas again, with all the guys screaming about their contracts. Dock Ellis was another guy who felt he should be getting more money. Dock was another guy who wouldn't take any shit from anybody, and he got into it with George, and I didn't want to lose Dock, but George got it into his head that Dock was gone, and by the end of April he was.

Dock liked to wear an earring, and one day he was standing in front of his locker wearing his earring when George walked in. George told him to take the earring off, and Dock told him that if George didn't watch out he'd wear the earring on the field when he was pitching. That was it for Dock. George had wanted to get rid of Stanley, boy, and without him we could never have repeated, because of all the injuries we had during the season. That spring George also wanted to get rid of Ron Guidry. He didn't like Guidry at all. He kept saying, "I got to get rid of him, he can't pitch, I got to get rid of that skinny kid. I'm telling you right now he can't pitch."

Gabe and I knew he was wrong. I had heard a lot about him when I first came to the Yankees, and when I saw him there was no doubt in my mind that he had a big arm. There was no question about it. He was used in relief, and every once in a while he started, and he was having trouble with his control. In spring training things went very badly for him. He couldn't get anybody out. He couldn't get the ball over, and when he did, they hit it nine miles. He'd ease up to get the ball over, and boom. I called Ron into my office and talked with him, and he told me he never had a good spring training, that it always had been that way. One day we had a two-run lead against the Detroit Tigers in Fort Lauderdale, and Ronnie went in and blew the game, and George really got down on him, started talking about getting rid of him. And I think if there had been a general manager from another club right there at the time, he could have gotten him for practically nothing. A few days later Guidry came in again and gave up a two-run home run in the ninth to Jim Rice to lose another game, and I thought George was going to have a stroke. He was sitting with Gabe telling Gabe that he had to get rid of Guidry, and Gabe kept telling him about his great arm, and the great speed he had. I tried to tell George what Ron had told me, that he never has a great spring training, that some guys you can't measure during spring training. Of course, George will deny this, and I don't think Ronnie felt I was behind him. After one game I was agitating him, and I told him, "You tell me one player you can get out, and I'll let you pitch to him." It was frustrating to see him go out there and get hit like that, and I was trying to get him mad, make him battle a little harder. Once the season got under way, of course, Ron Guidry turned out to be one of the best pitchers in baseball.

During spring training George was ranting and raving every day because we weren't winning, or because I wasn't doing something he wanted me to do. The man was driving me crazy. He wanted me to do all these things, and I knew they were wrong, and yet he was the owner of the team. It was a very uncomfortable spot to be in, but I felt that the team came before anything or anyone, including him, and I was going to do what was right, no matter what.

George's problem is that he looks at baseball like a football coach. He goes around telling everybody he was once assistant coach at Purdue, that he was the big man in college football. You know what his job really was? I heard he was in charge of getting tickets for the families of the football players! But he wants me to run the team like a football team. He wants all the players to eat dinner in the same dining room at the same time every night, and he wants the players in bed by ten, and he wants me to play my regulars a lot during spring training to get them ready for the season. Well, if you play everybody in spring training every day, they'll be burned out by July. A man can't play every day for 190 games. The mental fatigue alone of putting on the uniform and taking it off is great. Plus we're traveling all the time, and the time differences screw up your eating and sleeping, two days you're in one town, and boom, you're flying to the other end of the country, and it takes an awful lot out of a player. And these are things I don't think George will ever understand.

He thinks it's so important to win during spring training, and he's so wrong it's ridiculous. He's already got his season-ticket sales in. I told him over and over, "George, if we have a .500 exhibition season, everything is fine." He'd say, "No. We got to win down here. We got to win down here. It's important. Gotta have that momentum, that drive going into the season." I'd say, "George, forget about that." I played under Casey Stengel during the period when the Yankees won every year, and we never had a winning spring training. We didn't try to win. Casey would play us for four or five innings, give us an at bat or two, and he'd let us gradually work ourselves into shape. He knew we had a lot of games to play, and he wanted us strong all the way through September. That's why I don't push the players during spring training. I want them strong when it counts.

During spring training after a game if one of the players messed up, George would call down screaming, "You get him into your office and fine the son of a bitch." I'd say, "Okay, George, sure," and I'd hang up the phone on him. I wouldn't ever call the player in and humiliate him like he wanted me to. George didn't care who the guy was, whether it was Nettles or Munson, or a minor league kid, if he made an error or a stupid play, George thought he should be fined. If you do that, you end up losing your players. They're not going to bust their butt for someone who's fining them all the time. You want players to be relaxed and respect you and give you their best. What good was fining them? He'd be telling me, "You're not strong enough on this guy or that guy. Fine him." I said, "That's what makes you strong?" He said, "That's what we did in college. Straightened out those college boys." Sis boom bah.

George was always sticking his nose into things. One time I gave a few of the players permission to pick their wives up at the Fort Lauderdale airport. We were playing an exhibition game, and he wanted to know where Chris Chambliss was. I said, "He's picking his wife up at the airport." He said, "You can't let him do that." Or when a wife was leaving, I'd let the player take her to the airport, and that would make George madder'n hell.

It's amazing how he can be such a cutthroat when it comes to families. During spring training I'd let the players take their little boys out onto the field, and that would drive George up a wall. "Get those kids off there," he'd be screaming.

But the worst part of his being around was that I knew that when I said something, no matter what it was or whether he was knowledgeable or not, George would be sitting back there second-guessing. One time a player hurt his leg, and I didn't play him that day. When George saw he wasn't in the game he called down to the team doctor in the middle of the game and ordered him to check out the player right away. "Let us know right now how many days it's going to be," he shouted. The doctor looked at the player, and of course there was no way he could predict how long he'd be out. I thought his injury was pretty serious, and I told George he should be put on the disabled list, so we could bring up another player while he was recuperating. George, however, forced the doctor to give him an estimate of how long the player would be out, and the doctor estimated ten days. I said, "George, I've had that type of injury, and he'll be out two to three weeks." But George wouldn't listen to me. A week went by, and the player wasn't close to being ready, and another week, and finally George says, "It looks like we're going to have to put him on the disabled list." I told George, "It's too late to do that. You should have done that two weeks ago. Don't put him on now, he'll be ready in another week." And he was.

It wasn't bad enough that during a game George would sit in his box, and if a player made a mistake he'd throw up his hands and act like a murder had just been committed, and after a game he'd get on the phone and scream and yell about fining players—what would make me angrier than all his silly foolishness was his sending notes down to me during the middle of the game, telling me who to play, telling me what to do. Why the hell had George hired me? What did he need a manager for? If he was so smart, why wasn't he managing the team himself?

Cedric Tallis, the assistant general manager, would come down to the dugout, and he'd have a note from George with statistics on it. It would say: "Does Billy know that Nettles is 0 for 11 against Rudy May this year? Does he know Willie Randolph hasn't hit him? Does he know that Chambliss hasn't hit him? Does he know that Munson hasn't hit him? Does he know Rivers hasn't hit him?" I'd read this, and I'd say to Cedric, "Does George want me to take them all out of the lineup?" He'd say, "No. No, he just wants you to know this." One time I told Cedric to tell George to stick his statistics you-know-where. Him and his stupid statistics. What the hell did he want me to do, tell Thurman, "Excuse me, but you can't hit this guy. I got to take you out of there. George doesn't want you in there."

Finally, I told Cedric, "No more notes. Don't come down here anymore." He said, "I gotta, he's going crazy up there." I said, "Let him go crazy."

Cedric would leave and I'd take George's statistics and dump them right into the wastebasket. George would say, "See, Billy looks at my stats." But I wouldn't. I'd throw them away all the time.

A batting average doesn't always denote how good a player is. One year the Boston Red Sox had seven .300 hitters, and they came in second. What would George say about that? It doesn't matter to me what their average is. One year a batter could be 0 for 14 against a pitcher, and the next year he could go 10 for 14. It doesn't always follow a pattern. But in football, coaches send messages down to their assistants, and so George feels he has to always be sending messages down to the dugout. It's so stupid, him and his stupid statistics.

The other really big problem I had with George was that he decided that Reggie Jackson should bat fourth in the lineup every day. Reggie never gave me any problem with that. Oh, writers would come over and ask me, "How do you feel about Reggie complaining he isn't batting fourth?" I'd say, "I don't care what he's complaining about, I bat him where I think he should bat." Reggie never gave me any trouble at all. Sure, he didn't like it, but on every club I ever managed there were players who didn't like what I was doing, until we won at the end. When I pick a lineup, I'm doing what's best for the club. I wanted Chris Chambliss to bat fourth, the same spot he batted in 1976, because Chris makes good contact with the ball, he has a higher average than Reggie, he doesn't strike out nearly as much, and he isn't as likely to break up a rally as a result.

I had no dislike for Reggie Jackson. It wasn't anything personal at all, and if George would have kept his nose out of it, everything would have worked out fine. It's just that Reggie had it in his head that he was more important than the ball club, and I felt the other way. He was just one of twenty-five players, no more important than Thurman Munson, or Chris Chambliss, or even Fred Stanley. Look at the plays Nettles made, or Mickey Rivers, or Willie Randolph or Roy White or Lou Piniella. I could name every player on the club who did a good job, and that doesn't even include the pitchers. But here was a guy who wanted everyone to think he was the guy, period, and it didn't work that way. At least as the manager I didn't see it that way.

But I can't say it often enough that it was nothing personal. I understood how Reggie was, that whatever club he played on it was the same thing, a pattern he goes through, to let everyone know he's the best and most important. So it didn't bother me. All I asked him to do was play hard, and he did, and so long as he did, he was going to play. And if I wanted him to bat fifth, he'd bat fifth. If I felt he should DH, he'd DH. Reggie was not going to dictate to me how I should play him.

Neither was George. All the time George would be on the phone to me. "Billy, I don't know why you got Chambliss fourth." "Because I want him there, George." He'd say, "Reggie should be batting there." I said, "No, George, I don't think so, George." Who was it who hit the home run off Mark Littell to win the pennant for us the year before? George didn't remember that. But if Chris would strike out with men on base, that he wouldn't let me forget.

Every day I would make up a different lineup depending on who was swinging the bat really good and who was pitching against us. I'd consider which club was coming in, whether the other pitcher had ever faced us before, whether the pitcher was righty or lefty, experienced or not, who on our club hit him well. Those are the things you consider when making out a lineup, and I keep a record of all those things. Roy White may have gotten three hits the night before, but today we may be facing a pitcher he can't hit, so he sits. People wonder why. And these are the things I know when I'm managing a game, and this is why I didn't want George Steinbrenner, or anybody else, giving me stupid statistics or telling me how to make up a batting order.

It was the same thing when I was lifting our pitchers. George would be second-guessing me all the time. He has statistics for that, too. Again, averages don't tell you everything. When a team comes in, I want to know several things: Who's the hot hitter, on what count does the team suicide-squeeze, which batter does it the most, which batter hits-and-runs the most, what count does he do it on. When you're talking to your pitcher, you can't just say to him, "I want you to pitch to this batter by throwing the ball low." The pitcher might say, "But I only throw high. I can't get him out that way. I get him out this way." So what's the point of calling in the whole staff and telling them how to pitch to a batter? Instead you call in the catcher and that one pitcher, and the three of you discuss what you want to do that day. The pitcher tells me who he gets out easily and who he can't, and then in the middle of the game when there are runners on base, and I have to make a decision whether to take him out or not, I know what's going on. Also, a batter the day before could have gone 0 for 4. That means nothing. They could have been four line drives or some super catches could have been made. This is why it's important to know who's been hot. Sometimes a club comes in, and their best hitter has been in a slump, and they have a man on second and one out, and I'll pitch to him instead of walk him because I know he's in the slump. Next time the team comes in, he may have started hitting again, and the next time I'll walk him in the same situation. But with George, or any other general manager or owner—I wasn't hired to give baseball clinics, I was hired to manage a ball club. Maybe George didn't like the way I managed. I didn't care. What had he ever won? What had he ever done, except to sit up in the stands and second-guess? Now if it was Joe McCarthy or Miller Huggins or Casey Stengel sitting up there or somebody who had been successful in baseball, maybe I'd have listened. But I don't want to be listening to a guy who's a born second-guesser, somebody who doesn't know much about the game, somebody who knows just enough to make himself dangerous. You know it's so much easier to second-guess. The world is full of second-guessers. Every time I make a move, there are thirty thousand second-guessers in the stands, and that's fine. That's one of the fun parts about going to the ballgame, pretending you're the manger, seeing whether what the manager does works out or not. But when the guy who owns the team is always second-guessing, that's a different story. How would he like it if I was making judgments on every single thing he was doing? He should manage a team for one game and sit on that bench and have to make a decision during the middle of a game. He'd be down there about three innings, and he'd sing a different tune about second-guessing.

One time George called me after a game, and I got so mad I pulled the phone right out of the wall. George called the trainer to find out what was wrong with the phone, to find out why it wasn't working. The trainer said, "Billy just pulled it out of the wall."

George said, "Okay, tell him I'll call him tomorrow."

March hadn't even ended, when George and I got into it, and I was almost fired before the season began. George was always on me to ride with the players on the bus to and from the exhibition games. I told him, "I don't like riding on the bus. I ride with my coaches behind the bus, and after a game we can discuss the players, go over a young kid, decide whether or not to send him down, and I don't have to worry about who's overhearing my conversation, because if we go on the bus then we can't talk about the confidential stuff, and after we get back we have to go down to my office and do what we could have been doing on the way home."

George said, "You should be on that bus. I want you on it."
So finally he broke me down and I told him if it meant so much
to him I'd take the bus. We were playing the Mets in St. Pe-
tersburg, and we had scheduled a bus to take us to a practice
field where we could get in some extra batting practice.
George had donated lights to a college in the town, and he had
gotten us permission to practice there. Before the practice
George and I were talking on the phone about things, and the
bus was scheduled to leave at eleven-thirty, and I have a rule
that the bus leaves on time no matter who's late, including me.
Well, George and I were talking, and it gets to be later than
eleven-thirty, and the bus leaves without me, and I have to
drive to the practice field. I watched practice, and then I drove
in my rental car with the traveling secretary, Bill Kane, and
with Mickey Mantle, who was visiting me, to the stadium
where we played the Mets, and we lost on TV. Got shut out 6
to 0. He goes crazy when we lose to the Mets, even if it's
spring training. He feels we're going to lose fans to them if
they beat us. It's ridiculous, and it makes the players laugh at
him.

Apparently George found out I had driven to the game. He
didn't know why I had missed the bus in the first place. He
didn't know that I had driven to the practice field. All he
wanted to know was that I had driven to the game, and he had
told me not to.

At the end of the game George had told Kane, "Go get his
keys. Take that car away from him," and like a little kid he sent
Kane to the clubhouse to get them. Kane came into the clubhouse and said, "George is steaming, Billy. He wants me to get
your car keys." I said, "You're not getting any keys, Bill." He
said, "I know that." Mickey was sitting in my locker, changing,
and I'm sitting next to him when George and Gabe came
charging into the locker room. "You," George screamed at me,
"I want to talk to you." In front of all the players like I'm
nothing. I told him if he wanted to talk, we could go into the
trainer's room. We went in there, and he ran all the players
out, but they could still hear him because he was still screaming. "You told me you were going to take the bus," he said. He

was mad because we had lost to the Mets. I said, "Number one, I told you why I don't like taking the bus. Number two, I was talking to you on the telephone, and I missed the bus and had to drive."

He yelled, "I don't care. You lied to me. Get Yogi in here. I want to get this straight."

Yogi came in and George asked him, "Yogi, when you managed, did you ride in the bus?" Yogi said, "No." George was shocked. "You didn't ride in the bus?" Yogi said, "No. I liked to ride in a car with my coaches so we could talk, just like Billy does." George said, "I can't understand this. I don't know what I'm going to do, Martin. I'm fed up with all of this. . . ."

I knew the players could hear what he was saying, and I was starting to get really mad myself. I said, "I'm going to tell you something. I'm the manager of this team, and don't you be coming into my clubhouse again for any reason, coming in and telling me what I should do or not do and calling me a liar. You get your ass out right now! If you want to fire me, go ahead and fire me right goddamned now." I was standing right next to the ice bucket that the pitchers put their arms in after a game, and I took my fist and slammed it into that ice bucket, and the ice flew up into George's hair and into Gabe's pockets, and George said, "I don't know, Gabe, I think we ought to fire . . ." I screamed at him, "I don't give a shit if you do fire me, but you're not going to come in here and tell me what to do in front of my players. Now or ever."

Gabe didn't say anything, and they finally left, and when they walked out I figured I was gone. But after the notes during the game, and the second-guessing, and the silly nonsense, this was the straw that broke my back, his coming in and acting like a spoiled child, yelling at me over a stupid thing just because we had lost to the Mets in spring training, which is a joke as far as I'm concerned.

Mickey felt really bad. I had never seen him feel so down in his whole life. He thought he had caused my getting fired, because I had driven with him to the game. I told him, "Mickey, this has nothing to do with you. This is George's stupid way of acting up like a little kid." We went back to the hotel and had a couple of drinks, and Mickey was really depressed. He felt so bad he got on a plane and flew back to his home in Dallas. He said, "I just feel bad about this."

The next day Gabe called me on the phone. "George wants us to meet and have breakfast over at my house." I went over to Gabe's, and George had calmed down, which he does after he thinks about what he's done.

George said, "Sorry about yesterday, Billy. It was my fault. I shouldn't have done that." He said, "Geez, Billy, we talk about things, and you gotta be doing these things." I said, "George, can't you get it through your head that it's stupid to ride the bus." He frowned. I said, "If it makes you happy for me to ride a lousy bus, I'll do it." Another thing I promised him was the next spring training I'd stay at the hotel with the players instead of living in an apartment. "If that will make you happy, I'll do that, too," I said. "Once in a while, though, when we get near cutdown time, I'd like to ride in that car, because when we get back to the ball park everyone scatters and I'd like to talk with them when things are fresh in my mind. I want to talk to my coaches right then. Is that OK?" George said, "Okay, Billy, that's fine with me." We left on friendly terms. If he would only think before blowing up and acting like a little kid, it would be easier on everyone. He's like a little kid who keeps kicking on the door until he gets his way.

Spring training ended on a quiet note, but there was an incident with Reggie that left me a little shook. Reggie and I had sat in my office, and he asked if I would please give him a lot of playing time. He had come to camp overweight, and he wanted to work the weight off and get into playing shape. Every few games I'd have one of my coaches ask him if he wanted a rest, and Reggie would tell him, no, he wanted to play. Towards the end of the spring training games one of the New York reporters asked Reggie why he had been playing so much, because ordinarily the managers don't play the starters all that much. Reggie told him, "I don't know why I'm playing every day. Why don't you ask the manager?" That shocked the hell out of me, and it started me wondering about him a little bit, what motivates this guy, what moves him. One day he'd come to the park, and he'd be great, and the next day he'd say something like that. I got to thinking that sometimes there are really two Reggies. Sometimes he'd switch from one Reggie to the other so quickly. The good Reggie was there most of the time, but I found out that every once in a while the other Reggie would come out, and that's when there'd be trouble.

We opened the season losing our first two out of three to the Milwaukee Brewers, and after the third game I'll be damned if George didn't call me to ask why we had a losing record. Reggie had hurt his arm during the exhibition season, and he was having a hard time swinging, especially against certain lefties he had trouble against anyway, and it made my decision to bench him against certain pitchers that much easier. When we faced left-handed pitchers who came from the side with a big breaking ball, I preferred to play Roy White, who was a switch-hitter and who could bat righty against them. Against lefties who came over the top, like Vida Blue, usually I would play Reggie, because he had less trouble with them. One game I sat Reggie against Frank Tanana, for instance, and I had a meeting with George, and the next day I played Reggie against Blue, and everyone was saying it was George who made me play Reggie that day. That wasn't true, but I'm not about to explain to anybody why I do what I do. A reporter will say to me, "Why did you do that?" I'll say, "Because I wanted to." Should I have to be a baseball clinic every day? I did it because it was the move that gave us the best chance to win the ball game.

Sometimes George would call me and tell me I was at fault for not treating Reggie like a superstar. I'd say, "I treat him according to how he plays. If he doesn't hit, he doesn't play, and he's no different from any of the other players." You can't go around patting someone on the back who doesn't deserve it. The other players will laugh at you. They know what's bullshit and what isn't. They're men, not little boys. I had a duty to twenty-five men, including Reggie, to play the combination I felt would most likely get us a victory. And that's exactly what I did all the way through.

We weren't hitting, and in late April I did what I had done in Denver. Everyone was tense, and no one was hitting, and they were moaning about where they were batting in the order, so I wrote down the names of all the guys in the starting lineup on pieces of paper, and I threw them in a hat. I was sitting with Reggie at the time, and I told him to start picking names. "C'mon, let's do it," I said. He picked Randolph first, and Munson was second, and he was the third name out and then Nettles, with Rivers fifth, Roy sixth, Carlos May seventh, Chris eighth, and Bucky Dent, who we had gotten from Chicago for Oscar Gamble, batting ninth. Reggie got a big kick out of it. I told him, "The way you pick 'em, that's the way it's going to be." We won six straight games with that lineup, and in less than two weeks we were in first place. Batting in the eighth spot, Chris drove in more runs than anybody. I kept telling them, "See, where you hit doesn't mean a thing. It's just a reason to make alibis and excuses for your not hitting." Of course, Chris never cared where I batted him. I wish I had a whole town of Chris Chamblisses. Chris would say, "I don't care, Skip, bat me anyplace you like."

On April twenty-seventh George finally got rid of Dock Ellis. Gabe had suffered a slight stroke, but fortunately he was still well enough to keep an eye on what George was doing. As soon as Charley Finley saw Gabe was in the hospital, he saw the opportunity to deal directly with George. Finley knew George was anxious to trade Ellis, and he had a pitcher, Mike Torrez, who he wanted to trade because he hadn't signed or something. Finley told George he'd trade him Torrez for Ellis and Sparky Lyle. George and Sparky weren't on the best of terms, and George was willing, but Gabe and I talked him out of it. The next deal Finley proposed was Torrez and Bill North for Ellis and Mickey Rivers. George wanted to do that one, too, but again Gabe talked him out of it. Finley then tried Torrez for Ellis, Ron Guidry, and Mickey Kluttz, and George was really hot for that deal. Guidry hadn't done a thing except get banged around during spring training, and Kluttz was a shortstop who had broken his hand, and George figured he wasn't giving away a thing. Again, Gabe came to the rescue. They finally settled on Torrez for Ellis, Marty Perez, who became expendable when we got Dent, and a minor leaguer. Without

Lyle, Rivers, or Guidry, we never would have won the pennant. Thank God for Gabe.

After the trade Torrez had to see his wife, who was sick, and it took him a few days to arrive. George leaked it to the papers that I wanted to fine Torrez $500 a day for not reporting. But of course, it was George and his love for fining players, not me. Meanwhile, I didn't have anyone to start a game against the Seattle Mariners, and I decided to give Guidry a chance, and Guidry pitched a shutout for eight and a third innings and was as good as I could ever have hoped him to be. From then on it was just a question of getting Ron to finish what he started. George kept telling me, "He's too weak. He can't finish a ball game." I said, "That isn't true." He'd say, "Take a look at his past record" and all the stuff which means nothing. I was telling him, "He's going to be an excellent pitcher for us, George," and George would say, "He can't finish a game. Mark my words." You're dealing with a human being, not a machine, and his calculators and computers can't measure a guy's heart and his toughness, and if Guidry has anything it's heart and toughness. Guidry pitched about five games where he went until the eighth but couldn't finish. One day he had a big lead, and I decided that he was going to finish no matter what happened, even if it meant our losing the game. It was really scary at the end, too. The other team scored a couple runs, but Guidry struck out the last two hitters, and when he walked off the mound, I told him, "You're over the hump now." You have to do that with players, show your confidence in them, and once they feel confident they can do it, nothing can stop them. Guidry's as complete a pitcher as there is in baseball, and I'm as proud of him as anyone.

We were still in first place the second week in May when it became clear to me that Thurman Munson needed a rest. We had one other catcher, Fran Healy. Gabe had sent Elrod Hendricks, who we had gotten from the Orioles in the Holtzman trade, to Syracuse, and I needed him back with the Yankees desperately to give me added maneuverability. I called Gabe and told him Thurman was hurting and would he please send me Hendricks. Instead he sent me Del Alston, an outfielder. I said to myself, "How many times do I have to go through this? I went through it in Detroit and in Texas and now in New York. Why are they always fighting me over these utility players? Why won't they give me who I want?"

We were playing in Seattle, and a reporter asked me about Alston, and I gave the guy an honest answer. I told him, "I don't want an outfielder. I need a catcher." It came out in the paper, Martin Knocks Front Office, which was a lot of bullshit.

We flew back to New York the next day, and that afternoon I was talking to Gabe on the telephone for about two hours, and at the end of our conversation he said, "I want to meet with you tonight." I said, "I'm sorry, Gabe, but I have a seven-thirty appointment, and I can't meet you." He pleaded with me. "I'll drive across the George Washington Bridge, and you can meet with me for just five minutes. Please meet with me." It didn't make any sense. We had just talked about everything on the phone. Gabe said, "I've been told I gotta meet you, and if I don't it's going to be trouble." I said, "You want me to drive a half hour to the bridge just to meet you for a couple of minutes?" He said, "That's right." I said, "No, Gabe, I'm not going to do that." He kept insisting, "Please meet me, please meet me," but I wouldn't. The next day I was fined $2,500 for my comments in the papers about Hendricks and for not meeting with Gabe. I don't know which of them fined me, because when I asked Gabe, he said it was George, and when I asked George, he said it was Gabe. The way Gabe was talking, however, I'm pretty sure it was George forcing Gabe to do it. I don't blame Gabe. Gabe and I always worked very well together. Gabe's a very knowledgeable baseball man, and I've always had a great deal of respect for him.

The next week we were playing the Orioles, and in the middle of the game Lee May slammed into Thurman and knocked him out of the game. The score was tied, we had a man on second and one out, with Randolph, Rivers, and Fran Healy scheduled to bat. As I sat in the dugout, I was picturing the situation coming up. If Randolph struck out, Oriole manager Earl Weaver would be laughing at me. He'd walk Mickey Rivers because he'd know I didn't have another catcher and

Healy, who was hitting around .200, would have to bat. If Hendricks had been on the bench, I could have pinch hit for Healy. Sure enough, that's almost exactly what happened, and we didn't score. Two days later Hendricks was with the Yankees.

A couple days later we lost one of those games that come along every once in a while, a game that really gets to you. Ordinarily I'm very good about talking to the press after a game, but after this game I didn't want to talk to anybody. I told them, "Look, I'm really uptight right now. I don't want to give any interviews." I walked into the players' lounge, which is off limits to the press.

Dick Young of the *Daily News* came late. When he didn't see me, he walked to the door of the lounge, and he said to me, "Aren't you coming out to talk to us?" I said, "No, Dick, I just told the other guys that I'm not talking today." He said, "Come on, quit acting like a little kid. Come out and talk." I said, "Dick, don't be telling me how to act." You have to understand that one of Dick Young's pet peeves are my clubhouse rules. During the 1976 World Series the players had been complaining that the reporters were bothering them while they were taking batting practice, and so I had our ground crew put up a rope to keep the reporters back. Dick didn't like that, and he made a big scene. This time he began walking into the lounge, which is a no-no. I said, "Dick, get behind the door." He played dumb. He said, "What do you mean?" I said, "You know the rules. No reporters in the players' lounge." He said, "That's a silly rule." So I picked him up and bodily put him on the other side of the door. I said, "If you come through that door again, I'm going to punch you through it. You know the rules, and you know them better than any other writer, you complain about them enough, now keep your ass out of here." He went up to George, complaining. I tell Dick, "I'll let you in the lounge when your newspaper allows you to write your own headlines." Apparently they have a way of doing things. So do I.

Everything was fine until the June issue of *Sport* magazine hit the stands. It was the last week of May, and whatever the players thought about Reggie before that article came out, when they saw the terrible things he said about Thurman, there was certainly a great deal of animosity toward him after it came out. A couple of the players came to me and told me what was in the article and asked me if I'd read it. I told them no, I hadn't, and I didn't intend to. After it came out I talked to Reggie about it. He told me he didn't mean for it to come out the way it did, so hard and strong against Thurman. Reggie acted like he wished it had never come out. I went and talked to Thurman about it, and he made it clear he would never forgive Reggie for it, and I don't think he ever did. It always stuck in his craw. Right after the article came out, Reggie hit a home run, and when he crossed the plate he headed for the corner of the dugout and refused to shake anyone's hand. I'm sure he was mad because of the way the other players reacted to the article. Also, he had been in a slump, and I kept him out of the lineup a couple times, and he was probably mad at me. But those are the moods Reggie goes through sometimes. That's Reggie. And other times he'd come right up and put his arms around me and hug me.

My only complaint with Reggie really was that his fielding was beginning to hurt the team. When he had played against me, I never noticed that he wasn't a very good fielder because his bat was so noticeable, his hitting was what we had concentrated on stopping. But when the pressure after that article began to get to him, his fielding began to really hurt the team. In late innings I started putting Paul Blair out there for him. And I could tell when he was in the field, his mind wasn't on what he was doing, because he just wasn't hustling. He was telling me he was, but I could see he wasn't. I know a player who isn't hustling when I see one. He was getting a bad jump on the ball, and a couple times he kicked the ball around before he was able to field it, and line drives began falling in front of him, hits he should have caught. By mid-June we had fallen behind the Red Sox by a couple of games. It was nothing serious. We had a long way to go, but we were having a lot of trouble against left-handed pitchers. Teams were bringing up lefties from the minors just to pitch against us, and they were beating us. We were 25-11 against righties and only 10-15 against lefties, which was why I wanted Joe Rudi instead of Reggie. We desperately needed another right-handed bat.

We were playing an important series against the Red Sox June seventeenth, eighteenth and nineteenth at Fenway Park, and we were playing terribly. Our pitching just wasn't doing the job, and we got beat bad in the Friday night game. On Saturday the Red Sox hit five home runs, and we were losing 7 to 4 in the sixth inning and they had a man on first with one out. Jim Rice hit a soft fly ball out to Reggie in right, and after he jogged toward the ball, he fielded it on about the fiftieth hop, took his sweet time throwing it in, and made a weak throw in the general direction of the pitcher's mound. Rice, who was really hustling, made it worse when he raced into second on the throw. During the season I had yanked Mickey Rivers out of games when he didn't hustle, and I felt it should be no different with Reggie. I had told everybody what I was going to do in spring training, and I had to stick to my word. So I sent Blair in for him right then and there. Pulled Reggie right out of the game.

Reggie came back to the dugout, and he started making a scene. He was screaming at me, "You showed me up. You showed me up. How could you do this to me on television?" Television, what kind of person was this who realized the game was on television? Screw television. He was yelling something about my being a racist, just ranting and raving, and he yelled at me, "You're not a man." I ignored him, though I was steaming inside, and then he said, "Don't you dare ever show me up again, you motherfucker." I won't take that from anybody, because he was talking about my mother, and no one says anything about my mother. I tried to get him. I went right after him, and Elston Howard tried to stop me, and I threw him out of the way, but I couldn't get past Yogi. Yogi has those iron hands, and he grabbed me by the crotch and pulled me back. I swear if Yogi hadn't stopped me I would have beat the hell out of him. It's a good thing he grabbed me. It wouldn't have been any wrestling match, I guarantee you that. Reggie's big, but I wasn't afraid of him. He was lucky Yogi was there.

From what I learned George had been attending a funeral in

Cleveland, and he had watched the game, which we ended up losing, on television, and when he saw me go after Reggie, he wanted to fire me. As usual, George was taking Reggie's side. Fortunately, Gabe had the sense to understand the situation. I told him, "I'm the manager, and no one is going to tell me how to handle my players. He showed me up by not hustling, and I had told him if he did that, I'd show him up."

The next morning Gabe asked Reggie and me to meet him for breakfast in his hotel room. It happened that Reggie and I got on the elevator together, and he didn't say a word to me. We went to Gabe's room, and Gabe had breakfast for us, and while we're eating Gabe says, "We have to talk about this." Reggie was sitting there reading the newspaper, and he opens up the paper to the sports section, and he says to Gabe, "Look at how they're restraining Billy."

I was sitting there, and I stood up, and I said, "Nobody's restraining me now. You wanted to fight me yesterday. How about now? Right now."

Gabe said, "Now, wait a minute Billy." I said, "Wait a minute? You wait a minute, Gabe. I didn't come up here to listen to this guy pop off about me. Now or ever. He's just one man of twenty-five, he's not the whole ball club. It's about time he learns that." I started shouting at Reggie, "How about now? Want to get it on now? Let's get it going." Gabe calmed me down, and we started talking. I explained to Gabe, and to Reggie, that I didn't have anything personal against Reggie. I told him, "I treat you just like I treat all the rest of the guys. But you are not going to tell me off at the bench, and you are not going to show up the ball club by not hustling. All I ask of you guys is that you hustle, because if you hustle, I'll go through the wall for you. If you don't hustle, I'll embarrass you like you embarrass me."

Reggie said, "It was on television." I said, "I didn't know. I didn't care whether it was on television or not." Like I should manage differently because the game was on TV. I go out to argue with an umpire, I'm supposed to worry that the game's on TV?

When we left that meeting, as far as I was concerned, the incident was over. I'm not a manager who holds grudges. Every day is a new day. It was no different with Reggie than it was with Willie Horton or Mickey Rivers. It had happened, and it was old history.

Apparently it wasn't that way to George, though. As he was watching Reggie and me get into it on TV, all he could think to himself was that *I* was embarrassing him because I had lost my temper. At that point he really wanted to fire me. But George was very worried about the fan reaction if he did fire me, so instead of firing me on the spot he leaked a story to the papers to see how the fans would react. He was very worried about that, and the fans called by the hundreds backing me, for which I'll always be grateful, and George backed off for a while. George has such an ego, there's no way I could have won managing for him. When the team lost, it was my fault. When it won, it was his doing.

George flew into Detroit, our next stop after Boston, and we had a meeting. He said, "How could you have done a thing like that?" I told him what I told Gabe, that I had promised in spring training to take a player out if he didn't hustle. I said, "I thought he was dogging it, and I had to react the only way a manager should react, because if I didn't, I would have lost the whole ball club. The guys would have figured, 'If he can do it, we can all do it.' They'd say to themselves, 'Lookit, Billy says one thing and he does another.' " I said, "George, you can't do that. Your word has got to be as good as your bond."

Still, George didn't understand. He was siding with Reggie, and he was complaining that I wasn't doing my homework because I wasn't paying attention to his goddamn statistics, and finally he said, "It's up to Gabe. I'll let Gabe decide what to do."

He said, "As far as I'm concerned, you're gone, but I'll leave it up to Gabe." I said, "You're the boss, you own the ball club. If you want to fire me I'm not going to argue with you, but I would appreciate it if you would pay my salary because I need the money to support my family." George said, "Billy I would never hurt you that way, never." I said, "I appreciate that, George." I stood to leave. I said, "Whatever you guys decide to do, let me know," and I walked out.

When I left I was feeling terrible because I really didn't

know what they were going to do. I found out later that Reggie and Fran Healy and a couple other players spoke to George and asked him not to fire me over that incident, and that may have also had something to do with my not getting fired. That evening George came out to the ball park before the game and he gave one of his rah rah pep talks to the players. He told them he wasn't going to fire me, and he started yelling about how they weren't playing well, how they had stunk in Boston, and a whole lot of baloney the players don't pay any attention to. What the whole thing amounted to was that George was embarrassed by the way we got beat three straight in Boston. He's always panicking. If we're getting beat in spring training, he figures we've already lost the pennant. We get beat three games in Boston, and he's figuring there's no way we can ever recover. He was ranting about how embarrassed he was. Doesn't he think it's embarrassing for the players? Doesn't he think the manager gets embarrassed when home runs are flying out of the ball park? All he was caring about was how he was feeling.

When I went out onto the field before the game, the Detroit fans gave me a standing ovation, which must have really burned George's ass. The fans see through George. They know what type of man he is, and they can imagine what it's like to have to work for him. Actually, whatever they imagine, it's really much worse.

I didn't get fired because of Gabe, who hadn't been upset about what happened with Reggie nearly as much as George. The whole time Gabe was there, he was loyal to me. Once in a while a player would be complaining that he wasn't playing, and he'd go up to talk with Gabe, and Gabe would always tell me about it. And Gabe would make the players get permission from me before they would talk to him, which is the way it should be. A manager doesn't want to stop a player for talking to the general manager if the player wants more money, but it should go through the proper channels, so that if a player has a problem, it's only fair that the manager be told first so he can keep on top of things. I want to know what's going on all the time so I can help.

George, who's always talking about loyalty, was always talking behind Gabe's back when he wasn't around. He had told everyone that Gabe would be the one to decide whether or not I'd be fired, but after Gabe decided I would stay, George kept telling everyone he was the one who really decided. When Gabe found out, he packed his bags and quit. He flew home to Tampa.

George was always telling me, "I gotta get rid of Gabe. Gotta get rid of him." George kept telling me Gabe was getting senile. And all Gabe was trying to do was help George. Gabe was the one who had made those great trades that allowed the Yankees to win pennants and make money for George, but George was so jealous of Gabe, just the way he was jealous of me. He didn't want anyone else getting the credit. "Gotta get rid of Gabe. Gotta get rid of him." He wanted to get rid of Gabe so badly it was pathetic. Gabe, however, would never knock George behind his back. Gabe would say, "But this is the way George wants it, Billy. You have to do what George wants." I never heard Gabe run George down once. Gabe came back only after George flew down to Tampa and pleaded with him to come back. He told Gabe, "I'll never do it again, Gabe, I promise." He kept his promise for about a day.

With Catfish and Figgy out, I had run out of pitchers to throw against the Tigers in the second game. Ken Holtzman, who didn't pitch well when he played for us, hadn't pitched in a month, but I had to go with him. He got bombed. Fortunately we were hitting that day, and we beat the Tigers 12 to 11. It kept us from falling worse than five games behind the Red Sox, who had won 16 of their last 18. Meanwhile, all everyone was talking about was whether or not I was going to get fired, which to this day I can't understand. I had managed the Yankees to the pennant in 1976, and if the owner had some patience and wasn't such a worrier, he would have been able to sit back and see what was going to happen throughout the rest of the season. No other owner talks about firing the manager every time the team falls out of first place. If we took the lead on the first day of the season and kept in first every single day of the season, then I wouldn't have had to worry about my job. Except that I wouldn't pay attention to his stupid statistics, and maybe he would have fired me for that. Why couldn't he have been content enough to sit in his office, count his money, and leave the running of the team to the manager like every other sensible owner?

Plus George was still bugging me about where I was playing Reggie. We came home for a series against the Red Sox, and I benched Reggie against Bill Lee, because Reggie doesn't hit Lee very well. I played Roy White, and in the bottom of the ninth, losing by three runs, Roy hit a three-run home run into the seats to tie it up. I sent Reggie up in the eleventh against Bill Campbell, who's a righty, and Reggie drove in the winning run. The next day I kept Reggie on the bench again, and we played like it was 1976 again. We stole bases, executed a double steal, scored on a hit-and-run, and Paul Blair, who played for Reggie this day, drove in the winning run.

Reggie was in a terrible slump, and I felt that a couple days' rest would be best for him. I'd send one of my coaches over to tell him he wasn't playing. When a guy is in a slump, and there's a certain pitcher he can't hit, it's a good time to give a player a rest. A perfect time, in fact. Reggie, of course, didn't see it that way, but not many players do look at it that way. It's hard to explain to a player, because the player thinks you're putting him down, but what you're really doing is what's best for him and the ball club.

Baltimore was winning 14 of 16, but we had started winning again, and by July second we were back in first place. George was still second-guessing me every single day. One day he complained when I DHed Cliff Johnson and batted him fifth. He wanted him lower. Another day he got mad when I didn't bat Roy and Mickey at the top of the lineup. Any day I didn't play Lou Piniella I knew I would hear about it. He was always sending me statistics showing me not to play Carlos May. I also knew he was second-guessing me because the players would tell me. When a player would go up to see him, they knew exactly what to do when they wanted something. They knew it meant a lot to him that the players be friends with him, and so they'd go up there and lay it on thick, and they'd get whatever it was that they wanted. The players knew how to get the best of him. They're a lot smarter than George gives them credit for being.

You have no idea how difficult it is in life when you have somebody constantly second-guessing you, especially when the second-guesser isn't as knowledgeable as he thinks he is. If the man is so knowledgeable, what does he need me for? Why did he hire me? He sits up in his box and thinks he knows it all. He tries to dictate who should play and who shouldn't. That's the worst thing you can do to a manager. Baseball is an intuitive game. You have to make decisions right on the spot, and that's difficult enough without somebody's ghost right behind you making you ask yourself if you're doing the right thing. Sometimes I would do just the opposite of what George wanted me to do, because I won't let anyone tell me how to manage. If I'm going down the tube, I'm going to do it my way.

I would like to see George go into the dugout and manage for a week. Just a week. He'd be a nervous wreck, and he'd be such a maniac on the bench that all the players would be laughing at him. I'd like to see him manage one game. Not that he wouldn't like to. Let's see him make the first guess, know the right psychology to use with each pitcher, know when to hit-and-run, when to bunt, know the capabilities of each player, who *can* bunt and who can't. I'd like to be sitting up in the box as the owner waving my hands, screaming, "Oh, you dummy, how could you do a stupid thing like that? What are you doing?" See how he'd like it, always second-guessing him and calling him up on the telephone in the middle of the game.

Little things he'd call about. One time it was right before the game, and the players were warming up, and George called down. He said, "Thurman isn't wearing a cap. I want you to fine him."

Another time Cedric called down. He said, "Billy, Figueroa is in the bullpen, and he's not on the roster, and George says we're going to lose the game." Figgy was on the disabled list, and he wanted to sit out there. I said, "No, Cedric, wrong again. Tell George I've gotten permission from the visiting manager and the umpires that he can sit in there." He said, "No, Billy, it's here in the rules." I said, "No, you're wrong."

They checked it out and I was right. All the time George would be calling down with things, bothering the life out of me. Petty little things that didn't mean a thing. The game would be on, and he'd be calling down distracting everyone.

One game we were playing in Chicago, and it was the middle of the game, and the dugout phone rang. Nettles answered it. He said, "Billy, it's George." I said, "You gotta be kidding me." Graig had his hand over the receiver, and he said, "No, it's really George." I took the phone from Graig. I said, "Who is this?" He said, "George!" I said, "Don't be calling me during the game, you asshole." And I hung up. I said to Graig, "Imagine that, a guy trying to imitate George." Graig said, "That was George." I said, "Maybe he'll learn not to call down here anymore."

I was getting madder and madder because George was interfering so much. The players, even Reggie, had pleaded with George to let me run the team, and because of what George was doing I was starting to lose control over them. I'd have a problem with a player, and the player knew the management wouldn't back me, and it put me in a difficult position. At the same time all the time I would go up to George's office and have to listen to him scream and yell like a little boy, and it was really getting to me.

One day I was sitting on the bench real quiet, and Thurman came over. "Are you all right?" he asked. I said, "Yeah." He said, "Boy, I wish they'd leave you alone." I nodded. It was really getting to me.

At the same time the press was pitting player against player, player against manager, manager against management, and they'd go back and forth, back and forth, ask one player what he thought of another player, and then go back to the other player and tell him what the first player said and get a reaction, and then the headlines the next day would talk about the feud they were having. The New York reporters have a job to do. I understand that, that they gotta make a living, but the players should be smarter and know when to talk and what to talk about. I'd be telling the guys, "Be careful what you say. It's a game they have going, and they're experts at it. You have something to say to me, come tell me. Don't tell a newspaper reporter. We'll talk it out man to man. Don't be letting those guys use you like that."

They really worked us over, really raked us over good. Henry Hecht of the *New York Post* was the worst at that. He'd go over to the guys who weren't playing and get stories out of them, trying to give me a bad time. He has a job to do, but I wish he'd do it with a little more dignity. I understand he works for Rupert Murdoch, who's like George in that he keeps his employees nervous all the time, but after a while you see what's in the paper day after day and you wonder whether they'll ever let up.

Dick Young was another guy who ripped me bad. Tried to get me fired every chance he could, and then after I was fired, kicked me a few more times. What I don't like about Dick is that he isn't one of the regular reporters. He shows up every other week or so, and sometimes he digs something out and he doesn't check the facts, doesn't do his homework, and he makes an incident worse than it really was. In Texas, for instance, when I slapped Burt Hawkins, Dick wrote that I had beat up an old man. That really upset me.

Another thing that upset me was hearing that George was monitoring my phone and listening in to my phone conversations. I was told he had had the Yankee Stadium phone system installed privately in such a way that he could listen in to anybody's phone call anywhere in the stadium. At first I didn't realize it, but I'd be talking to friends or my agent, and later George and I would be talking, and George would make it clear that he knew what I was doing. Business dealings and financial matters, even personal matters. He knew where I was going, where I'd been, and I couldn't understand how he could possibly know because I keep my private life as quiet as possible. I even called a friend who worked at the stadium and asked him to check to see if my phone was bugged. He said there was no bug, but he told me about George's special phone system. I couldn't understand it: Even when George was in Florida, he'd find out what I was doing. It was spooky. Finally I got tipped off by one of the telephone operators at the stadium that George was listening in on my phone calls.

What George was doing was building a case against me. He

wanted to keep a fear in me that he could fire me at any time, leaving me without the money I needed to support my family. One secretary, who he since fired, told me, "Watch out for George. He's keeping a file on you, every word you say, everything you do."

The first time my agent, Doug Newton, met with him, George pointed to his file cabinets and said, "I have a file on Billy Martin. I have dates, I have names, I know everything about the man's private life, and let me assure you I won't hesitate to use it and make it public, and I'll destroy this man if he pushes me too far."

Things with George got ridiculous. Thurman had complained to reporters about George's interference, and there were big headlines in the papers, and George called me and told me I had to call a press conference to announce in no uncertain terms that George was absolutely not interfering in any way, which was a joke and everyone knew it. I wanted so badly to bar the press from the clubhouse, especially Henry Hecht, but I knew that never would have sat very well with Commissioner Kuhn. I felt that certain writers were out to get my job, trying to hurt me, and I should have some way to stop them, but there was no way, not as long as the players would keep talking to them.

Things came to head in mid-July. We were playing in Milwaukee, and though we were only a few games out, morale was shot, what with George interfering and the papers screaming about everyone feuding and not getting along. I went back to the hotel, and my suite was next to George's, and as I walked by his door I could hear loud voices. It sounded to me like Thurman and Lou Piniella. I stood in front of the door, and I listened for a little while, and I knocked on the door. George said, "Who is it?" and I told him. He said, "What is it, Bill?" I said, "Do you have a couple of my players in there?" He said, "No." I pushed opened the door, and I didn't see anyone but George, but then I went to the door adjoining the two rooms of George's rooms, and I opened it, and there were Thurman and Piniella. They said, "Billy, this isn't what you think it is." I knew that. I trusted Thurman implicitly, and even though

Piniella and George were close, I never questioned Piniella's loyalty to me.

Thurman and Lou were up there defending me to George. They were telling George, "Either take the restrictive clauses out of his contract, or fire him, because no one in this whole world can stand up to the kind of pressure you're putting on him. If the manager is always worried about whether or not he's going to get fired, he's not going to be able to do his job," which was exactly the way I felt. I had to spend more time thinking about George than about who we were playing against on any given day.

George agreed to take out the clauses and let me manage, and then he went over to a blackboard he had in the room. On the blackboard he wrote down the starting lineup of the Yankees, the Red Sox, and the Orioles and their hitting averages. He was comparing Mickey Rivers to Fred Lynn, and was saying how Lynn had a higher average, and I was sitting there thinking that you don't compare teams that way at all. Batting averages are deceiving. He goes by them, lives by them, because maybe statistics are what he uses to run his shipbuilding business. But baseball's got a heart and a stomach and a brain, and averages don't reflect any of those things, and you can't measure those things by what you read in the papers.

When he got finished comparing the teams—and quite frankly I'm still not sure what conclusions he drew from the comparisons—he said to me, "Well, what's wrong with the team?"

I said, "You, George, you're what's wrong with the team. You're meddling all the time, you're creating problems leaking out stories in the newspapers. When you get mad at a player, you call the newspapers and leak out a story on him. You're the problem. That isn't like the New York Yankees. We don't leak stories and do things like that. That's unlike any Yankee I ever saw in my life."

He said, "I'll take out the clauses, but I would like you to try my batting order." He had Piniella batting fourth, Rivers and White first and second, Jackson in right batting sixth, and White as DH. I used his lineup for exactly one game. Then I went back to what I was doing. Exactly ten days after our meeting where he promised not to interfere, George had been asking around whether Walter Alston would make a good manager. The next day he asked Dick Howser, my third-base coach, whether he would take over as manager. Howser refused out of loyalty to me.

There were more rumors that I would be gone and Dick Williams was going to take over. I wasn't at all anxious to call George and ask him. I thought back to the time I called Brad Corbett to ask him whether the rumors in Texas were true, and when it turned out they were, I was out of a job.

Another day later Gabe Paul called, and I went up to his office to see him. Gabe said I was still the manager. He also said George was showing up the next day to hold a press conference. We were playing Kansas City at the stadium, and that day more people bought tickets at the gate than for any other, and when I went out onto the field, the fans cheered and cheered. I couldn't help thinking to myself, "If only I could make George feel the way they do."

When George arrived he called a press conference to defend himself against those who said he was treating me lousy. Once again he told the reporters that it would be up to Gabe as to whether I was fired or not, though no one really believed him. Then he handed the reporters a list of seven rules under which he was to decide whether I'd be fired in the future or not.

Here's the list:

1   Won-lost record

2   Does he work hard enough?

3   Is he emotionally equipped to lead the men under him?

4   Is he organized?

5   Is he prepared?

6   Does he understand human nature?

7   Is he honorable?

It was such bullshit. Gabe had made that list up before I was hired. It was Gabe's list for hiring a manager, not for firing one. Actually, Gabe's list was only the last six items. George added the top one so the reporters would think the list was made to apply to me. But hadn't I led the Yankees to the pennant the year before? And at this point in the season we were only about three games out. What was so terrible about that? I dare anyone else in the world to work under the conditions I was working under. Here was a felon setting himself up as judge and jury to decide whether I was good enough, moral enough, and a good enough student of human nature to manage his team. I was trying to win another pennant, but it wasn't easy with all this crap going on around us. I couldn't help thinking how the players were reacting to their manager having seven rules thrown at him. If I was a player, and it was my manager, I wouldn't be very happy about it.

We had a crucial three-game series with the Orioles toward the end of July, and I decided that it would be best for Reggie to DH. I was hoping that with his not having to go out into the field, it would take some of the pressure off him, and his hitting would pick up. We were losing the first game 4 to 2 in the ninth, and with a runner on first I sent Cliff Johnson to pinch-hit for Bucky Dent, and Cliff homered to tie. The next batter was Reggie, and he followed Cliff's homer with a homer of his own to win the game. The next game we got beat by Jim Palmer, and in the finale against Rudy May, I benched Reggie completely this time, and as it turned out, we didn't need him, because we won 14 to 2. Mike Torrez pitched a four-hitter that started him on a seven- or eight-game winning streak. Thurman, who hit everything in sight against the Orioles, had three hits including his hundredth career home run. After the game George sent Thurman a bottle of champagne. I offered him a beer. He drank the beer.

Thurman was very upset at how George was treating me. He told a reporter, "I don't like being laughed at. When a manager gets seven rules thrown at him, people laugh. The Yankee uniform stands for more than that." I couldn't have said it better.

Thurman decided to show George what he thought of his

rules by growing a beard. There's a dress code on the Yankees, and growing a beard is against the rules. We were on a western trip when he first started growing it, and once the papers got ahold of the story, Thurman's beard became headlines for a week. Such pettiness. That was the most ridiculous thing in the world. Here's a championship baseball team, and what were the writers worried about? They were calling George every day about Thurman's beard. What was this, a soap opera? I asked Henry Hecht and Joe Donnelly of *Newsday*, "Why is this so big?" "People want to know about the Yankees, about Thurman," they'd say. I'd say, "Why can't you guys just write about baseball games anymore?"

George and Gabe got all upset, and Gabe called me and told me I would be responsible, that if the beard wasn't gone by the exhibition game with Syracuse, that there'd be trouble. The final series before we flew to Syracuse was in Seattle, and we started out by losing the first two games to the Mariners to drop five behind the Red Sox, who had won nine in a row. There were rumors that Frank Robinson was going to take over as Yankee manager, and my nerves were frayed right down to the end. After the second loss, for some reason George thought it fitting to apologize to the fans of New York for the way we were playing. It wasn't enough for him to embarrass me, he had to embarrass all the players, too. The way he was acting, he should have apologized, to us, not to the fans. It was still early in the season. We still had plenty of time to regroup and win a pennant. The day before we were to arrive in Syracuse, I asked Thurman if he would please shave the beard. I wasn't about to force him to do it. I had too much respect for him to do a thing like that.

In Syracuse before the game Thurman came in, clean shaven. He said, "I'm not going to talk to the press anymore." I said, "Okay, you don't have to talk to them if you don't want to. Just treat them politely." He said, "I will." And from that day on Thurman stopped talking to reporters. He saw what they could do after he started growing the beard. He was going to make sure it didn't happen again.

Chris Chambliss was in an awful slump, and the day of the Syracuse exhibition game I decided that Reggie was going to be my new number-four hitter. The next day was an off day, and George called me into his office for a meeting. He offered me a two-year contract. He said, "Billy, you're doing a great job, and I'm going to give you a nice raise." I told him I appreciated that, and I told him he could fill in the numbers. I knew he'd be fair and generous, and he was generous. He wrote in $90,000 for each of the two years, which was really flattering, and I told George I was going to bat Reggie fourth every day, and play Piniella regularly, which he liked, and while we were talking he was talking about our pitching staff, asking me what we could do.

I said, "George, if you want to get the whole thing turned around, get me Art Fowler. There's no one better to work with the pitchers." George said, "I understand Art's a heavy drinker." I said, "Art never in his whole life drank as much as Bob Lemon, but even so that has nothing to do with whether a guy's a good coach or not. Give me Art Fowler, and I can turn it around. I need a guy who is loyal to me first and the pitchers second, someone I can work with. Give me Art, and it'll all straighten itself out." And George said okay.

I called Art and told him he was my new pitching coach. He said, "Billy, there is no way with Gabe still there." I said, "Yeah, you are. Get on a plane and get out here."

Art came in and went into the clubhouse, and I told him to go up to see Gabe to sign his contract. Gabe didn't ask him how much he wanted. He merely told his secretary what the contract called for, and Art had to take it. Art looked up at Gabe without saying a word, signed the contract, and walked out. It had been many years since Cincinnati, but he had never forgotten the way Gabe had treated him. Gabe had gotten George to think that Art wasn't a good pitching coach, but Gabe was wrong this time. Art showed up, and from that day on we won 40 of our last 50 games to win the pennant. He did some job with those pitchers. He wasn't there but five weeks, and at the end of the season the players voted him $6,500 as his World Series share. They appreciated the work he had done and let him know it.

With Art there Guidry won seven games in a row by the scores of 2–1, 1–0, 4–0, 4–3, 4–2, 5–0, and 6–5, and in the

6–5 game he was leading 6 to 0 going into the ninth. Torrez pitched seven complete games in a row, and with Don Gullett out we decided to start Dick Tidrow, as gutty a pitcher as a manager could ever hope for. The whole time Tidrow had bone chips in his elbow, and he pitched in terrible pain, and in the seven games he started down the stretch, he won five and Sparky Lyle won the other two in relief.

The Red Sox, as they often do, folded. In one of the key games, Reggie made a great catch of a ball George Scott hit. He leaped up and grabbed it out of the stands. On another play Reggie made a diving catch of a blooper to save a run, and we went into the ninth inning tied 0 to 0. In the bottom of the ninth Thurman got on, and I gave Reggie the bunt sign. The pitcher threw a ball. I took the sign off. He fouled off the pitch. I put the bunt back on again, and the pitcher threw another ball. Again I took it off. The pitcher wound up, and Reggie homered into the bleachers to win the game.

When he came back to the dugout, I said, "Sorry I gave you the bunt sign." He said, "I understand why you did, Skip. No problem." In the pennant-clinching game, Don Gullett pitched a shutout, and Reggie hit a grand-slam home run. When the Red Sox and Orioles knocked each other off, the pennant was ours. On the final day of the season Thurman drove in his hundredth run for the third year in a row, the first American League player to accomplish that since 1952, '53, and '54, when it was done by Cleveland third baseman Al Rosen.

We had won against all odds. George had done everything he could to keep us from winning, but he had failed. During the stretch run he wasn't completely silent. Every chance he got he was telling people how he had won it for New York, and he down-played the role Gabe and I played whenever he could. He was asked whether I'd be fired after the play-offs and World Series. Instead of saying no, he told a reporter, "We'll have to wait and see." I thought to myself, "In two years, we've come in first two times. How much better could I possibly do? What does this man want from me?"

As it had been the year before, the play-offs against Kansas City went the full five games. We were behind all the way, losing the first and third games, with Guidry pitching a three-hit shutout and Sparky Lyle pitching five innings of scoreless relief to win games two and four.

After game four I went to my hotel room. I knew Paul Splittorff would be pitching for the Royals the next day in game five, and I knew it would be in the best interests of the team to play Paul Blair in right field and not Reggie Jackson. As I sat on my bed, I wrote down different lineups, some with Reggie playing, others with Blair. There was just no way I could play Reggie and feel good about it. I knew George would go through the ceiling if I played Blair, but if I played Reggie and we lost, I would have felt I had let the rest of the players down. If I'm a rubber stamp for George I'd have been cheating those other ballplayers, and I'd have been cheating myself. I'd even be cheating Reggie and George. You can't run scared. I knew all the while that George didn't like me, and that was a terrible feeling. When he'd leak statements to the press about me, and when I'd read in the papers what was being said, I'd feel it down to my gut. But I had a job to do, and I had made up my mind to try not to pay attention to the things in the papers, and I had sworn to myself that I wouldn't run scared, even if I ended up getting fired. As far as Reggie was concerned, I had no beef with him at all. I wasn't trying to show him up. I wasn't trying to make him look bad. I simply had to do what was best for the team. There were other guys I had to think about other than Reggie. Also, I was hoping that if we beat the Royals without Reggie and got into the World Series, Reggie would take his anger with me out against the Dodgers. That way, we'd be a winner both ways.

The afternoon before the game I went with my friend Judge Eddie Sapir from the Crownson Hotel, where the team was staying, to the old Muhlenberg Hotel, where I could get some peace and quiet. We were eating peanuts and drinking beer, and I was looking over the statistics of our players against Splittorff. I knew this was a tough decision, probably the toughest I had ever had to make as a manager. Now, as I said before, statistics don't tell the whole story, but Catfish Hunter and Ken Holtzman had told me that Reggie, when he was with Oakland and Baltimore, hadn't had much success against Splittorff, and

I knew he didn't do well against him with the Yankees. Making it more difficult, Paul Blair, a right-handed batter, was hitting four hundred something against him, and Reggie in the field can't compare to Paul. I needed another right-handed bat in the lineup and I told Eddie, "I've got to take a chance tomorrow. I've got to do what I think is best for the team. I'm going to play Blair in right and bench Reggie." I said, "If we get to Splittorff and they bring in a righty, Reggie would be a perfect pinch hitter for us."

Eddie made a face. He knew that Reggie was George's boy and that if we lost, it would be a perfect excuse for George to fire me. I was leaving the door wide open. Eddie said, "If that's the way you feel, that's the way you gotta go."

We walked to the local Catholic church, I offered my prayers, and we walked to the park.

That evening in the clubhouse I ran into George Steinbrenner and told him what I was going to do. I told him I had stayed up all night, and given it a lot of thought. As we were talking, Catfish Hunter was walking by us. George said, "Hey, Cat, you played with Reggie at Oakland. Can Reggie hit Splittorff?" Without breaking stride, Cat looked back at George and said, "Not with a fucking paddle," and kept walking. George said, "You do it, but if it doesn't work, you're going to have to suffer the consequences." I said, "Fine, as long as if it works, I get the credit."

We were playing at a disadvantage in that the game was in Kansas City. Also I was pitching Ron Guidry with two days rest against Splittorff, who seems to beat us every time out. We started badly. The Royals scored two in the first, we each scored one in the third, and it was obvious Guidry's arm was too tired for him to be effective. I relieved him with Mike Torrez, who had started and lost the third game, and Torrez was outstanding, pitching shutout ball until the eighth. By then Splittorff was gone, replaced by manager Whitey Herzog, for which we shall always be grateful. In fairness to Whitey, he had been going with the percentages in the late innings all year long, and after Willie Randolph singled, with Thurman coming to bat in the eighth, he brought in right-handed reliever Doug Bird. Bird struck Thurman out, but Piniella singled Randolph to third, and with a righty pitching, it was a perfect spot for me to send Reggie up to pinch-hit. Reggie had told me he wasn't a good pinch hitter, but when the pressure is on, he usually will get the job done, and against Bird he hit a single up the middle to score Randolph, and we were a run closer at 3 to 2.

In the ninth Herzog relieved Bird with Dennis Leonard, a 20-game winner. Blair did not have a high average. He had been hit in the face by a pitched ball a few years earlier and since then had been gun shy. It was very hard on Paul, and I knew how he felt because the same thing had happened to me at the end of my playing career. I knew how tough it was to stand in there when your heart told you it would be better not to. Still, during the season Paul had come through with six game-winning hits, and I didn't even consider pinch-hitting for him. Leonard got two strikes, and then Blair fouled off two hard sliders away. Leonard came back with a tight fastball, and he blooped a single to center. I knew right there that we'd be winners.

I sent Roy White up to bat for Bucky Dent, who was having a poor season at bat, and with the count 3 and 2, Roy fouled off a couple pitches and walked. I don't know why Roy never got the credit he deserved from the New York press and the fans. He may not have had the greatest throwing arm, but he was a guy who could do so many things for you, and in the tough situations he *always* came through. Herzog took Leonard out and brought in my old pal, Larry Gura. I wanted Mickey Rivers to bunt, but he'd refused to take lessons from Phil Rizzuto in spring training, and he wouldn't improve, and when the pitch came in he fouled it off. I figured, "What the hell?" and I took the bunt sign off and Mickey, bless him, singled hard over second to tie the score. Herzog brought Mark Littell into the game. He had thrown the home-run ball to Chambliss the year before. Randolph, who was up again, hit a long fly ball to the outfield, and Roy scored to put us ahead. It was the ninth inning of the fifth game, and for the first time we were ahead.

Sparky Lyle, who had won the game before, was on the mound, and I knew there was no way they were going to score, and they didn't, and we were champs of the American League for the second year in a row.

After the game I grabbed a bottle of George's champagne and poured it all over him. "That's for trying to fire me," I said. George said, "What do you mean 'try.' If I want to fire you, I'll fire you." I didn't doubt it for a second. In all the years baseball has been played, I wonder whether a manager going into his second straight World Series was still fighting for his job?

After Kansas City the Dodgers were a piece of cake. My toughest decision for the Series was in deciding on a rotation. Gullett was fresh for the first game and won, but Torrez and Guidry were tired from the play-offs, and I needed someone to pitch in game two, and I settled on Catfish. I was throwing him to the wolves, because his arm was hurting him and he wasn't as sharp as he should have been, but by my pitching Cat, I was giving Torrez and Guidry enough rest to have them come back and be sharp. My only other choice was Tidrow, but I needed him in relief. Catfish was a man about it, as he always was. He was willing to go out there and pitch the best he could, and though he ended up giving up four home runs in three innings and we lost that game, we were set for the Series, and Torrez won game three, Guidry won game four, and Torrez won the sixth and final game. Reggie was complaining to the press about how Cat hadn't pitched in a month and how could I do something so stupid as pitch him, but he was just sticking up for Cat, who didn't need anyone sticking up for him, and there was no sense trying to explain it to Reggie.

Before the final game Gabe called me into his office and told me that George was giving me a substantial bonus, including a Lincoln Continental, and that he was going to pay the rent for my apartment. He also told me I'd be back in 1978, which was nice of him. I'd only won them two pennants in two tries.

The sixth game belonged to Reggie. We were losing 3 to 2 in the fourth when Thurman singled and Reggie hit a line drive into the lower right-field stands for the lead. The next time he got up he hit another home run. He was so high his feet were barely on the ground, and when he came to bat again he went up there with so much concentration that I would have been surprised if he *hadn't* hit another one. Charley Hough threw him a knee-high knuckleball, and Reggie hit the ball over 475 feet into the center-field bleachers, the longest home run he had hit all year. For the Series Reggie hit five home runs, and nobody had ever done that before. Nobody was more happy for him than I was.

After the game Reggie told reporters, "I'm not a superstar, but I can always say that on this one night I was." He was certainly right about that. Oh, yes, we won the game 8 to 4.

When we won the World Series, it hit me like a sledgehammer. When the game had ended, I sat at my desk in my office, and I was never so tired in my life sitting there. After all the problems we had had all year long, after fighting to win a division title, fighting to win a pennant, fighting to win a World Series, fighting against an owner who doesn't respect you, doesn't honor you properly, all year long battling for players against him, and he's telling the players just the opposite. It was tearing me up, making me sick, and it was a miracle I didn't have a stroke or a nervous breakdown. If I had been an older man or if I hadn't had a strong constitution, I might have had one, because of all the hassle and bullshit from him, petty bullshit, harassment. Not every once in a while. Constant harassment. Every day, whether or not he was in town, he'd call and cause problems. Somebody was on the field without a hat. Make him put his hat on. One player was wearing a red shirt under his uniform, make him take it off and put a blue one on. A player was sitting on the railing talking to the fans. Billy, go down and get him away from there. He'd ask me why I wasn't on the field. I was talking to a player in the clubhouse. Oh. One day he sent two of his goons down to run my kid off the field. We got no insurance to cover it, they said. Petty shit, every day, every single day.

Afterwards we all went to the Sheraton Hotel in Hasbrouck Heights for a party, and I was so exhausted I couldn't even enjoy it. My wife and my son had come up for the Series, and I was at the party, and people were going crazy trying to get in, and as I was trying to get to the bar people were pushing, shoving me against the wall, wanting to talk baseball, and when a woman would come over and say hi, my wife would give me a bad time about it, and I don't think she realized what I was going through at the time, but after arguing with George and arguing with the players and arguing with the umpires, to have to come back and argue with her became too much. I tried so hard not to let everything get to me, but I guess finally it did. I grabbed my glass, threw it to the floor, and I left. I drove to a little bar nearby all by myself, and I sat there and rested where no one could bother me.

As I sat there I thought how happy I was for Gabe Paul, because all the years in baseball he had never won a Series before, and he had been so good to me in so many ways. And I was happy for George, because George wanted it so bad. I said to myself, "Now he can really have fun at the 21 Club. He'll go around and give rings out to his friends, and he'll be able to talk about this one as long as he lives."

CHAPTER 4

During my entire playing career as a Yankee I never once felt secure because the whole time I knew that Yankee general manager George Weiss hated my guts. It didn't matter how well I played, or how many pennants we won, I always knew that as soon as Weiss could find a way to get rid of me, he would.

I came up to the Yankees in 1950, and though I felt I should have been the starting second baseman, I was on the bench and Jerry Coleman was playing. I'd play every once in a while, and when I got in, I'd drive in a couple runs or make a good play in the field, and so in late April when our manager, Casey Stengel, told me the Yankees were sending me down to Kansas City, I was a little upset.

Casey called me into his office, and he said, "The reason we're sending you down is that we have George Stirnweiss on the club, and we're trying to sell him to Cleveland, but until we do there isn't room on the club for you. Go down to Kansas City, and you'll be back in about thirty days, and when you come back you'll stay here." That sounded reasonable enough to me, and I said okay. He said, "Aren't you mad?" I said, "Sure I'm mad, but what can I do about it?" He said, "Well, you can go up and tell Weiss off."

Everybody at the time thought that George Weiss and Casey

Stengel were friends, but the truth of the matter was that they were really rivals, really didn't like each other. George Weiss had built the Yankee farm system, and while he was very protective of the players who came up through his farm system, he didn't have as much enthusiasm for the one or two other guys who he bought or traded for. I had been bought in 1949 from the Oakland Oaks where Casey had managed before he started managing the Yankees, and it was Casey who had told Weiss to buy me. Casey was the one who didn't like it that I was being sent down, and he was letting Weiss know it through me.

Weiss was a very serious, humorless man. He ran the Yankees like a Hitler. Dan Topping and Del Webb were the owners, but they hired Weiss to run the team, and they gave him a free hand. Weiss made it clear that he was the boss, and it was rare when anyone dared challenge his authority.

I went up to his office and entered the room. He growled at me and asked me what I wanted. "How can you send me down?" I said. "Look at my batting average. Why do I have to be the guinea pig?"

He became furious. "You're going to go down there, son. You've got to learn." I started crying, feeling really down, and I started shouting at him. I told him, "You'll be sorry. I'll show you," which was the worst thing I could have said to him because he never forgot it all the years I played on the Yankees. From that day on he just hated my guts. In the 1952 World Series I caught a tricky pop fly with the bases loaded to save the final game. You know what his comment was? "That fresh little kid, he just tried to make it look hard." That's how much he disliked me. It was such a shame he didn't let me get to know him better. But he would never let me get to know him.

Fortunately I did have Casey to protect me against Weiss. When I was playing baseball in high school, Red Adams, the trainer for the Oakland Oaks, would have me come down to the Oaks' field. Red would buy me a hamburger, and give me a locker, and he'd make sure I got a ride to and from the field, and I'd work out there. Red would keep telling Casey, who was the Oakland manager, about me. They wouldn't let me hit, but I'd go out into the field, and Casey would hit grounders to me, and Red would keep telling Casey, "How'd you like him? See that kid out there. He's going to make it." Casey would say, "That skinny kid?" Red'd say, "You watch, Casey." Well, Casey kept hitting me grounders. I bet he hit between eighty and a hundred grounders, and I'd catch most of them, but some would bounce up and hit me, and I'd just throw them back ready for some more.

Casey told Red, "That little son of a gun. I've hit him so many grounders, I think he's trying to wear me out. He doesn't catch them all, but he doesn't back off from any, either."

That was the spring of 1946. After I graduated, I didn't get a single offer from a major league team. Nobody wanted to sign me because they thought I was too small, although I had led my high-school team two years in a row. I could run like heck, and I had a fantastic arm—erratic, but fantastic. One time I'd throw the ball over to first with such speed that you could hear the ball whir. The next time I'd throw it fifteen rows into the seats.

I'd been working out with Oakland, and I was playing in our local playground, James Kenney Park, and I remember the date—it was July twenty-eighth—and a man by the name of Jimmy Hole came down and asked if a kid named Billy Martin was around. I told him I was Billy Martin. He told me an Oakland Oaks scout by the name of Eddie Leashman had sent him. Leashman had watched me in high school for two years. Holt said, "I saw you play a little bit, son. Leashman kinda thinks you can make it, and we wanted to know if you would come down to the Oakland ball park and talk to us about it. We're thinking of sending you to Idaho Falls. Do you want to go?"

I said, "Oh, yeah." Of course I wanted to go. I was eighteen years old, and I had worked in a slaughterhouse, worked in a pickle factory, done all sorts of odd jobs. My whole life I had wanted to be a baseball player. Did I want to go? Is the Pope Catholic?

I signed a contract for two hundred dollars a month to play for Idaho Falls, which was in the Oakland organization. Oakland was in the Pacific Coast League, which was like the majors to the people living in California. Each of the Coast League teams had it's own chain of minor league teams. There were three rungs to the Oakland organization. Idaho Falls was its bottom rung.

When I signed, I was asked whether I had any clothes. "I had a suit," I said, "but my uncle just died, and they buried him in it." I was asked whether I owned a suitcase, and I said no. "Here's three hundred dollars, kid, go out and buy yourself a suitcase and some slacks." I went home and bought a couple pairs of slacks and a nice suitcase, and I went over to the park to get a glove. I didn't own one. I used to borrow one at James Kenney Park, where I played on the team. They had gloves with JK stenciled on them, and before I left for Idaho Falls, I signed out a glove. I told them I was going to play pro ball and that I'd return it at the end of the season. It was kind of a raggy glove, but I'd been using it for quite a while, and I really had become attached to it.

I said good-bye to my family, and I got on a train for Salt Lake City, where I was to meet the Idaho Falls team. I only played in thirty-two games, because as soon as I got there I developed the damndest charley horses you've ever seen, and I could barely walk. I hadn't had a spring training, hadn't played for a while, and when I ran all out, I pulled muscles in both legs. The muscle in one of my legs is still pulled away from the bone because of what happened. And at that time they had a theory that if you got a charley horse, the way to cure it would be to run on it. I'd run, and it would just kill me it hurt so bad, and the trainer made me walk to and from the ball park after the game. Towards the last month of the season my legs started coming around, and I began to play regularly, and I must have played well because the next spring I was in training with the Oakland team, and that's where I really got to know Casey. He really took a liking to me. I was such a fresh kid, very pushy, and he liked that. I had been working out during the winter playing semipro ball, so when I came to camp, I was ready. The Oakland players were older guys, they had been around before, and when I got there I made it clear that I was going to take somebody's job away. Casey had me at third, and during practice right from the start I was really firing that ball, wanted to show them I had quite an arm. A fellow by the name of

Hardy was their regular third baseman, and the other players were saying, "Hey, Hardy, the kid's trying to take your job away," which was exactly what I was trying to do, and though they were getting mad at me, I really didn't care. I was there to win a job.

At the end of spring training the managers from the Oakland chain began to split up the players, and Johnny Babbit had the Stockton team and Arky Biggs had the Phoenix team, and Babbit decided he didn't want me, he wanted another kid, so I drove with Arky in a station wagon to Phoenix and when the season started Arky had me batting eighth. The pitcher batted ninth. The first exhibition game we played I had 6 hits, and the next day I had 4 hits and drove in 5 runs, and he moved me up to seventh in the order. By the time the regular season started I was batting sixth, and in a couple games I drove in the winning run, and he moved me up to fifth, and half the season I batted fifth until our catcher, Clint Courtney, broke his arm, and then I moved up to fourth. I almost hit .400 that year. The last week of the season I dropped to .393.

When the season ended, I went home. We didn't have a phone, and a couple days after I came home there was a knock on the door. It was an Oakland club official. "What are you doing here?" he said. "You're supposed to be in Portland." "Portland?" He said, "When the Phoenix season ended, you were supposed to report to Casey up in Portland." "I didn't know," I told him.

I went up there right away, and Casey put me in, but I didn't do too hot. In my first game Casey put me in against a pitcher by the name of Tommy Bridges. Casey told me he had a good curveball. It wasn't the whole truth. The first time I faced him he threw three fastballs by me for strikes that I didn't see. The next time up I went up looking for the fastball, and he threw me three curveballs that broke off the table— there was no way I could have hit them. I felt really overmatched, no question about it. I'd never seen anyone like that guy. Fortunately the rest of the pitchers weren't as good as he was.

By the next spring I had adjusted. Casey shifted me to second base, and after a couple months I began to play regularly.

In 1948 I hit .277, which wasn't too bad, and it was that spring that I got my first indication that I was going to make the majors.

We had played the New York Giants in a couple of exhibition games, and I'd put on the hit-and-run and executed it successfully a couple times, and I must have impressed Giants' owner Horace Stoneham, because he tried to buy me. Casey, however, wouldn't do it. Even though Casey was only the manager, he had complete control over who played, who was sent down, who was traded, and he told Stoneham that he was going to go to the Yankees the next year and that I was eventually going to go with him.

When the season began, however, I wasn't a starter. Dario Lodigiani was the regular second baseman, and Casey played him, and every day I would be pestering Casey to put me in there. One day he called me off the bench. "Grab your glove, kid," he yelled, and I ran over to him ready to go in. He said, "Stick around. I may need you to umpire!" A couple times I'd play and Casey would pinch-hit for me, and I'd be all over him, but Casey never seemed to let it bother him. He enjoyed my brashness, because though he was an old man even when he was with Oakland, as a kid he had been as brash as any of them. Casey had a reputation for being a clown—the story of his going up to the plate, taking off his cap, and having a bird fly out from his head is famous—but behind that image was a very tough, hard-driving competitor. He hated to lose, too, almost as much as I did. Casey and I became very close.

All the while I watched how he did things. I was amazed at his loyalty to his players. One time our whole team was involved in a fight on the field, and I turned around, and I couldn't believe it: Casey was right behind me out there ready to go at it if he had to. A couple times he went out there and got shoved to the ground. I saw the way he treated each player differently. He never had a doghouse. If you got in a fight with him, by the next day it was forgotten. And he would talk to me all the time, even when I wasn't playing. He made everyone feel right at home, and when I did play, he was always bragging on me, giving me confidence. He was tremendous to me.

Casey was always telling me to be more aggressive. The 1948

Oakland team was known as the Nine Old Men—all the starters were ex-major leaguers or long-time Coast League players, and I was just a kid—in fact I got my nickname Billy the Kid playing with all these old-timers—and Casey wanted me to be more of a leader even though I was so young. He wanted me to go to the mound and talk to the pitcher if he was in trouble, wanted me to take charge of the infield, things I wouldn't have done ordinarily because I was so young compared to the other guys.

For two months I played second, and when Lodigiani returned, Casey had me starting at shortstop and third as well. He had always believed in platooning his players, figuring that if the infielders could play more than one position, he'd be that much better off if somebody got hurt. He'd have the same number of players as everyone else. He'd be able to do so much more with them.

Casey roomed me with Cookie Lavaghetto, who was another extremely intelligent baseball man. Cookie had played for ten years with the Pirates and the Dodgers. Just the year before he had broken up Bill Bevens's no-hitter in the ninth inning of the World Series. Bevens was leading 2 to 1 in the ninth, and after two Dodgers walked, Cookie doubled them home to win it. Casey had Cookie work with me, and I learned so much from him. He taught me how to make a double play and what to expect from the runners. He taught me to learn who could run fast and who couldn't, to know when I had to hurry on a play and when I didn't. He'd make me sit in a restaurant and stare at a wall without blinking my eyes. I'd practice that for hours. Try it sometime. It isn't easy. He had me do that because he felt that when you were up at the plate, the ball would go by so fast that if you accidentally blinked, that fraction of a second would be enough of a distraction to make you miss the ball. He taught me how to get the ball out of my glove, showed me how to circle the bases, taught me how a slower guy could circle them faster than a fast guy by cutting the corners right. So many things he taught me.

Another teammate of mine who I loved was Ernie Lombardi, who should have been in the Hall of Fame years ago. In 17 years in the majors Ernie hit over .300, and I can't imagine a better catcher. He'd stay in his squat, and he'd still throw guys out stealing second. The only thing Ernie couldn't do was run. The shortstop used to play him in shallow left field, and he'd hit a grounder on fifteen hops and still get thrown out. Imagine what he would have hit if he could have run!

Ernie would sit behind that plate, and when the pitcher would throw it in when he wanted a new ball, Ernie used to catch it with his bare hand. One day he was throwing a runner out at second, and I was the second baseman, and the ball tailed into the runner, and the runner cut my knee wide open. They were going to bring the stretcher out, but Ernie was so upset he came running out from behind home plate, picked me up like I was a toy, and carried me all the way into the clubhouse. He felt so bad. Felt it was his fault.

I had twenty-eight stitches. The doctor sewed me up right in the clubhouse. He said, "Do you drink, son?" I was twenty at the time, and I had taken a vow that I wouldn't drink until I was twenty-one. "No," I said. He said, "We don't have anything to kill the pain. You're going to have to take something." He called for a messenger to run out and get me a double bourbon. I drank it, and did it burn inside. He said, "I'm going to have to sew up your leg right here," and fortunately I have a rather high tolerance for pain, but as he was sewing the leg, I could feel that pain knifing through me. Four teammates had to hold me down. He finished the job, and he said, "I want you to get up and walk on it." Everyone was telling me I'd be out at least two weeks, but I bet 'em it wouldn't be a week, and it wasn't. I had won a starting job, and I wasn't about to give it back. We won the Coast League pennant that year, the first for Oakland in more than twenty years. I had been driving around in a '34 Chevy with one fender off and the driver's side so mashed in that you had to get in on the other side. At the end of the season Oaks' owner Brick Laws bought me a black 1948 Chevy convertible. Oh, I was hot stuff.

I was disappointed Casey didn't take me to the Yankees in 1949, but it wasn't too bad because he told me it wouldn't be long before he called for me. I had another good year for Oakland in '49, hit .286, drove in 92 runs, and all during the season I kept hearing how different major league clubs wanted me.

Jackie Jensen had been a football and baseball star at the University of California, and he had signed a big bonus contract and was playing for the Oaks that year, and at the end of the year it was announced that the Yankees had bought me and Jensen. I was ecstatic, until I found out Jensen was getting $60,000 to sign with the Yankees. I got zero. In fact, when I went to see George Weiss to talk about my salary for 1950, he offered me $7,500, which was fifteen hundred dollars less than what I had been making with the Oaks. Again, because I was Casey's boy, Weiss made my contract negotiations as tough as he could possibly make them. He fought me for every penny.

While Casey was managing the Yankees to a pennant in '49, he had been bragging to his players about me. He was telling everybody how fresh I was, and Ralph Buxton, who had played with me at Oakland, was in camp in '50, and he was telling the other Yankee players what a fresh little bastard I was. I had barely arrived, and they were calling me "Casey's Little Bobo," "The Dead End Kid from Berkeley," and "Billy the Brat." They were making me out to be like Eddie Stanky.

Maybe I was a brat, but in my whole life I had never taken any crap from anybody, and I saw no reason why I should start just because I was on the Yankees. One day I was pitching batting practice, and Jim Turner the pitching coach yelled at me to get off the mound. He wanted his pitchers doing the throwing. I turned and yelled at him and said, "Are you the manager of this club? I thought Casey was the manager." And Turner and I got into it. Turner had been the manager of the Portland team in the Pacific Coast League, and when we played against them he used to ride me, call me "Big Nose" from the sidelines. Just because he was now a Yankee coach, he didn't think I forgot how he used to agitate me, did he? My memory wasn't short.

I hit over .350 in spring training, showed the guys I could play, and that helped my getting acceptance. I'll never forget George Stirnweiss, who's job I was taking away. He never resented me. In fact, he tried to help me all he could. It was the Yankee way of doing things, teammates helping teammates. Phil Rizzuto was nice to me, helped me a lot. One day I was sitting in my locker, and Joe DiMaggio walked by. DiMage was from the San Francisco Bay area, where I was from, and he had been a big Coast League star and then a major league star ever since I was a baby. At the time he was spending a lot of time by himself, he had become a loner, but he came over and said, "Billy, would you like to go out to dinner with me tonight?" I was awed, in shock. I said, "Sure, Joe." I got up to go out for practice, and all the guys started really hoorahing me. They were really on me. "Guess who's going out to dinner with the Big Dago?" Johnny Lindell and Cliff Mapes kept asking. I finally said, "Do you know why he's taking me out?" They said, "No, why?" I said, "Because he likes to go out with people who have class. That's why he isn't taking you bums with him." Oh, did they let me have it.

I was the only guy who could tease Joe and agitate him. For some reason, when he got undressed, he would take his pants off first. He'd be wearing a tie and a jacket and even his shoes, and the first thing he'd take off was his pants. He'd take them off and sit in his locker, and he would say to Pete Sheehy, the clubhouse boy, "Hey, Pete, how about a half a cup of coffee." Joe had a spittoon in his locker, and he would sip the coffee, and spit a spray of coffee into the spittoon.

When he walked into the clubhouse, it was like a United States senator walking in. Everyone would be saying, "Hi, Joe," "Hi, Dage," "Hi, Clipper," and as he walked in, I would come walking in right behind him. Our lockers were next to each other, and he would walk over to his and take his pants off, and I would take my pants off, and he would sit down, and I would sit down, and he would ask for a half a cup of coffee, and I would ask for a half a cup of coffee. We'd both get our coffee, and he'd spit into his spittoon, and I would try to spit, but I could never do it. He'd look at me and say, "You fresh little bastard."

Remember those fountain pens that used to squirt ink that would get all over you and then disappear? One day Joe came walking into the clubhouse, and I yelled over to him, "Hey, Joe, would you sign this ball?" He said, "Sure, Billy, I'd be glad to." When he came over I shot that ink all over his shirt, and he gave me such a dirty look that if there was a way I could have run out of the clubhouse, I would have. It was the dirtiest look I ever got in my life. I was saying, "Joe, it'll disappear. It'll disappear, Joe." Later he laughed. But at first he didn't think it was too funny.

I started going out with Joe, and a few of the other veterans, and third-base coach Frank Crosetti cornered me. He said, "I want you to be careful. I don't want you staying out late and getting into bad habits. You got a future ahead of you." I thanked him. On the Yankees they were always watching out for the younger kids, making sure they didn't get into trouble.

I had always listened to the Yankees when they were playing in the World Series. We didn't have a TV, only a radio, but the announcers would talk about Yankee Stadium, and one of my most memorable moments came when spring training broke and we took the train to New York and I saw the stadium for the first time. When I was a boy I had read a book about Lou Gehrig, called *A Quiet Hero*, by Frank Graham, and here I was playing on the same field as Gehrig, and Babe Ruth, and Joe DiMaggio. I stood out on the field. I was in such awe. I stood there for the longest while, staring into the grandstands and the bleachers and the dugouts, looking at the monuments, noticing how beautifully the grass was cut, looking at the latticework of the overhang on top of the grandstand.

I walked over to the visitors' dugout, where Ruth and Gehrig had sat before the Yankees changed dugouts, and I reached down and touched the steps where they used to walk up and down. I was just so happy to be a Yankee. Just happy to be there.

It wasn't easy for me the first couple of years because I had to sit on the bench most of 1950 and '51. I had been a regular player all my life, and I wasn't playing. I'd bug Casey about going into the game, just the way I did when I first came up to the Oaks, but Coleman was in front of me and I couldn't get him out of there. Having Joe there made everything easier. He would talk to me like I was a little brother, tell me that my chance would come and that I had to be patient.

I remember opening day that year, we were getting beat 9 to 0 in Boston, and Casey put me in figuring that the game was lost. I came up with two men on, and DiMage, who was in the on-deck circle, was yelling, "Come on, Billy, come on," really rooting for me, which was unusual because Joe was so quiet most of the time. Mell Parnell, who had won 25 games the year before, was pitching, and he threw the first pitch almost over my head and I swung and missed. He was crazy enough to throw me a strike, and I hit a double off the left-field wall. Joe Di was screaming with joy. He then got up and bombed one over the wall to make it 9 to 6. I came up again in the same inning with the bases loaded, singled in two more runs, and we ended up winning the game 15 to 10.

The game was over, and we were in the clubhouse, and all the writers were around Joe. I had just established a major league record, getting two hits in my first two at bats in the major leagues, and the publicity didn't mean anything to me, never did, but when they went over to talk with Joe, he told the writers, "You think I had a good day. What about that kid?" And he pointed to me. "He's the one you should be talking to." Other days he'd hit a home run, a triple, and a couple of doubles, and I'd get a couple humpback singles, and he'd come over and say, "Great day today, kid. Great day." He was so good to me.

I didn't play for a couple weeks after that, and then Coleman hurt his knee and was out for a game, and I played and drove in the winning run. I didn't get to play for another couple weeks. We got back to New York and I pinch-hit a single to drive in two runs and win the game, and Weiss sent me down. After I came back up a month later, I spent the rest of my Yankee career looking over my shoulder.

In October of 1950, right after the World Series, I got married. Her name was Lois Berndt, and I had known her since I was in the ninth grade. We dated in high school, and then she broke up with me, and went out with a guy named Nivarro. He had a car and I didn't. When I started playing minor league ball she started liking me again, and when I came back from Phoenix in '47 we started hitting it off real good.

Lois was a doll. She was a really pretty girl. My best friend was Howard Noble, and Lois was the best friend of Howard Noble's girl friend. They used to hang out together, and Howard used to tell me how ideal it would be if I took Lois out. So I started dating her.

We got married because Howard and his girl friend got married, and Lois kept telling me how depressed she was with me away from home playing ball, and all that same old baloney you always hear. To be honest with you, I didn't want to get married. I was twenty-two years old and in the major leagues. But when I got back home at the end of the season, I felt sorry for her, and we ran off and got married.

The Korean War started in June, and I got my draft notice about a week after we were married. I went to Fort Ord, California, as a private. My stepfather had had a heart attack and couldn't work. My older brother, Tudo, who wanted to go into the service, was turned down, and I was supporting a brother and two sisters who were still in school, my wife Lois, my stepfather, and my brother Jackie, who was suffering from dysentery and couldn't hold a job. All on a private's salary.

I was trying to get Army allotments for them, and when I applied I was told that I wasn't making enough money to support all those people. I had passed the officers'-school test—I have trouble opening a garage door but they decided I was mechanically inclined—and they told me if I wanted to make more money I could go to Fort Benning, Georgia, and become a second lieutenant. But there was a catch: I had to spend an extra year in the service. I said, "Can't you just make me a second louie without my having to stay in the extra year?" They said no. I was told to apply for a hardship, which I certainly didn't want, because I had put in five and a half months, and I wanted to get my service obligation out of the way. But they told me I had to apply, didn't have a choice, and after they checked out my story, I was released in late March of '51. That was all right with me at the time, but if I had realized what it was going to mean later, I would have fought it.

Meanwhile, while I was at Fort Ord, I was driving with three other soldiers late at night back to the post when a car ran a red light, sideswiped me, and took off. I chased after the car to get his license-plate number, and we tailed him to a dead end, where we had him cornered. He jumped out of the car, and the four of us jump out, and one of the other guys tackles him and pounds him. The two stopped fighting, and the guy who hit us got back into the car and drove away. I wasn't within ten feet of him at any time. We turned in his plate number to the police, and when the guy found out who I was, he filed an assault suit against me! I couldn't believe it. When the case comes to trial, the three other guys who were in my car were all in Korea. I couldn't bring in a single witness, and so it was his word against mine, and he won the case. I ended up having to pay almost three thousand dollars to a guy who sideswiped my car, a guy who hit-and-run me, a guy I didn't even punch.

When I went back to the Yankees in '51 I was again making all of $7,500 a year. I was staying at the Concord Plaza Hotel, up the hill from Yankee Stadium. I didn't have enough money to go anywhere, and I was lonely. Lois was in Berkeley and I was in New York, and she must have been terribly lonely, too.

It was also a tough year for Joe DiMaggio. Joe was depressed quite often. Injuries and age began taking their toll, and it was a well-kept secret, but for the last couple years Joe couldn't throw. No one said anything, he kept playing, with the second baseman running as far out into right field as possible to take the throws. Everyone admired his arm so much from before that they never caught on that his arm was bad. He was also starting to struggle at bat. His back muscles were hurting him, and he was having a hard time holding his bat up, they hurt so much, so he had to drop his bat down a little, and he was hitting balls to the opposite field, which he never did before. When he hit a home run to right field, he would complain about his "piss home run." He'd say, "Anybody could hit a piss home run to right." I knew '51 would be his last year. He didn't feel he was Joe DiMaggio playing anymore.

If Yankee Stadium wasn't the shape it was, with its short right-field porch and its 457 feet to left center, Joe would have hit eighty or ninety home runs a year. Every year he'd hit thirty or forty balls to the warning track that were 430-foot outs. Joe would have broken every home-run record ever set, and not Hank Aaron or anyone else would have come close.

Also, Mr. Weiss used to take down the center-field net on

Sunday doubleheaders so he could squeeze a few thousand more fans into the park. He'd take down the black screen that would allow the batters to see the ball, and if you went one for eight on a Sunday, you'd be having a good day. That had to have cost Joe twenty points a year on his batting average.

Yankee Stadium separated the men from the boys when it came to right-handed hitters. It was the reason we were able to beat the Dodgers in the World Series so consistently. The Dodgers would come in with all those right-handed home-run hitters like Hodges, Robinson, Campanella, and they'd hit balls nine miles for outs. The ball park defeated the Dodgers.

Despite Yankee Stadium, Joe DiMaggio retired with a .325 average, 361 home runs, 131 triples, 389 doubles, more than 2,200 hits, and remember, he missed all of 1943, '44, and '45 when he served in the military. I wish I could have seen him the year he hit in fifty-six straight games. That must have been something.

Wherever Joe went, people would grab at him, crowd him, take away whatever time he had away from the park. Sometimes when he was eating dinner, people would grab at his arm, and that would make him mad. That makes a lot of players mad. They don't mind signing autographs at the park, or in the hotel, but they have to have certain places where they can have some privacy. It got so Joe and I would eat dinner in our room. We had many dinners in the room, and I would root for Joe to get three or four hits in a game, because then he'd feel happy enough to go out to eat, and we'd go someplace where the owner would protect us from the public. When he was happy, I'd be happier than he was. When he was down, I felt terrible for him.

I saw Joe starting to get happy again when he was going out with Marilyn Monroe. He blossomed. He was a changed man, and I was very happy for him, happy for them both. A couple times the three of us went out to dinner together. Usually I begged off and got out right away, because I didn't want to feel like a third wheel. I remember when we were together, I was very impressed with her. She seemed bashful and shy and sensitive. She was polite, and she was much more beautiful in person than she was in the movies.

They got married, but their marriage lasted about as long as mine did. It didn't work out. Joe never talked about it, and I never asked him. Never would.

Mickey Mantle came up to the Yankees that year. He came up as a shortstop, the funniest shortstop I ever saw. Every once in a while he'd catch a ball, and when he did catch it, he'd throw it into the stands more often than not. But, oh, he could run, and he could hit. We trained in Phoenix that year, traded camps with the Giants, and though he only weighed about 160 pounds, in batting practice he was hitting the ball nine miles over the center-field fence batting from both sides of the plate.

At first Mickey thought I was fresh. One day Frank Crosetti was talking to me about making the double play, and I was telling Crosetti, "No, I was taught to do it this way." I disagreed with him, and Mickey couldn't believe I could act like that. But after a while we started palling around together, and we found out we had a lot in common. Neither one of us were heavy drinkers, so we'd go to the movies a lot. He would sit and listen to country-and-western music, and at first I didn't like it at all, but he got me to sit and listen to the lyrics, and I fell in love with it. We'd fish, play golf together. Neither one of us were good golfers, but we had a lot of fun. We'd hunt.

One time we were hunting in his hometown of Commerce, Oklahoma, with his twin brothers Roy and Ray. They were big and could run, and they had been great athletes in high school, and the day we went out ducks weren't in season. We were walking along with our guns, and a long distance over rows and rows of dirt from a plowed field, there were a bunch of ducks sitting in a pond. Mickey and his brothers crawled around to one side of the pond, and I went around to the other side, we crouched down and started popping those ducks. After I shoot, I look up, and I see Mickey, Roy, and Ray running just as fast as they can back to the car. They were running so fast their feet were barely touching the top of the clods of dirt. I looked around, and there was the game warden coming toward me. It was cold, and I had layers and layers of clothes on, and as I ran, it felt like I was running in quicksand. I was hardly moving at all. I couldn't catch up with them, and here the game warden kept coming toward me. I wasn't going to shoot him, but I dropped to the ground and pointed the gun at him to scare him, and when he saw that, he turned and started running the other way. Then I got up and ran to the car, and we got away. When I joined up with them, I said to Mickey, "It was awful nice of you to warn me."

Mickey would always be playing tricks on me. We'd go into a restaurant, and I'd see a face I recognized, and I'd say to Mickey, "Who's that?" He'd say, "Fred." The guy would come up, and I'd say, "How are you, Fred?" and the guy would say, "My name's Al, Billy." Mickey used to tell me the wrong name all the time. He could remember names, and I couldn't. He'd stand there and giggle.

One day we were going hunting. He said, "We're going down to south Texas, about a five-hour drive. I have a friend I went to school with there, he has a big ranch, and we can go deer hunting." I said great. We made the trip, got down there, and Mickey said, "You stay in the car. I'll go in and talk to my buddy, and we'll go right out and hunt." Mickey went into the house. I didn't know this, but the owner said to Mickey, "Heck, Mickey, you can hunt all over my place, but would you do me a favor? I have a pet mule who's going blind, and I don't have the guts to kill the poor fellow. Would you kill him for me?" So I didn't know he had asked Mickey to kill it.

Mickey came out, and he slammed the door like he was mad. I said, "What's the matter?" Mickey said, "He won't let us hunt here." I said, "You got to be kidding." He said, "No, I'm not, and I'm so mad that I'm going to go by the barn and shoot his mule." I said, "Mickey, you can't shoot that man's mule." He said, "The hell I ain't. I'm gonna kill that mule." We drove through the barnyard, and there was the mule. Mickey got out of the car with his rifle, and crack, he shot the mule and killed it. He turned around, and he saw that my rifle was smoking. He said, "What the hell are you doing?" I said, "I got two of his cows."

Ahh, that cost us some money.

Mickey never once let his baseball fame affect him. He was always the same, a down-home country boy. We were young kids. He was nineteen and I was twenty-two. Everyone thought that because we were major leaguers that we were mature adults. We weren't. We were kids. When we traveled from town to town, we went by train, and we'd be in our private car and we'd have a couple drinks, and we'd wrestle. He let me get my favorite hold on him, and I'd get as tight a grip as I could, and he'd throw me against the wall like I was a toy. I'd come back and grab him again, and he'd flex his muscles, and I'd go flying again.

One time I said, "I'm going to beat you on the train today." He said, "You're going to beat me?" I said, "Yes, today I'm going to beat you." He said, "You don't have a chance." We started wrestling. He said, "Get your favorite grip." I put my arm around him, and when he went to throw me, I got ahold of his gums with my fingers, and I held on for dear life. He couldn't eat for two days!

We'd bring water guns into the clubhouse, and we'd squirt water at each other and at everyone else. When Polaroid cameras came out, Joe Collins would be sitting on the toilet, and we'd open the stall door and take a picture of him. We'd play darts in the clubhouse.

We didn't have much money that year. The other players did, and they'd rush off to go someplace, and Lois and I and Mickey and his wife Merlyn would go back to our apartments next to the Concourse Plaza. We were told the apartments had a nice breeze in the summer. Cross ventilation, we were told. Our apartments adjoined one another, and the cross ventilation turned out to be a window in my bedroom taking the air to a window in his apartment. It was so hot that we had to watch television in bathing suits. Because our bedroom windows were adjoining, it was possible for each of us to crawl outside and peek in and see what the other was doing in bed. Lois and I were always teasing Mickey and Merlyn about doing that, and they'd be teasing us, and one night I went outside, and it was absolutely pitch black, and I started crawling over to Mickey's bedroom window. I was down on my knees, and as I was making my way, bang, I hit heads with someone. It was Mickey. I said, "What are you doing?" He said, "What are you doing?" We caught each other.

Mickey was so naive when he was a kid. We were staying at

the Chase Hotel in St. Louis. We had a midnight curfew, and it was about eleven-thirty, and you know how young guys are always hoping that some women would show up. There were five of us, Mickey, Whitey Ford, me, Hank Bauer, and Ralph Houk. We all hung around together. Suddenly five girls came out from the lobby. I started talking to them, and they were friendly, and just then five guys came out, guys who were with them, and they weren't too friendly. One of the guys wanted to fight. He was mad. I don't know why he got so mad, but he did, and Hank Bauer and Ralph Houk started arguing over who was going to fight the guy. Houk said, "I'm not playing regularly. If I get hurt, it won't hurt the club." We knew Ralph could handle himself. He had been a Marine and had won a couple medals in the war, and Mickey was watching this, and he was in awe. He had never seen a fight in his life. Everyone in Oklahoma is a cousin. Very gentlemanly, Ralph and the guy squared off, and Ralph proceeded to knock the guy down. Just as soon as he hit the pavement, Mickey ran over, took a hand-kerchief, wiped the blood off his face, and picked him up like he was a toy. The guy again squared off with Ralph, and again Ralph knocked him down. Again Mickey wiped off his face and picked him up. Ralph knocked the guy down a third time, and Mickey ran over to him. The guy was lying on one elbow, and he turned to Mickey and said, "Buddy, I don't know who the hell you are, but would you mind staying out of this fight?" He wanted to stay down.

Ralph got involved in another incident in St. Louis. Ralph, Charley Silvera, Gene Woodling, Mickey, and I and a few other guys were sitting in a bar, and there was a woman bar-tender, and somebody said something to her, you're cute, nothing bad, but she took exception and got mad. The next thing we knew, the bouncer came over to one of the players and started to give him a bad time, and we all came together, and four or five other bouncers showed up, too, and it looked like all hell was going to break out. One of the bouncers pulled out a gun, and quickly Ralph took a whiskey bottle and broke it on the bar and he put the broken bottle up to the neck of the guy who had the gun. Ralph said, "I'm not afraid of guns. You put that gun away, or I'll cut your throat." He said, "Okay," and using him as a hostage, we walked backward out of the bar with the bottle to his throat. Did you ever see eight guys get into a cab? We all jumped in one cab, got the hell out of there, and went back to the Chase Hotel.

I loved the guys I played with on the Yankees. Old Timers' Day means so much to me because I get to see them again. We used to spend so much time together, not like today. Now you get on a plane and land in a city, and everyone rents his own car, and everyone goes off in a different direction. We spent hours with the other guys on the train or on a bus, and we'd come to the clubhouse early and sit and talk baseball or play cards. There was so much more closeness then, more respect and admiration for each other than there is now. You'd get to know the other guy's good points and bad points, better than you knew anyone else, sometimes better than your own wife.

We had so many good players on those Yankee teams, and everyone pulled for each other. There was no airing out of feelings in the newspaper. If there was criticism to be made, it would be constructive. A player would go up to another player and tell him privately what he did wrong and what he should do so it wouldn't happen again. Sure, there were players on the club we didn't like, but we kept it to ourselves. That was the Yankee way of doing things. Also, on those Yankee teams, whatever the manager said went. Casey ruled with an iron hand, and he was always on top of everything. He liked players who were just like him. When a player blew a game, he'd watch to see who he hung around with, wanted to see how the player reacted, whether he acted like he cared or not, wanted to see if the guys he hung out with cared or not. He hated it when we lost and someone would be laughing or joking after the game.

I was the one guy on the team who could agitate the old man, and what was so great about him was he never built a doghouse. We'd scream and yell, and the next day it would be forgotten. Casey loved Mickey and me, and on spring-training trips he usually made Mickey and me go with him. This one day, though, he decided to leave Mickey behind. It was a couple spring trainings later, and we had to take a bus from St. Pete to Orlando, which was a long ride on bumpy, narrow roads as the big highways hadn't been built yet. It was a three-day road trip to Orlando, and when we got there, we knew that the field, where the Washington Senators played, was really terrible, hard and rocky. No one liked to play there.

Mickey was in the clubhouse with his son, Mickey Junior, who was about five then, and he started teasing me: "Have a nice trip on that bus going over to Orlando. You're going to really enjoy that nice bus ride and that beautiful park over there." He was really teasing me. I said, "I'm telling you, Mickey, you better get off my back." He said, "Aw, I think I'll take Mickey Junior home, and maybe we'll take a nice walk, go down to the beach and catch some trout." He was really pouring it on. Our bags were packed, and we were ready to get on the bus, and I walked into Casey's office. I said, "Casey, I can't stand this any longer." He said, "What's the matter?" I said, "Mickey's hoorahing because we have to make this trip, and he gets to stay behind. I don't think that's right. He shouldn't be doing that." I'm putting the old man on, right? I didn't know he was going to get mad. Real quick, Casey says, "Oh he is, is he?" He walked into the clubhouse. Mickey had his jeans on, and he had his kid by his hand and he was about to walk out when Casey stopped him. "Put your kid in a cab," he said. "You're going on this trip. You're not going to be making fun of the guys who have to play." Mickey had to put Mickey Junior in a cab and make the trip. I laughed the whole way there. He kept saying, "You son of a bitch. You son of a bitch."

Casey didn't miss much. Nothing went by him. One night Casey and I were at a banquet, and he was talking to a few people, and this girl came up to me, she was a real doll, and we got to talking, and I told her, "After the banquet Casey and I have to go over to some people's house, but when that's over, I'll meet you back here, say at midnight." She agreed, and Casey and I went to the people's house, and he was talking, and he had my right arm locked in his left arm as he talked. It was getting to be eleven, and he was talking and still had me by the arm, and then it was eleven thirty, and I wanted to go real bad, and I started to pull away, but he held me so tight I couldn't. He said, "Stay here with me and listen. You might learn something." What could I do? Midnight came and went, and it got to be twelve thirty, and I knew I had blown it with the girl, and finally Casey lets go of my arm and says, "You can go and see that girl now if you want to." The bastard had heard us arranging our meeting, and he was making sure I'd get to bed on time for the next day's game.

He sure knew how to handle players. He'd leave Yogi and Rizzuto alone, because when he got on them, they'd pout and wouldn't play as good as they could, but he would ride Mickey and me, because he knew we responded to that. He was always doing things to me. One day he posted a lineup that had our pitcher, Tommy Byrne, batting eighth and me batting ninth. I blew my top. I took that lineup, and I thumbtacked it to the wall upside down, so now I was batting first. Turned out he was just agitating me, and in the game I batted leadoff, as I did sometimes.

The same guys played year after year. Yogi was behind the plate almost twenty years and Mickey was in center for eighteen years, and at shortstop he had Rizzuto, who had played there since 1941, and he had Coleman and me at second.

Casey had kept me on the bench most of '51 as he had in '50, but when I came to camp in '52 I was ready to step into a starting role, because Coleman had been drafted, and I knew he'd be gone by the end of April. I was excited about getting my chance.

Joe DiMaggio had retired, and in '52 he was doing a pregame TV show, and he asked me if I'd like to do a commercial for Buitoni macaroni. In the commercial I was supposed to slide into second base to break up a double play while Rizzuto was leaping over me to make the throw. I was to get a hundred dollars. I agreed, and we did the commercial. The next day I got a phone call. Would I please shoot the commercial one more time? They didn't like the way it had come out. I was doing it for Joe, so naturally I agreed. That day I had put on a brand-new pair of spikes. To break in spikes, you wear them maybe a half an hour a day until they're broken in. I had just started wearing these spikes, and when I did the commercial a second time I slid in, tucked my leg under, and as I hit the bag my spikes caught, and I could hear "crack, crack" from my ankle. I laid there, and Rizzuto said, "C'mon, get up." I said, "No, I think I've ripped up my leg." He said, "C'mon." He thought I was kidding. Again he told me to get up. I tried to get up, and I fell down, and I said, "I think I've broken my leg." Finally he believed me. I was brought into the clubhouse, and they were trying to stick my foot in an ice bucket, and they couldn't get it in there, and it was killing me. The doctor is telling me I had a sprained ankle, and Mickey was getting madder'n hell. "Can't you see it's not just a sprain," he was yelling at him. "You're hurting the guy." He and the doctor, Sidney Gaynor, almost got into it. Gaynor said, "I know what I'm doing." Several players had to restrain Mickey. It's the maddest I've ever seen him get.

They took me to the hospital, and Mickey was right. Two ankle bones were broken. Fortunately they had cracked in place. Gaynor put my leg in a cast that night, but he put it in too soon. He didn't wait for the swelling to go down. That night the governor of Florida was having a banquet, and the Yankee executives were there, and Dr. Gaynor was there, and because I didn't want to stay in the hospital, a special room was set up for me in the Sorena Hotel. I was rooming with Mickey, and my leg started throbbing. I took pain pills, sleeping pills, nothing that night seemed to work. I couldn't stand it much longer. I told Mickey, "Call the banquet. Get Dr. Gaynor down here immediately." Mickey called him, and he came back to the hotel.

I said, "Doc, this leg is killing me." He said, "It might have swelled a little bit. He cut open the cast, and my leg sprung out of it a bright red. He looked at it and said, "We have a lot of swelling here, a lot more than we thought we were going to get." I always wondered who the "we" was. He left the leg out all night, and the swelling went down, and the next day I was all right, and he put it back in a cast.

I broke the leg on March twelfth, and I was playing by May twelfth. This was my opportunity to win the second-base job, and here I was hurt. While I was in the cast, I would do two hundred heel-and-toe lifts, and did that hurt. After a couple weeks I was out of bed, and I would walk with my walking cane around the ball park, and as my leg got stronger I would jog some until I could run, and I would keep running until the pain wouldn't let me run anymore.

Meanwhile I was so worried, I couldn't eat, and my weight dropped from 160 to 131. I didn't eat breakfast, didn't eat dinner. I was living on bread and a cup of coffee and a lot of lemonade. I couldn't keep the food down. When I ate something, I'd throw it up.

I started playing regularly, and I was doing okay, and then in June I hurt my knee making a head-first slide. Again I was out, and again I worried. My career had just started, and I was getting hurt all the time. I had seen too many players whose careers had ended before they began because of injuries. I was also worried about George Weiss. I knew he had been worried about my knees before he signed me. There was another thing: My marriage to Lois wasn't going so well. It's tough being married to a ballplayer who's away so much, and she and I were starting to fight with each other. She was pregnant, too, and I didn't want what happened to my mom and dad happening to Lois and me. I didn't want my baby to grow up not knowing her father.

All these worries kept me at the edge. We were playing the Red Sox at Fenway Park, and Jimmy Piersall, who unknown to everyone was mentally ill at the time, began needling me while we were having infield practice. He was calling me busher and dago, and finally I got tired of it, and I challenged him to fight me under the stands. He yelled, "Yeah, ya little dago, let's go." He went into his dugout, and I went into mine, and we raced under the stands to meet behind home plate. Our coach Bill Dickey was right behind me, and Boston pitcher Ellis Kinder was running after Piersall, but we got into it before they could stop us, and I managed to cut his cheek and bloody up his nose a little. Dickey tried to grab me, and I knocked his cap off. Two days later Piersall was shipped back to the minors, and a couple months later he ended up in a mental institution, which made me feel terrible. I didn't know he was sick, otherwise I never would have gone after him. But he didn't know how I was feeling about things, either. The men in the white suits weren't too far behind me, either.

I got into another fight a few weeks later, but that had nothing to do with my state of mind. I had been watching catcher Clint Courtney spike players all through the minors. One time when I was with Phoenix, he threw a body block at Arky Biggs, who was our manager and second baseman, and he broke Arky's arm. I went after Courtney, but I wasn't able to get to him. Later that year I had an infected toenail and couldn't play, probably the one game of the season I missed, and a little kid by the name of Eddie Lemade was playing third— Lemade and I went to high school together; he was killed in Korea—Courtney jumps into him with his spikes and puts thirty stitches into his leg. I was watching the game from the stands, and I came running out, jumped over the railing, and I yelled at him that I would get him if it was the last thing I ever did.

Courtney and I both started on the Yankees, but he was traded to the St. Louis Browns, and in this one game he slid into me with his spikes high. I sidestepped him, and I planted the baseball right between his teeth full blast. Knocked him colder than a cucumber. I stood waiting for him to get up, but he didn't, and I figured if I stood out there any longer I would get in trouble with the umpires, so I started running to the bench. Our pitcher, Allie Reynolds, yelled for me to look out, and Courtney threw a right hand that just missed me. If he had connected, he would have landed me in the upper deck. I swung around, and I belted him a couple of times. The umpires knew who had started the whole thing. They threw Courtney out of the game but not me. But I was still fined $150, and everyone was saying how bad it was that I had gotten into a fight. What did they want me to do, stand there and let Courtney deck me?

We battled the Cleveland Indians down to the wire to win the '52 pennant, and we met the Brooklyn Dodgers in the World Series. It was the beginning of probably the greatest World Series rivalry in history, two of the greatest teams in baseball history playing each other four times, in 1952, '53, '55, and '56, and to make it even more exciting, every year the Series went the full seven games.

I was really looking forward to playing the Dodgers. When I was a kid I went to a Dodger tryout. I went with three other kids down to San Mateo. We didn't have any money, so we hitched to get there, and when we arrived we didn't have anyplace to sleep, so we went to the park and fell asleep on the top of the dugout. It was about nine at night, and the cops came. They wanted to know what we were doing there.

"We're ballplayers," we said. "We're trying out for the Dodgers tomorrow." One cop said, "You can't sleep here. Why don't you spend the night in the station house? We'll let you sleep on cots in the cells." That sounded good to us, and after spending the night getting a good sleep, we went to the tryout. I got four hits in a squad game, played well in the field, and the scouts took my name and address and phone number. It was the old "don't call me, I'll call you" routine. Of course, we didn't have a phone—still . . .

Another reason I enjoyed beating the Dodgers was the competition with Jackie Robinson. There was a black lawyer in Berkeley by the name of Walter Gordon, who helped my mother when I was a kid. He had also helped Jackie, so when we played in the Series, I always wanted to show Walter that I was a better second baseman. That was my real challenge. And always I outhit, and always I outplayed him. Every Series we played in.

In the seventh game we were leading the Dodgers 4 to 2 in the seventh inning. Vic Raschi had pitched the day before, but Reynolds had gotten tired, and Casey brought Vic in to start the inning. He got an out but gave up a hit and two walks, and the Dodgers had the bases loaded. Casey went out to the mound and brought in Bob Kuzava, which surprised the heck out of me, because we were playing in Ebbets Field with that short left field, and Kuzava hadn't pitched much, and the next two batters were Duke Snider and Jackie Robinson. Duke popped out. Two down.

It was getting toward the end of the game, and the sun was real bad on the right side of the infield, and when Jackie hit a sky-high pop-up between Joe Collins and Yogi, I turned to see whether Joe could see it. Yogi was calling for him to make the catch, but I could see that he didn't know where the ball was, and I knew if I didn't get it, the ball would drop and two, probably three runs would score. I was playing deep, almost on the outfield grass, and as I started after the ball, I could tell that the wind was taking it toward home plate. I didn't realize how long a run I had to make until I watched the play on the motion pictures. I had to run past the pitcher's mound almost to home plate, and I got it just as it reached knee level. Kuzava held them the rest of the way, and we were champs again.

When the season ended Lois and I returned to Berkeley. She was pregnant with Kelly Ann. After my great World Series, I went to about four banquets a week, and I guess I didn't spend as much time with Lois as she would have liked, because something was coming between us. She was pregnant and had to stay at home, and it has always been difficult for me to sit in one place. I had to be on the go, and I just couldn't sit home. I had to get out.

The day Kelly was born, I was at the hospital, and she was having labor pains. She was screaming for me, and I started to go to her, and the nurse said, "You're better off if you don't go in." I figured she knew what she was talking about and I didn't go in. Maybe she was hurt because I didn't go in there. But I felt funny and awkward being in there. Who knows?

When she came home from the hospital, I could see that she hated even to see me. She hated everything about me. I accused her of having a boyfriend, and one time I did catch her on a date when she told me she was going out with her girl friends, but looking back, it really didn't matter. We never should have gotten married in the first place.

I was living with her and her parents in their home, and there was a knock at the door. She said, "Go see who it is, there's someone to see you." I opened the door, and this guy handed me my walking papers. Lois had filed for divorce. I couldn't live home anymore. I flew out to Kansas City and spent the winter there.

All through the 1953 season I had an empty, terrible feeling. I loved Lois, probably more than I realized, and I wanted her back and I wanted to be able to be with my baby, and I could not accept the reality of her wanting a divorce. I wouldn't give her the divorce right away. I held back quite a while, because I was praying she'd change her mind. I guess I should have realized there was no way I was ever going to get her back.

During the season when we were in New York I went to St. Patrick's Cathedral every day to say my Hail Marys. I used to say this one prayer to the Virgin Mary to "help me in this need." I was hoping through my prayers Lois would come back to me. Throughout the entire 1953 season, which was my best in the majors—I hit .257 with 15 home runs and 75 runs batted in—I was on the verge of a nervous breakdown. Only my friendship with Mickey saved me from going over the edge.

He'd see me call and try to talk to my wife, and she'd hang up on me, and I'd be upset and crying, and he'd be there to console me. It got so bad that one day I tore up just about our whole hotel room.

That year I also got into another fight with Clint Courtney. We were in St. Louis, playing extra innings, and Gil Mc-Dougald tried to score from second base on an infield single. The throw home had him beat, but Gil bowled over Courtney, who was catching, and scored. Courtney led off the bottom of the inning against Allie Reynolds, who he hit like he owned him. I found out later that he had sworn to Yogi that he was going to "get somebody." He singled to right, and with no chance of making second, rounded first and headed there for the express purpose of spiking somebody, in this case Phil Rizzuto, who was covering the base. It was funny, because Hank Bauer in right, Joe Collins, the first baseman, Allie Reynolds, the pitcher, and Gil McDougald, the third baseman, all ran toward second knowing exactly what Courtney was going to do. He jumped feet-first at Phil, gashing open his leg with his spikes, and bowling him completely over. Before he hit the ground, Collins, McDougald, Allie, and I all were on top of him. After the fight Whitey Ford said, "I threw the best punch." I said, "I didn't see you throw any punches." He said, "No? Look at this." Whitey had stomped on Courtney's glasses and shattered them into a million little pieces. He was standing there holding up the twisted frames.

The Browns fans started throwing pop bottles at our out-fielders. Gene Woodling complained to umpire John Rice. Rice told him, "Just ignore it." When another bottle landed near him, Gene picked it up and threw it at Rice. "Now we can ig-nore it together," he screamed at Rice.

We won the pennant so easy it was a laugh. Whitey Ford came back from the Army and won eighteen games, and he, Mickey, and I started hanging around together. The night we clinched the pennant we were all at the Stadium Club where they were throwing a victory party for us, and it was a really dull party, no music, no nothing, a dud. Mickey, Whitey, and I, and a couple other players, decided we'd go down to the Latin Quarter. We listened to the music and ate and were having a good time, and when the check came, I had enough to pay for it, and I said to Mickey and Whitey, "I'll get it, and we'll square up tomorrow, and the others will be our guests." Whitey said, "Tell you what. Let me sign it, and they can send the bill to the stadium, and we'll square up when it comes in." That sounded okay to me. He wrote his name, Mickey's name, and my name, and the waiter said, "For us to send it to the ball park, you have to put your boss's name on it, too," so Whitey wrote Dan Topping's name down there along with ours. The bill went to Topping, and boy, was he mad.

Mickey and I were staying in a downtown New York hotel, and usually in the morning I'd pretend I was sleeping so Mickey would always have to answer the phone, but this day the phone rang, and it was George Weiss. He said, "If you two are not in our office in a half an hour, it's going to cost you five thousand dollars." I said, "Okay, yes, sir." I hung up, and Mickey was still sleeping, and I go into the shower and start getting dressed. He raised his head up out of the bed and said, "Where are you going?" I said, "You better get out of that bed, pal, because if we're not in the Yankee office in fifteen minutes, we're both getting hit with a five-thousand-dollar fine." You should have seen him fly out of that bed. He didn't shower or even brush his teeth. He said, "Thanks a lot, boy."

The office was on Fifth Avenue, and when we got there I said, "Mickey, you do the talking," because in situations like this for some reason whenever I say something I only make things worse. Topping said to us, "Really cute, you guys." He threw the meal check at us. "What is this?" he asked. Mickey said, "It wasn't supposed to go to you." Topping said, "Don't tell me where it was supposed to go. My name was signed to this." He said, "Both of you are fined a thousand dollars." I was hoping Whitey was going to tell him how it happened, but Whitey wouldn't play their game. He didn't even show up. At the end of the month I got my paycheck. It came to twenty-eight dollars. I gave it to Pete Sheehy. Topping, and George Weiss, too, I'm sure, never believed we hadn't done that on purpose. I had nothing to do with signing Topping's name to that check, but Weiss, I'm sure, blamed me anyway.

In the '53 World Series we beat the Dodgers again. I hit 12 for 24, hit two home runs, two triples, and drove in eight runs and won the Babe Ruth Award as the Series' Most Valuable Player. In the final game the score was tied 3 to 3 in the bottom of the ninth, and we loaded the bases against Clem Labine. He threw me a fastball, and I lined a single up the middle to win the game and the Series. My career average may have only been .257, but my one for four would kill you. I was a regular in four World Series, hitting 33 for 99. In October my one for three would kill you.

After the Series I went back to Berkeley, where my friends gave me a brand new baby-blue 1953 Cadillac convertible. I was invited to a ton of banquets, but I didn't go to very many of them. I kept trying to get Lois to take me back, but she still insisted on divorcing me. I went to Japan for a couple weeks to play with the Eddie Lopat All Stars, and when we got back, instead of staying in Berkeley, I decided to spend the winter with Mickey in his home in Commerce. I drove all by myself from Berkeley to Commerce, and when I got there I couldn't believe any town could be that small. He was always telling me it was small, but I never pictured it could be that small. The town had one street, about four stores, if that, but there was plenty of hunting and fishing, and for the first time in a long time I was able to calm down.

Mickey had always bragged to me how great the Oklahoma people were, what an honest town Commerce was. I was there one hour, and my car was ripped off! When I was in Japan, I bought pearls, and little statues, silk jackets, and Nikon cameras, and I'd put them in the back seat of my car. After I arrived in Commerce, Mickey took me to a neighboring town called Miami. Oklahoma was a dry state, but in Miami there was a place called The Stables, which was a stable out by the racetrack where you could sneak a drink. We drove there in my car, and I went to lock the car doors, and Mickey said, "You don't have to lock your car in Oklahoma, people don't steal here." We had a drink each, two drinks at the most, and when we went back to the car, somebody had gone inside and cleaned me out. Took the pearls, the jackets, the cameras, everything. It's a good thing my trunk was locked or they've have gotten my clothes, too. I looked at Mickey. He said, "The guy had to be from another state. Okies don't do things like that."

Despite that it was a wonderful winter I spent with Mickey and Merlyn. I gained about twenty pounds. Merlyn would cook quail for breakfast. She fattened me up, was nice to me, made me feel right at home. It proved to me that a man and a woman can get along wonderfully if the woman would just feed the man, do the housework, and try to understand him. I've never had much luck with that, really haven't. Of course, I may have been at fault a little bit myself.

After spending that winter with Mickey and Merlyn, I was looking forward to the '54 season. I never felt better physically, and for the first time in my life I was making a little money. I was up to $17,000, and even though I owed the government some tax money from the year before, I didn't figure I'd have much trouble paying it off with the money I would be making. However, after all the publicity I'd had, my draft board reclassified me in March, and in April I was drafted. My brother Jackie was eligible, and he couldn't get a job because he was draft age, and so he volunteered, and they wouldn't take him. Even though I still had seven dependents, including my daughter Kelly Ann, they were determined to draft me, not him. It was deliberately done against me. If I had been in the service just two weeks longer the first time I was in, they couldn't have redrafted me. Also, I was thirty days short of being too old to be drafted. The draft board sped things up so I wouldn't get away.

At the time I really blasted my draft board good. They said I should sell my car if I was such a hardship case. How do you sell a gift that was just given to you? You don't do that. So they drafted me again. I made up my mind I would go into the service, put in my two years, and no matter what, I'd serve right to the day.

I was sent to Fort Ord again, and I drove there in my new Cadillac, which I was so proud of. The general in charge of the fort was named McClure. He was one of those generals who liked golf so much he had the government build an eighteen-hole course right on the fort. He saw my Cadillac, and naturally he got a little jealous because here was this private with a brand new Coupe de Ville Cadillac. He popped off in the papers about it. He said, "He doesn't look like a hardship case to me. Why doesn't he sell his Cadillac?"

He and I got into a few words. I told him, "How do you sell a present? That's like telling those people, 'Thank you but no thank you.'" When I went out for the post baseball team, he wouldn't let me try out. This was around the same time as the David Shine incident, where the Army was being accused of coddling athletes. I wasn't going to let him discriminate against me, however.

I went right to the adjutant general, saluted him, and said, "I have a complaint to make." He said, "Against whom, Private?" I said, "Against General McClure. He won't let me try out for the post baseball team, and I am entitled to the same rights as any other soldier." I also contacted Senator McCarthy's committee about this.

Apparently all this got to McClure, because three days later I was transferred to Fort Carson, Colorado. He moved me right out of there.

I drove to Fort Carson in my Cadillac, and when I arrived there I was immediately put in a KP unit. KP sounds terrible, but it happened that there was a group of Italian cooks who really took care of me. I did my work washing pots and pans and peeling potatoes, doing whatever it was I had to do, but it wasn't bad duty because you had one day on and two days off.

I worked KP for two months, but I guess somebody found out I was having it too good, so they moved me to a line company, mountain climbers who got up in the morning and ran around the airfields with guns over their heads being gung ho and climbing mountains.

I remember one two-day climb we had up a mountain. We were supposed to carry extra socks, shorts, and winter gear, plus the stuff you need if you're in a battle, in our knapsacks, but it was so hot at the bottom none of us packed that stuff. As I said, the dago cooks were friends of mine, and they rode on trucks ahead of us to set up the camp. We would have to walk an hour, and then we'd get a five-minute rest, and what I did, I carried beer the cooks gave me in my knapsack for my buddies. We'd stop for a break, and I'd take a beer out and drink it, and I'd go up the hill refreshed. A second lieutenant came over and said, "You think you can make it to the top like that?" He was barely making it. I said, "Sir, easy." I had hunted all my life. Walking a long ways was no problem. We'd stop again, and the cooks would reload me, and we'd climb some more. The climb itself was no problem at all. However, when we got to the top, there was three inches of snow on the ground, and none of us was dressed for it. We were in pup tents, sleeping out in the snow, and we had to wrap newspaper around our legs because we were so cold. The next day they trucked us all down the hill.

Around this time, would you believe, I got into another fight. I went into my barracks, and I went to my bed, and there was a guy sleeping in my bed. I said, "Excuse me, buddy, you're in my bed." He said, "Get lost, mac, you're in the wrong barracks." I said, "You're in my bed." The lights went on, and everybody woke up, and he got out of bed and found out he was the one who was in the wrong barracks. He reached in his pockets, and as soon as he did, I belted him. The MP's came running. They said, "Why did you hit him?" I said, "He was reaching into his pocket for a knife. And besides, he was in my bed." The guy said, "I don't have no knife." The MP reached into his pocket and found a switchblade. They grabbed him and threw him out.

Everyone was very nice to me in that line company. I was there about a year, and then they moved me over to special services. I was in charge of the post gym.

The MP's continued to give me a bad time on account of my Cadillac. They'd harass me when I drove up to the gate, make me get out of the car, inspect my trunk, instead of asking for my pass and seeing me through. I was a corporal by this time, and with others they would just look at the sticker on their car, salute, and let them through. Me, it was always an ordeal. Finally I got tired of it. The colonel in charge of the MP's came down to the gym and asked, "We have gym time scheduled, don't we, corporal?" I said no. "What do you mean? We're scheduled for it," he said. I said, "No, your gym time is over. I got it slated for someone else." He said, "I'm going to see Colonel Gilbert about this." I said, "Go and see Colonel Gilbert. See if I care." Colonel Gilbert was in charge of the athletic program on the post, and he was a wonderful man, one of those guys who you could talk to about any problem you had and he would understand. He was the kind of guy who gave you a job to do and then left you to do it and respected you for what you did, and most important, when you went to him, he backed you all the way. He would have made an ideal general manager on a baseball team.

Colonel Gilbert called me in about the MP's' gym time. He said, "What's the story, Corporal?" I said, "The MP's keep harassing me at the gate, sir, and as long as they do that, they're not going to get gym time." He said, "It's your gym. You run it your way."

I left, and later that day I got a call from the colonel in charge of the MP's. He said, "What can we do to correct this, corporal?" I said, "Just get off my back at the gate." The next day I drove downtown, and when I returned I stopped at the gate, and I got a salute like I was an officer and I was told I could drive right through. I called the colonel up and said, "You have gym time, sir."

Before I got out of the service, I was involved in one more fight. I talk about these fights, not because I'm proud of them, but because I want people to understand that I'm never the one who starts them. For some reason I'm the type of guy people like to pick fights with. One evening I went to the movies on the post. There was a rule that when you went to the theater, you had to wear your Army outfit, including a tie. It was the middle of summer, one of those days when it was so hot you couldn't stop sweating, and when I got into the theater I took my tie off. Almost immediately a sergeant walked over and said, "Put your tie on, soldier." I said, "Geez, Sarge, I'm not bothering anybody. It's so hot in here." He said, "Put your tie on or I'm throwing you out of here." I said, "You're not going to throw me out of here." He was a great, big, tough guy with a couple rows of ribbons. I stood up to leave, and he grabbed me by the neck and swung me around towards him. I guess he was going to whip my ass. He started swinging, but I landed a hard right and decked him, and I picked him up and decked him again, and I went to pick him up and I started to swing again, when a lieutenant said, "Corporal, he's out. That man is out. And I'd suggest you get out of here before the MP's come." I said, "Thank you, sir." I saluted and left.

The next day I went right to Colonel Gilbert and told him what had happened. He said, "Thank you, corporal, for telling me about it. I heard about it. I heard how he grabbed you and threw you." He said, "There'll be no punishment." I said, "Thank you, sir," and I left. I guarantee you, if I was six feet six, that sergeant wouldn't have dared try to throw me out of there, or even bothered me about my tie. Why couldn't he have just left me alone?

My barracks was right across the street from Colonel Gilbert's office. Because I was in charge of the gym, I lived in a barracks all to myself, the barracks where the visiting teams stayed when they came to the post. My quarters was a room away at the end, and inside I had a little stove in there, and the Italian cooks had gotten me a little refrigerator, and it was like I was living in my own apartment. I kept it locked so no one would see what I had there. One day a major decided to inspect the barracks. I always kept the rest of the barracks clean, but I never cleaned my own room because it was always locked. This time the major saw the locked door. He said, "I want to go in there." I said to myself, "Uh oh." I opened the door, and he looked in and saw my wardrobe hanging there and my refrigerator and stove, and the place was kind of a mess, and I was really afraid he was going to write me up. He looked in, and he started laughing. He said, "Is this yours, corporal?" I said, "Yes, sir." He said, "Not too shabby," and he walked away laughing.

Meanwhile I was the manager of the post baseball team, and we had a good ball club. We had a 25 and 4 record. I made up the schedule. We played Albuquerque, we played the Colorado Springs Sky Socks, a Class A team, we played a number of professional teams, and we beat them, and of course we beat all the service teams we played. I had no aspirations to be the manager, but I was the only major leaguer. The other guys were a bunch of guys who wanted to play. I had captains and majors on the team, but at my first team meeting, I told them, "Gentlemen, there is only one boss here. I'm not going to address any of you by rank or call you sir, and I don't want to see anybody try to pull rank on me. All of you will get an equal shot at making the team."

I played first base and was a relief pitcher, and once in a while played center field. I had a second baseman, Dick Dickerson, and I had other guys who could play the infield, so I played where I felt I would be needed most. I did a lot of relief pitching. I could throw real hard then, and when the starter got in trouble I'd go in and blow the ball by everyone.

I was playing on the post team, and to make some money I played two or three nights a week for a semipro team in Goodland, Kansas. It was about a six-hour ride, and a couple of the guys on the post team and I would get into my Cadillac, and we'd drive out to Goodland and play the game, and we'd come back to the base just as reveille was sounding. I would pitch at Goodland, and I was hitting home runs like I never did before. It was a small park, and even though the other team was always gunning for me because I was the pro, the harder they tried to get me out, it seemed, the farther out I would hit the ball. I led the Goodland team to the semipro-ball world series at Wichita University. We came in second, and it was in the championship game that I decided that if I ever did manage, I would never let a pitcher talk me out of taking him out.

I was playing center field, and a fellow by the name of Jock was pitching for us. Jock gave up a couple of hits, and I walked in from center and was intending to relieve him, because this was a game for the championship, and I felt I had a better chance to get us out of it. I got to the mound, and our catcher says to me, "He's doing okay." Jock then said, "I'm all right,

Billy," and I go back to center field, and the next pitch, boom, a three-run home run. I came in and stopped them, but it was too late. The home run cost us the game. I won the Most Valuable Award for the tournament, but it still upset me that I had let that pitcher talk me out of taking him out. We should never have lost that game. We should have been the champions. Now when I go out to the mound, my mind is made up, and there's no way that pitcher can change it.

I was in the service until August of 1955. I had saved up my leave time, I had thirty days coming, and when I met the Yankees at the stadium they were in second place, about a game out, and when I got back there Casey let me give a talk to the players, and I told them exactly how I felt. All my money was gone. I had won a car for being MVP of the '53 World Series, and I had to sell that car. I had been making about six dollars a week in the Army, and I still owed the government back taxes, and Lois had just divorced me, and I had to pay her off, and I was down to about zip. All I had left was the Cadillac my friends in Berkeley had given me. I stood up and said, "I don't know about you guys, I don't know how hungry you guys are, but I'm hungry. I need the money. I want to win this pennant real bad." We were going to go to Japan after the season, and everybody was looking forward to going, and I was feeling that some of the guys cared more about the trip than winning the pennant, and I said so. "I had three cars when I went into the Army, and now I'm broke, and you're playing like you're trying to lose. We got to get into the Series. We gotta."

I played shortstop the last eleven games of the season. I got two hits my first game back, and we won the pennant, and the players awarded me a full share, which made me feel very proud.

Against the Dodgers, however, we lost the Series. I honestly believe we lost it because the players were more concerned with all the things they had to do to get ready to go to Japan than with playing in the Series. We should have won that '55 Series easy. Johnny Podres was sensational, you can't take anything away from him, but it was a streak of luck that allowed them to beat us. The Dodgers were winning 2 to 0 in the seventh inning of the seventh game. I was on second, and Gil Mc-Dougald was on first, and Yogi Berra was the batter. First of all, Yogi was a pull hitter. He batted lefty, and he almost always hit the ball to right field. Second of all, Dodger manager Walter Alston had just pinch-hit for the regular left fielder, and in his place he put Sandy Amoros. With Yogi up, Amoros was playing Yogi almost on the left-field line, which was ridiculous. Yogi didn't hit the ball there three times in a season. Of course, that's where Yogi hit it, and because Amoros was so far out of position, he was able to race to the fence and catch it, and after he caught it, he threw a perfect peg to Pee Wee Reese, who was standing on the third-base line, and Reese fired the ball across the diamond to double up McDougald. Gil had done the right thing. If the ball had fallen, he would have scored the tying run. But Amoros caught it, and sometimes when you're aggressive, you get caught like that.

I still thought we were going to win, and I was very disappointed when we didn't. When Podres got the final out, I started crying so hard I couldn't stop myself. When I went into the locker room, I pounded my fists so hard against the wall I was bleeding. I went and hid in the trainer's room so nobody could see me. Crosetti came over and put his arms around me. He said, "Too bad a lot of the other guys don't feel the way you do. If they had, we would have won it." It was the first time I had ever lost a World Series, and I couldn't accept it.

After the Series the same thing that had happened to me happened to Podres. His draft board reclassified him 1-A and drafted him. If we had won that last game, he never would have been drafted.

I was only on a thirty-day leave, and though I didn't realize it, when I didn't rush back to Fort Carson after the Series I was technically AWOL. I was a couple days late, and when I got back to the base, a major came up and said, "Corporal, do you realize you're AWOL?" I gulped and made a funny smile. "I didn't know, sir," I said. He said, "Don't worry. We'll have to fix that. By the way, I want you to take a look over there," and I looked, and there was an honor guard waiting for me. I was a corporal, and they had an honor guard for me! I asked the major, "What do I do?" He told me, and I shook everybody's hand, and it was one of the proudest moments of my life.

Usually it takes two weeks to get processed out of the Army. They processed me in a day. They stamped everything in sight, and during the last week they asked me if I'd like to be a sergeant, and I told them I didn't. I didn't want people second-guessing me, saying I was getting something I didn't deserve, saying I was getting a promotion just because I was a baseball player. I said, "I'll go out as a corporal, that's good enough." I went out a corporal with a good-conduct medal. About a week later I joined the Yankees for their goodwill trip to Japan. We spent two weeks in Hawaii, and then more than two weeks flying to the Philippines, Guam, and then to Japan, where we played more than twenty games.

Before the trip I told Mickey not to get any of the shots the Yankees wanted us to take. I had been to Japan earlier, and I knew what they did to your arm. I told him, "You don't have to take them. Your arm will swell up and it'll hurt so much you won't be able to lift it high enough to brush your teeth." So Mickey and I didn't get the shots. The other guys took them, and for two days were in a lot of pain. Mickey and I were walking around, punching them in the arm, hoorahing them, and when they saw us coming, they started running for it.

During our stay in Hawaii, we played a couple of games on the island of Kauai, where my father is from. My father was living in California then, but all my relatives on his side came and they gave me a day, the only day I've ever had in my life. That day I hit a home run in the game, too.

While we were in Hawaii we played the meanest volleyball games you've ever seen. Hank Bauer and I were up front, and you're not supposed to touch the top of the net, but we were reaching so far over to spike the ball that our underarms were raw from the top of the net. We played touch football, and we were tackling each other, and we were like a bunch of kids. We never had so much fun in our lives. When we got to Japan, Mickey and I went to a movie theater, and as we were sitting there two Japanese guys were sitting behind us setting off these poppers that shoot confetti into the air, and the confetti was coming down on our heads. Mickey whispered for the usher to come over, and he bought a hundred dollars worth of these things. We had a giant box of them, and Mickey was firing them point blank at the two guys like it was a war. The two guys and their dates were covered in a mountain of confetti.

When the movie ended the lights went on, and an announcer started to announce the members of the New York Yankees present, and we were so embarrassed that we had fired so much confetti at these people that we snuck out of the theater on our hands and knees.

One evening Mickey and Whitey and I were sitting in a lounge, and sitting near us was a sumo wrestler, a great big guy, must have weighed three hundred pounds. He was talking to another guy in Japanese, and we figured he didn't understand English and Whitey looks at him and says to me, "If that big fat son of a gun says one word, I'm going to slap him out." I said, "Let me handle that Jap slob, Whitey." Mickey said, "No, I'll do it. I'll kill him. I'll tear him to pieces." We get up to leave, and the guy says, "Good luck in the game tomorrow, guys!" I said, "Let's get out of here quick!"

Another time we were playing in Hiroshima, and that was sad. It was only ten years after the atom bomb leveled the place, and they hadn't really begun rebuilding. There would be one little building, and everything around it for blocks would be flat. It was an unbelievable sight. That was the quietest crowd that I ever played before. The only sound I heard was the whiz of the ball being thrown. We were playing, and the home-plate umpire was calling everything against us. He was calling pitches over our heads strikes, and we didn't know whether he was doing it on purpose or what was going on. Mickey got up, and he called him out on a bad pitch, and when he got back to the dugout I told him, "Mickey, the next time tell his ass off. Don't just walk back here. Give it to him good. The guy doesn't understand English. Let him have it."

The next time up the umpire called a bad pitch a strike, and Mickey started in on the guy. He said, "You dumb Jap son of a bitch, boy I'm glad we bombed your ass." Really laid into him. The ump says, "Geez, Mickey, I thought it was a good pitch."

Mickey came back to the dugout swearing at me. He had felt about an inch high.

We were at one of the northern Japanese islands at an Air Force base, and Whitey and I were sitting at a bar very late at night talking with the Air Force pilots, really hot jocks, and everybody got up to leave, and Whitey says, "Let's have some fun." I said, "What do you want to do?" He said, "We'll pick up the phone and call the other guys, and I'll say your in a fight down here, and I'll break a glass and we'll see who'll come and who won't."

We paid the bar owner fifty dollars for some glasses, and we started calling the guys one by one. We called everybody. Bill Dickey came down in his robe. Casey came down in his red pajamas. The old man was ready to fight. Everyone had his pajamas on, and when somebody came down we'd applaud and buy him a drink, and he'd sit down and wait for the next guy. Only two guys didn't come down, Moose Skowron and Bob Cerv, our two biggest guys—and they got hoorahed about it from that day on. They wished they had come down. We loved Moose. Mickey and I thought the world of him. We'd love to agitate him. "Big, tough Moose." We wouldn't let up.

The first game we played in Japan, I was on first, and there was a ground ball, and as the second baseman was making the double play, I tore into him and bowled him over, knocked him clear out into left field, and he couldn't make the throw to first. It had been the Japanese way of playing for the runner to get out of the way while the fielder was completing the double play. The Japanese were very polite when they played. After the game the players asked me about what I had done, and I explained that it wasn't being dirty, it was good, hard baseball.

The last game we played in Japan, we were playing the same team, and I was playing second, and there was a ground ball, and the guy I had dumped came into second and sent me flying. It was beautiful. We both got up, faced each other, and bowed. From then on the Japanese players learned to knock the fielders down on a double play.

○ ○ ○

In 1956 Mickey Mantle had a fantastic year, a sensational year. We opened the season against Washington in Griffith Stadium, and Mickey hit two shots that went about 450 feet for home runs. Later that spring against the Senators in the stadium, Mickey hit one off Pedro Ramos that missed going out of there by about two feet. The ball was still going up when it hit the façade, and had it not hit there, it would have gone more than 600 feet!

What was so great about Mickey was that even though he was a star, no one pushed himself harder than he did. He ran the bases hard, hustled all the time, played hurt, just pushed himself every minute. Coming from nothing, he appreciated having something for a change, and he wanted to stay on top. He had four sons, very young, and he had a lot of responsibility because he was taking care of a lot of people, just like I was. He always took care of his mother and his sisters in addition to his wife and kids, and there are a lot of other people who owe Mickey money. Mickey loves people, he always overtips, and he's bighearted. He's got a heart as big as Yankee Stadium.

Mickey won the Triple Crown that year, led the league in home runs (52), runs batted in (130) and batting average (.353), and we won the pennant in a walk because of him. When Mickey went to Baltimore after the season was over to pick up his Triple Crown Award, I went with him, and I was just as happy as he was about it. I knew how much pressure he went through, saw how he was hounded by the press every single day, saw how hard he was on himself if he didn't play well one day. I was so happy for him. I wouldn't have been happier if I had done it myself.

For myself, I didn't do too badly. I hit .264 with 9 home runs. Obviously it was a lot harder for me than it was for Mickey. Every day for me was a struggle out there. With Mickey, when he knew he had a pitcher, he would take him out of the ball park. I had to fight to get my one for four.

This was also the year the Yankees were spreading rumors about me that I was leading Mickey astray. How badly could I have led him astray if he won the Triple Crown? I wish someone would lead me astray that way. The rumor that I was a bad influence on Mickey Mantle followed me wherever I went.

When I went out to manage for the first time at Denver, people said, "How can he manage a ball club when he can't manage himself?" That hurt me, still does, for someone to say that about me. And if it isn't that rumor, it's some other rumor like I fight too much or I drink too much. There's always something.

Maybe everyone would like it better if I kept my mouth shut, let everyone walk all over me, and finished eighth. They'd say, "There goes a real nice guy. Isn't he nice? Isn't he a nice person?" It's like Leo Durocher said, "Nice guys finish last."

We avenged our loss to the Dodgers from the year before. Remember the famous picture of Don Larsen throwing the final pitch of his perfect game? There's a player standing behind him. Know who it is? It's me. I was the second baseman in that game. Twenty years from now no one'll even remember I was there.

The Dodgers had us down two games to one, and I was more concerned with winning the game than with his perfect game. We were all conscious of the fact he was pitching a no-hitter, but I wasn't all that concerned about it. Winning it was all that mattered to me. I made a point the last couple of innings of concentrating on getting right in front of any ground ball that came to me. If I booted it, I wanted the ball to fall in front of me and not bounce off to the side. In the eighth inning I called all the infielders together. I told them, "Nothing gets through." Nothing did.

The last pitch to Dale Mitchell, the one that ended the game, was a strike. He thought it was high, but it was close enough and he should have swung at it. He didn't think it was a strike, but nobody does when they get called out on a third strike.

When Don got the final out, I was happy for him because he was such a good person, but to be honest, I wasn't all that excited or thrilled about his pitching a perfect game. I was just glad that we won.

We split the next two games, and after we lost 1 to 0 to Clem Labine to tie it at three games each, we were riding on our bus from Ebbets Field to the stadium when I sat myself next to Casey. Casey had played Enos Slaughter in left, and he had misjudged a fly ball to give the Dodgers their run, and I was very angry. I told Casey, "If you play that National League bobo out there tomorrow, we're going to lose this thing." Casey asked me who he should play. I told him he should play Elston Howard, and I told him to play Moose Skowron at first instead of Joe Collins.

Casey did just as I told him, and Ellie hit a home run, and Moose hit a grand slam, and we won the final game 9 to 0 behind Johnny Kucks, who was a great competitor. I hit .296 in that Series, and during the winter I spent much of my time going to banquets and having a good time.

That winter I lived at the St. Moritz Hotel in New York. There was a party over at Toots Shor's. A hospital wing was donated in memory of Mickey's father, and we were there, and Jackie Gleason was there, and good old lovable Toots was the host, and while we were standing around, Gleason got into a discussion with Phil Rizzuto about how good a bowler he was. Gleason said to Phil, "I'll bowl you for any amount you want." Phil said, "I won't bowl you, but Billy will." I wasn't a bad bowler, used to average around 185. Gleason said, "Okay, I'll bowl you." Toots said to me, "Play him, and don't worry about losing. If you lose, I'll pay it." I said, "Thanks, but I'll pay."

We went to Gleason's bowling alley, and he bet me three hundred dollars on the game. The first game I just barely beat him, and he asked if I wanted to bet double or nothing. The next game I bowled 215, and he bowled 180 something. He asked to double it again. I was really staring at the pins now. I was wondering how long we'd play, till I lost one. I opened the third game with a spare and three straight strikes. The last strike went down, and Gleason said, "Away I go," and he walked out. He paid me, too. I'll never forget that. "Away I go."

After my good year in '56 I went to spring training, and George Weiss called me into his office. There were those rumors that I was leading Mickey astray, the same old bullshit, and here Mickey had the greatest year of his whole life. Mr.

Weiss said, "You better not stay out late once, you better not make one false move, because if you do, you've had it."

I told Mickey and Whitey what Weiss had said and whenever they were planning to stay out late, I'd say, "See you later. I gotta get in." A couple times I found myself past curfew, and instead of going back to the hotel and taking the chance they'd see me coming in late, I slept over with Whitey and his family. He had a bed over the garage, and I slept there. Even if it was one minute past twelve, I didn't dare go back to the hotel. Weiss had a detective in the lobby watching, but they didn't check beds.

The day before we broke camp Mr. Weiss called me into his office again. I was saying to myself, "What the hell have I done now?" Mr. Weiss said, "Martin, sit down." He said, "Well, you haven't done anything in spring training. You've been real good. But I want to tell you something. One thing goes wrong this year, you're gone." I said, "What have I done, Mr. Weiss?" He got mad. He said, "Don't you talk back to me. I'm just telling you." I figured there was no sense in saying anything more, so I didn't.

I left his office, and I told Mickey about what he had said. I said, "I gotta really watch it."

In May we had two days off in a row, May fifteenth and May sixteenth, my birthday, and Whitey and Mickey decided to throw a birthday party for me on the fifteenth, knowing we had a day off the next day. Unfortunately one of our games was rained out and a game was scheduled for the sixteenth, but the married guys had made arrangements with baby-sitters, and they decided to hold the party anyway. We began the evening at Danny's Hideaway, where we had dinner. Our group consisted of Mickey, Whitey, Yogi, Hank Bauer, Johnny Kucks, and their wives, and me. After dinner we went to an eight o'clock show at the Waldorf, where Lena Horne was singing, and after her show the wives wanted to see Sammy Davis, Jr., and we went to the Copacabana for the midnight show.

We were toward the back, and all the women were seated, and we were standing around the table behind them, and next to us were five guys doing the same thing with their wives. The guys were members of a bowling team, and in the middle of the show one of them made a loud racial remark about Sammy Davis. Hank Bauer got hot when he heard that, and he said something to the guy, and the guy said something back, and pretty soon they were ready to fight. Bauer turned to me and said, "You with me?" I said, "Sure I'm with you. I'll back you." Because if there was a fight, Bauer would be the first one to back up a teammate. The brother of the guy who was giving Hank a hard time came over to me and said, "Billy, can I talk to you?" I said, "Yeah." He said, "Let's get out of here so we can talk." He and I went out into a private room. He said, "I don't know what's between my brother and Bauer, but you calm Bauer down, and I'll calm my brother." I said, "No problem." Just then the guy's wife came in, and she was yelling, "Don't you fight with Billy." I told her, "We're not doing anything. We're settling the thing out here." She said, "Oh, I'm glad." Just then, I heard a boom over in the coatroom, heard a crash on the floor, and when I went out to see what it was, here was the guy who'd been bothering Bauer lying out cold on the floor. Mickey came running over, and he must have thought it was me lying there, because he was yelling "Billy, Billy, Billy, Billy." He knew I was missing, so he thought I was the one on the floor. I said, "Mick, I'm over here." But when the reporters came snooping around, everyone had heard Mickey call my name, and as a result some of the people evidently thought I had hit the guy.

We never did find out who hit the guy. Hank didn't hit him, never touched him, and I certainly didn't, I was talking to his brother. We think that a bouncer must have followed him back and decked him.

The next day it came out in the papers, Yankees In Brawl At Copa, and it wasn't true. Not one Yankee was involved.

We all had to testify before the New York Supreme Court, and Mantle was testifying, and he had gum in his mouth, and the judge asked him to take it out of his mouth. The district attorney asked Mickey, "Did you see the fight?" He told him no. The DA asked him in his opinion how it happened. Mickey said, "I think the Lone Ranger came in on his horse, and the horse kicked him." I don't know why he said that, it just came out of his mouth. Everybody laughed. They called Yogi in, and

Yogi said, "Nobody did nothing to nobody," which was the truth. But the next day I went to the stadium, and I packed all my stuff. Mickey said, "What are you doing?" I said, "I'm gone." He said, "Aw, come on." I said, "Remember in spring training what Weiss said to me. This is just the excuse he needs to get rid of me. You watch. I'm gone." I told Pete Sheehy, the clubhouse guy, "I'm probably going to be gone by the next road trip, but I'm going to pack all my gear now." Pete said, "Billy, they can't blame you for what happened. You didn't do anything." I said, "I'm telling you. You watch."

It was a Saturday in Kansas City, the day of the June fifteenth trade deadline, and we were in the clubhouse, and Jerry Coleman was scared to death. Cutdown was that night, Coleman was worried. He said to me, "Billy, I'm gone." I said, "Jerry, there's only one way to find out if it's you. Look at the lineup card. If my name is on it, it's you. If your name is on it, it's me." He said, "Aw, they're not going to get rid of you." But I knew they would, because Bobby Richardson was on the club, and he had looked very good, and I knew Weiss wanted him instead of me.

We went out and looked at the lineup card in the dugout, and my name wasn't there. Casey didn't allow the players to sit in the bullpen, he wanted them with him in the dugout, but before the game I got my glove and went out there, hoping, I guess, that if they couldn't find me the day would pass without my getting a call that I was gone.

Around the seventh inning the old man came out to the bullpen to talk to me. We went up the runway under the stands. Casey said, "Weiss says he's trading you to Kansas City." He told me that the Kansas City owner, Arnold Johnson, was coming over to talk to me. Casey said, "I'm going to tell him what a great person you are and a great player. . . ." I said, "Casey, you ain't going to say shit. I don't want you bragging on me or saying a word. When I needed you, you let me down. So you ain't saying shit for me." Casey said, "Now wait," and at that point Johnson came over. I said, "Mr. Johnson, I don't want to hear him bragging about me or saying anything. I'll give you my best. That's all you want, isn't it, sir?" He said, "Yes." I said, "Thank you," and I left to go to the clubhouse.

After the game Mickey and Whitey found out, and we were all crying. We couldn't believe it. I had helped them to five pennants. The only one they didn't win was when I was in the Army. I couldn't understand why Casey didn't stick up for me. The other guys had told him I had nothing to do with that Copa fight. He had let me down, and I made up my mind I wasn't going to speak to him ever again. He was like my father, and he let me down like that. And I didn't talk to him for seven years. Just ignored him completely when I saw him. I don't know what was between him and Weiss, but I guess Weiss swung Casey over to his side, and Casey went along with him. Oh, Weiss hated me. My whole time when I was with the Yankees, whether as a player or as a manager, there was always a George trying to hurt me.

The next day I was wearing a Kansas City uniform. I had cried all night, couldn't sleep one hour. Johnny Kucks was pitching for the Yankees, and my first time up I hit a ball up against the left-field wall for a single. Yogi threw it back in real quick, and later the score was tied, and I hit a home run. It was the funniest feeling in my life. I was running around the bases, and I wasn't even happy. The Yankees tied it in the ninth, and they went on to beat us in extra innings. Lou Boudreau was the Kansas City manager. After the game, he was telling the other players, "That Martin can play. Isn't it great that he's here," and he's giving them a bullshitting pep talk. I couldn't believe it. Players don't pay attention to that stuff. They never did, never will. I was so unhappy not being a Yankee anymore.

After I was traded, I wasn't the same player. I tried and tried, but I couldn't get my heart into it. It felt like my heart was broken. Mickey told me, "You're like another player." But I just couldn't generate it anymore, and I'd try, but I couldn't get anything going anymore. From then on, I was through. It was all downhill.

In four years I played for six teams. At the end of the 1957 season I was traded to Detroit in a big player deal. Jack Tighe was the manager, and he put me at short and moved Harvey Kuenn to center, and though we had a couple of good players like Al Kaline and Kuenn, we couldn't do anything. They were a bunch of selfish players, and then Tighe was fired and Bill Norman came in, and the ball club didn't do a thing. At the end of the year I was traded to Cleveland with Al Cicotte for Don Mossi and Ray Narleski, and I had a tough year there because I was having trouble physically and because the manager, Joe Gordon, didn't like me at all.

I was playing second for Cleveland when an outfielder by the name of Al Pilarcik bunted the ball past the pitcher's mound. I came charging in, fielded the ball, and fired it underhand to Vic Power at first, and after I threw it, I fell hard on my shoulder and separated it. My arm was put in a sling, and I couldn't play for a couple weeks, and then when I came back, I was playing catch before a game, and before when I threw I could really make that ball jump, but this time I threw it, and nothing. I had no velocity. I threw it again, as hard as I could, and again, nothing. I couldn't understand it. I had lost my arm. It happened just like that. I couldn't believe it. I said to myself, "What is this, some kind of a joke?"

Another problem I was having was my left knee would give out on me every once in a while, I guess from getting knocked down at second base so many times. I'd go for a ground ball, and it would cave in on me. It didn't have the strength it used to. It didn't hurt at all, but if I put too much pressure on it, I'd collapse right to the ground.

Despite these problems, I was still the best second baseman Cleveland had, and if manager Joe Gordon had played me right, we would have won the pennant instead of Chicago that year. I was having a good year at bat, hit .260 and hit a few home runs, but the only reason I was playing was that the Cleveland general manager, Frank Lane, forced Gordon to play me. Gordon had been a Yankee second baseman like I had, and I had always admired him because he was a super player, but when I came to Cleveland a lot of people were comparing us, arguing who was better, him or me, and this must have bothered him, because he just didn't like me. I'll give you an example. We were tied in the ninth with the bases loaded and nobody out, and I was the batter, and Gordon sent up Hal Naragon to pinch-hit for me. Hal Naragon's best shot is a weak single. Also, he was slow, he couldn't run. I came back to the bench, didn't say a word, because I was taught you don't say zip to the manager, that you honor him whether he was putting you down or not. Gordon said, "I guess you're wondering why I took you out." I said, "Yeah." He said, "You've been hitting too many long fly balls." I said, "What do you want in this situation, a ground-ball double play?" A fly ball wins the game. On the first pitch Naragon hit a weak grounder to the pitcher, who threw home for the force, and the catcher threw to first for the double play. Our next batter struck out, we were out of the inning, and we lost the game. Then he benched me.

He and Lane really got into it after that. They're screaming at each other in the papers, and finally he puts me back in, and we climb back into first place. We were in front by three or four games, and we were playing a doubleheader against the Washington Senators in Cleveland. I drove in the winning run in the first game. I was the leadoff batter in the second game, and Tex Clevenger threw a fastball right for my neck. I lifted up my bat to let the ball go by, and instead of turning my head, I watched it come in, and the ball sailed in until I was staring at it. It struck me in the head right in front of my ear. When it hit me, I saw bright lights, and I dropped to the ground, and I started bleeding out my nose and my ears. My jaw was broken, my eyebone cracked, my cheekbone was knocked toward my chin, and my face blew up so you wouldn't have recognized me. They put me on a stretcher and drove me to the hospital on a stretcher. I figured I had had it.

Doctors X-rayed me, and one doctor asked me what I thought I had. My jaw was broken and I couldn't talk, so I mumbled, "Broken jaw." He said, "Yeah, you have that." And then he told me all the other things I had. He told me the damages were so extensive that a specialist had to be called in.

The specialist came to see me. He said, "If we have trouble with the bleeding, we may have to cut your throat." I shook my head no. I was thinking, "Whatever you do, please don't cut my throat."

They operated, and when it was over I was in the worst pain I had ever been in. The next day I couldn't see out of my eyes, my face had swelled up so much. Poor Tex came to visit, and when he saw me he started crying. You wouldn't have recognized me, wouldn't have known me, my face was so swollen you would have thought I weighed five hundred pounds. After two days I was able to see again, but my eyes were black and blue for a long while. They had pushed my cheekbone back up, wired all my teeth shut, cut out some fat around my eye.

I remember when I woke up after the operation, I could see a little bit, and I was able to make out this guy, a Catholic brother—it was a Catholic hospital—toweling my face. I could hardly speak, and I asked him who he was. He said, "I'm your nurse. I'm assigned to take care of you." I said, "A male nurse. My luck is really horseshit." He laughed.

I had to be on morphine. I'd take the pain as long as I could, and then they'd shoot me. You'd feel like you were peeing in your pants, and then it would knock me out, and I'd sleep for a couple of hours, and then I'd come to, and I'd stand the pain for as long as I could and then get another shot. The doctor said, "Billy, if you can just stand the pain five or ten minutes longer each day, we'll gradually get you off the morphine." And that's what I did.

That winter I made a comment in the papers that I didn't know whether Tex had thrown at me deliberately or not, though to be honest I don't think he did, and I said that nobody's going to throw at me ever again or they'd pay.

I was traded to Cincinnati along with pitcher Cal McLish in December, and when I went to spring training I was determined not to let my getting beaned affect me. I had never been afraid at the plate, never. I'd been hit many times by guys deliberately throwing at me. I'd been hit in the ribs, hit in the head, and remember we didn't wear helmets in those days. It was different this time, I found out. I'd get up to the plate to swing, and my rear end would fall out, like I was scared. I couldn't believe it. I said to myself, "Hey, this isn't like you." I put on four jackets, and I had pitchers Cal McLish and Joe Nuxhall deliberately throw at me and hit me with pitches, but no matter how hard I tried, I guess the shock was so bad, even with my heart I couldn't overcome my fear. It took me almost two years before I started to lose it, and by then it was too late.

Combining that with my weak arm and my bad leg, I knew I wasn't the same player I used to be. It was scary knowing my playing days were coming to an end. It's like dying almost because playing was something I had been wanting to do since I was a child, and subconsciously on some level you know you're not going to be able to do it much longer. You never, ever admit to yourself that one of these days you're going to have to quit. You never think you're going to be through. You feel you'll be able to play forever. You don't want to admit you're losing it. You just don't want to. That's the toughest thing in the world for a player to do. And now for me, the toughest thing for me as a manager is to tell a player I don't think he can play anymore, to release him. I hate to do that. I hate to even go up and tell a kid he's going back to the minor leagues. I always have someone else tell him. I don't like to do it, to see a kid cry, to break his heart. I know how it feels, an empty feeling, a hurt feeling. To tell a player he's through with baseball, that he's going to have to find another way to make a living, that's very hard.

The year with Cincinnati was difficult. I had married Gretchen, and so I had family responsibilities again, and at the same time my career was slowly slipping away from me. Also, pitchers didn't stop throwing at me, and every time I got hit, I'd remember how it felt when Clevenger hit me. I had promised in the papers that anyone who threw at me would be sorry, and I kept my promise, and that led to a couple of fights.

We had a pitcher by the name of Raul Sanchez. Before a game he was to pitch, he was told he was being sent to the minors, and during the game in his anger he hit three guys in a row. The last guy he hit was Gene Conley, the Philadelphia pitcher. Gene stands about six foot eight. He used to play professional basketball, and he's so strong he used to tear up dashboards of cars with his hands.

Conley didn't say anything, because fortunately he's basically an easygoing guy. He just trotted down to first. Gene Mauch was the Philly manager, and it was Mauch who was hot. He came running out of the dugout and headed for the mound to hit Sanchez. I came running in from second base to stop him, and as I grab hold of Mauch, all of a sudden I got hit so hard I got knocked to the ground. It was Conley. When I revived, I felt my face. It was the same side where I had broken all those bones the year before, and I yelled, "Who hit me?" Conley, someone said, and I was so mad I jumped up in the air to try to hit him in the jaw. I couldn't quite reach him, and I gave him my best shot against the neck, and boom, down he went. The guys all grab me, and Conley comes to, and other guys grab him, but all he wanted to do was shake my hand because he felt bad about hitting me. I yelled, "Leave him alone. He wants to shake hands." I told him there was no hard feelings. He said, "I'm with you, pal. Let's forget about it," which is the way most baseball fights end.

Later that year we were playing the Chicago Cubs in Wrigley Field. Darrell Johnson, a good friend of mine for many years, was in the stands scouting. After the first game of the series, Darrell said, "They knocked you down quite a bit today. It looks like they're trying to get that fear back into you." I told him, "I'm not going to take it anymore."

The next day Jim Brewer was pitching for the Cubs, and I had been watching him. I saw that he was a control pitcher, and I was at bat looking for a low pitch, and he threw one about two inches behind my head. There's no more dangerous pitch, because the batter's natural reaction is to fall back when a ball is being thrown at his head, and if the ball is thrown behind you, you pull back right into its path. Fortunately I got my elbow up, and the ball hit me in the elbow. The ump, though, said it hit my bat, and called the pitch a strike. I had started for first, but when the umpire called me back, I said to myself, "I'll fix him," meaning Brewer. One thing a batter who's thrown at can do is make the pitcher skip rope on the next pitch by slinging his bat at him and pretending it had slipped out of his hands. I had never done this before, the next pitch came in, and I let fly with the bat, only my aim wasn't so good and it landed nearer to first base than the mound.

I waited at home plate for someone to bring me the bat, but no one did. The bat boy didn't get it. Their first baseman didn't get it. I had to go out and get it, and as I ran out to pick up my bat I see Brewer out of the corner of my eye coming toward me. He was yelling, "You little dago SOB," and as he got close to me, I can see that he's got his left hand in a clenched fist, and he's going to punch me. The newspapers took a picture of his fist. It was in all the papers. It showed that when he swung at me, I punched him in the jaw. He went down. I didn't get another punch in, because their catcher and first baseman, Elvin Tappe and Frank Thomas, jumped me and started taking cheap shots at me. Meanwhile Cal McLish, who was my roommate, had been pitching that day, and he had come out to the mound and started pulling people off me. Brewer finally came to, and he gave Cal a kick that broke a couple of his ribs, and Cal punched Brewer five or six times in the face and broke some bones around Brewer's eye.

I figured this was just another baseball fight, that nothing would come of it, so I didn't say to anyone that McLish had thrown the punches. I figured the whole thing would blow over like it usually does.

Of course, it didn't happen that way. The Chicago papers wrote up the fight like I had come out of an underground tunnel to hit him. Here was poor, defenseless six-foot-four, 215-pound Jim Brewer being attacked by five-foot-ten-inch, 160-pound monster Billy Martin. The papers really made it sound bad, and I got a lot of hate mail. Guys wrote they were going to knife me, shoot me, and when I got called in by the National League president, Warren Giles, he had already made up his mind I was guilty, and he suspended me five days wthout pay and fined me five hundred dollars in addition.

The next time the Reds played in Chicago, a guy walked up to me and said, "Are you Billy Martin?" I said, "Yeah," and he handed me a paper, and I opened it, and it was a summons and complaint from Brewer. He said, "Excuse me, here's another one." This one was from the Chicago Cubs. I totaled them up, and in all I was being sued for more than two million dollars. I looked at it and said, "Ask Mr. Wrigley how he'd like it, cash or check."

I thought it was funny at the time, but it didn't turn out to be too funny. I was traded by the Reds to Milwaukee, and I was there for about five minutes, then they traded me to Minnesota, where I became a scout and coach. Years had gone by since they had served the papers on me. Cincinnati had hired a lawyer for me, but after I was traded they dropped the lawyer. The Reds by now had a new owner, and the new owner didn't have any interest in Billy Martin. I got a call about a deposition, and I found out that Brewer was pursuing the case. I called the commissioner of baseball, General Eckert, who had just been appointed, and he said he had not been in baseball at the time and it wasn't his business, and I had no choice but to go to court.

We had a jury trial, and I'll bet the twelve people on that jury never saw a baseball game in their lives. They didn't know that when a pitcher walks off the mound toward the batter that means he wants to fight. They ruled against me. I wasn't making any kind of salary at the time, and they ruled I had to pay Brewer about $25,000. Later they made it less, but it was still a lot of money, and I had to go to the bank. A friend of mine in Minnesota by the name of Joe Duffy cosigned a loan for me, I borrowed the money, and for years I was paying it off. It really strapped Gretchen and me bad, really hurt us. Anyone who wants to can read about the case. It's in the law books. Brewer versus Martin.

CHAPTER 5

After winning a pennant and a World Series in my last two years, I would have thought that 1978 would have been easier for me, that George would have trusted me to do what was right and that he would have left me alone more. Instead the demands and the pressure he put on me were worse than ever. For one thing, Gabe Paul was no longer with the Yankees. A friend of his had bought the Cleveland Indians, and it was a good opportunity to run a team where the owner wouldn't be criticizing and running him down behind his back. Also, to get away from George had to be a help to his health.

The man George picked to replace Gabe was another of his Cleveland cronies, Al Rosen, who used to play third base for the Indians in the early fifties. Rosen had been working in a casino in Las Vegas, and the money they offered him was good, and Rosen wouldn't fight George like Gabe did, so Rosen seemed to George a perfect choice. I liked Al, always did, and I was sorry he took the job, because I knew George would make him crazy before he ended up quitting, as just about everyone who works under George ends up doing sooner or later.

Reggie and his big salary didn't create enough problems in '77. George went out during the winter and signed relief pitcher Rich Gossage for a couple million, relief pitcher Rawly Eastwick for more than a million, and starting pitcher Andy

Messersmith, who was coming off a bum arm, for three hundred and thirty-three thousand a year. He also traded for first baseman Jim Spencer, another left-handed first baseman to play behind Chris Chambliss, who George never liked for a minute. What the hell was I going to do with Spencer, who I've always liked, but on this team had no room to play? I had plenty of left-handed DH's. And what about the pitchers who had won for us the two years before? How was Figueroa going to react to a washed-up pitcher like Messersmith getting all that money? How was Sparky Lyle, who had just won the Cy Young Award in the American League, going to react to Gossage's getting all that money when he was already fighting with George over money?

We got to spring training, and I watched Eastwick throw, and it wasn't the same Eastwick I had seen pitching for Cincinnati. I didn't like the way he threw, and I told George that. He was reaching back for a little bit extra, and he wasn't cutting it. I wasn't overly impressed with the way Messersmith was pitching, either. He was throwing a lot of off-speed pitches, and it was clear he didn't have his fastball any more. I was hoping he'd do well because he was such a fine competitor. After he pitched his first game against Cleveland, the writers asked me what I thought of him. "Oh, I thought he did a good job," I said. I didn't want to tell them that I thought he couldn't throw his fastball any more. That certainly wasn't the Messersmith I had seen with the Dodgers. George and Rosen asked me for my opinion about these guys, and when I gave it to them, they got mad at me. I told George, "Just because you got these guys, don't compound your mistake by keeping them. Admit you made a mistake. Trade them."

George would say, "We're trying, Billy, we're trying, but we just can't get rid of them right now." He'd make all sorts of excuses and alibis, and anyway I would never know if he was telling the truth, it's so hard to tell. When they finally traded Rawley to Philadelphia, they got Jay Johnstone, who wasn't much help to us, either. He was another guy George wanted me to play. "I want you to play these guys, Billy," George would tell me, and I'd tell him, "They can't do it, George. They can't cut the mustard," and he'd get mad at me. He'd hold on to them, and I was always two or three players short. My God, it was tough enough trying to win the pennant without an added handicap, without having more players sitting on the bench complaining about not playing. He got Johnstone, Spencer, Gary Thomasson—he was filling me up with a club of DH's.

I never knew what George was going to do. For instance, he got Eastwick and didn't ask anybody. He got Messersmith the same way, just went out and did it himself. One time he was talking to Pittsburgh about trading Thurman for Dave Parker. I kept telling him, "George, no way we can part with Munson."

It seems that everyone I liked he got rid of. I liked Mickey Kluttz very much. He wasn't a shortstop, but I really liked him at third. He traded him. He got rid of Mike Heath. I liked him. He got rid of Paul Blair. Who could have been more valuable than Blair? He later got rid of Dick Tidrow. His trades were driving me crazy, and I knew with Gabe gone, here was this unknowledgeable man making these deals, and I'd be the one who had to keep all these guys happy.

Making things worse was a steady stream of injuries. When the season opened, Ron Guidry and Ed Figueroa were the only healthy pitchers I had. Catfish was in pain, and so was Gullett and Messersmith, and the job Art Fowler did juggling around the pitchers was amazing.

By mid-May we were about two games behind the Red Sox, which to George meant we were going to lose the pennant, and he'd be calling me on the phone, constantly complaining about my lineups, second-guessing like he did the year before, leaking things in the papers about me, making me look bad to my players, promising players things in their contracts he had no intention of honoring, just making it hard as hell for me. Guys were mad because they were talking contract, and they'd have a session with George, and they wouldn't want to play anymore. Mickey Rivers was one. Sparky Lyle was another. Munson was very angry with George about his contract.

In May, Mickey was going through some contract troubles and some money troubles, and we were in Kansas City, and we lost 10 to 9 because Mickey messed up a couple of fly balls in the outfield, messed 'em up bad. It looked like he didn't care out there.

After the game I was walking up the runway to the clubhouse, and Lou Piniella said to me, "Why don't you bench the son of a bitch so we can win this damn thing? We don't need a guy like that playing."

We got on the plane to fly to Chicago, and one of the hostesses came over and told me that she was having some trouble with a couple of players who were in the aisle. I walked back there, and guess who it was? It was Piniella, who was playing cards with Rivers. I was mad, because we had lost a tough game, and I said to Lou, "Here you're mouthing off about how you want to get rid of him, how he's no good in the field, how he isn't catching the ball, and here you are playing cards with him. That makes a hell of a lot of sense." I was hot. I said, "Why don't you tell him what you told me going up that runway."

Now, Lou and I are very close. I wasn't happy about embarrassing him, because he's one of the good guys as far as I'm concerned. George was always trying to tell me that Lou spoke against me behind my back, but I found that hard to believe. I thought the world of Lou Piniella, because he was one of those guys who doesn't bother you. He just does his job, and he does a hell of a job.

I went back to my seat. Understand that Lou and Thurman Munson were very close. Also Munson loved to tease me. Thurman was a fun-loving, good-natured kid who loved to agitate me. After an inning, he'd come running into the dugout, and he'd throw a ball at me and then run up the runway like a little kid. On the plane Thurman walked up to me and said, "Is Billy mad at me? You mad at me, too, Skippy?" But I was in no mood for his kidding around. I said, "Thurman, cut the shit." Took him aback. His timing was wrong, and his back went up, and he got mad, and I was standing there screaming at him, but despite what it said in the papers, there was nothing to it at all. He was teasing me, and we both got hot, that's all.

The next day he came over and said, "Skip, I wasn't trying to yell at you." I said, "I know it, Thurman, but your timing was wrong. I was mad at somebody else, and you come up agitating me. That had nothing to do with you." He said, "I wouldn't do anything in the world to hurt you. You know how I feel about you." I said, "I love you, too, pal, but your timing was off, that's all." But the papers wrote it differently. They had it that we had had a shouting match with each other, which is ridiculous. You have to know the people involved before you write something up. Two people can be yelling at each other, but if they like each other, it doesn't mean anything. Thurman would agitate me and tease me every day, but that was his way of relieving tension. I never once had any malice toward him when he agitated me. I used to enjoy it, and he used to get such a kick out it. I wish he was alive to do it now.

The next day in the papers it also came out that I blasted Kenny Holtzman, which wasn't true. I liked Kenny, but I was mad at him for going with Mickey Rivers to the track all the time. Looking back, if it hadn't been Kenny it would have been somebody else, so I was wrong there. As I said, I really liked Kenny as a person. I just wasn't overenthused about his pitching, and maybe that was my fault, too. Most of his problem was that I didn't pitch him enough. Though he didn't have the live fastball he used to have at Oakland, he would have been a lot more effective if I had pitched him regularly. However, I had five other pitchers who my coaching staff and I felt were better, and that's the way it falls sometimes. Sometimes a pitcher suffers under certain managers, and apparently he suffered under me. To this day I don't know whether he could have made it on the Yankees if I had pitched him more. He just happened to be the sixth pitcher on a five-man staff.

I called Mickey into my office to talk with him. I told him, "You have too much class, little man. You're too good of a ballplayer. We don't want to get your teammates mad at you." I said, "You have problems, don't you?" He said, "Yeah," and he told me about his problems. He owed some money, and when he went to George to get some more, either George put him off or he didn't want to give it to him because he knew Mickey was already way overextended, it was something, and Mickey's head wasn't into the game.

Mickey never meant to do anything wrong. Just every once

in a while, he'd lose his motivation in the field, and he'd get a couple of our pitchers real mad, and it would make the rest of us mad, too, because we knew that balls had fallen in front of him that he should have caught.

I benched Mickey for a couple days. I talked to him, never screamed or yelled at him. I told him, "You're too good of a player to be letting your teammates down. There's no reason for you to be doing this. I want to see you bust your ass." He said, "All right, boss." And he carried the team for the next couple weeks.

We arrived in Chicago to play the White Sox, and in the middle of our opener I told our trainer, Gene Monahan, that something was wrong, that I felt faint and that he should sit next to me. I was getting cold and then warm and then cold, and I had begun to shake. It was the worst I had felt in a long time. Maybe George was finally getting to me. He was always meddling. Sometimes after he'd call me with his cock-eyed lineups and suggestions I'd be so upset that I couldn't eat. Other nights I wouldn't be able to sleep. He was driving me nuts. I'd sit there and listen to him, and I'd say to myself, "Do I really have to listen to this junk all the time?" But I'd have to, because of the clauses in my contract. If I didn't put up with his bullshit, he could fire me, and he wouldn't have to pay me. I had a wife and kid to support. It was a lot of money on the line for me. The team was doing well despite the injuries, but everything was building up inside me, what with his phone calls, and his making comments about me in the papers all the time. And I got very tired talking to the press all the time about whether or not he was going to fire me. It got stale after a while. Getting fired was on my mind all the time, though I still continued to manage the way I felt was best. It was always on my mind. It was just like when I was playing second base for the Yankees, and Mr. Weiss would sit in his private box, and I'd look up there knowing he hated my guts. I still had to play, but it made it tougher.

The trainer called in a doctor who came to the bench. He thought I was having some sort of heart problem. My doctor in Minnesota had just checked out my heart, and he said it was fine. I told the doctor, "I don't have a heart problem." He said, "We should get you to the emergency ward at the hospital right away." I said, "I can't leave this ball club. There ain't no way. I gotta stay with this club." He said, "Well, I'm not responsible if anything happens." I told him I understood. I told him, "I'll be all right," and the next day I was a lot better.

I managed to keep that from the press for a while, but there wasn't much else they missed. It was so different from when I was a player. Back then most of the writers were older guys who had been around baseball twenty, thirty years. They were all looking for a scoop, but they weren't interested in sensationalism. And they couldn't go to Dan Topping or Del Webb, the owners, and they couldn't go to George Weiss, the general manager, for quotes, and no one in the front office would dare leak out quotes against Casey Stengel or against any of the players. The Yankee way was to keep things out of the papers. Now it's like a sieve. George picks up the phone and calls a writer with a story. The next day you read about a "reliable source" high in the Yankee organization. That's George. Or if there's dirty work to be done and he doesn't want to look like the bad guy, he'll call Al Rosen or Cedric Tallis and make him say it.

George thinks he's buying the writers this way, but they're on to him. When George calls one writer, the writer calls the rest of them with the information. They know how George tries to use them, and they stick together.

The press made it so much harder for all of us. Henry Hecht of the *New York Post* was the worst. He'd go around and talk to the guys who weren't playing, the bench guys who normally griped, and they'd complain because they weren't playing, and Henry would write it. Or he'd try to pit player against player, like he did with Thurman and Reggie—until Thurman refused to talk to any writers anymore—like he did with a player against me, or me against George. He'd come over and ask me a question, and I'd answer, and he'd then take my answer back to the player—he'd do this especially with Reggie—so the player would have a reaction. He'd do that all the time. I kept telling the players to quit giving out information to these guys, to just talk baseball and let them do their game stories. They have an important job to do, and I admit that sometimes I was too helpful, I gave them too much myself, and sometimes I got in trouble because of it. I was being too friendly with them.

On the one hand there are some guys who know me well. If I'm saying something controversial, they assume it's off the record, and they don't write it. In a way they're protecting me, and I appreciate that.

On the other hand, some guys when they heard one single thing I might have said in jest, they'd take it out of context and write it, and there'd be big headlines in the papers: Martin Knocks George. I may have been teasing. I used to tease George a lot in my conversations. The phone would ring, and I'd say, "It's George. He's calling with another one of his lineups." Most of the time it wasn't even George on the phone. I'd be teasing. But a writer who didn't know me, he'd turn to the guy next to him and say, "Did ya hear what he said? Ooooooooh," like he really had a big story or something.

Little things would happen, and the press would blow them all out of proportion, like the incident with Thurman on the plane. When this would happen, the player quoted in the papers would come over the next day and tell me, "I didn't say it the way he wrote it, Billy." I'd tell him, "I know you didn't. Don't get upset about it. Just go out and do your job."

The only time I'd get angry with a writer was when he'd ask me a stupid question, try to second-guess me. It would never be a regular writer. They knew better than to ask me a question like "Why didn't you bunt in such-and-such situation?" "Why did you try a steal?" It would always be a guy on a one-day assignment or a guy from a tiny radio station—how they got the pass to get in there I don't know—and I'd look at him like, "Did you really say that?" And the guy would get annoyed that I had ridiculed him, and right away the guy would be mad at me. The regular writers never asked questions like that. They wrote what they saw on the field, which is what they should do. If they want to second-guess in the paper, that's their prerogative. But don't come and ask me to help second-guess myself. I understand their making a living, but I'm not going to help them that much.

To give you a good example of how the press made it harder:

We were in Seattle, and I was sitting in my office, and Al Rosen called me on the phone to tell me that the Yankees had brought up catcher Mike Heath from Tacoma. The day before I had given Al specific instructions as to my whereabouts, that I was fishing and I'd be back at a specific time, and he had had plenty of opportunity to call me to tell me about Heath. Instead, I found out he was being brought up on the local news show. I just don't like to be surprised. I don't like a player to come up to me out of the blue and say, "Hey, Skip, here I am," or even worse, "Hey, Skip, I'm gone." I don't like that. It's embarrassing for a manager.

So when Al called me to tell me, I already knew and I was hot, and I slammed the phone down on him. I shouldn't have done that, but it would have been forgotten the next day if three writers hadn't been there when it happened. You should have seen the headlines the next day. You'd have thought I'd just bombed Pearl Harbor.

A day hadn't passed before I got in trouble in the papers again. During spring training, Murray Chass of *The New York Times* had asked me about George's signing all these free agents, and I made a comment about their being "George's boys." On June first my comment about "George's boys" turned up in the *Times*, and George had an apoplexy. For the umptyumphth time, George was going to fire me.

My agent, Doug Newton, had been sitting in the press box when he was called into George's office in the middle of the game. He told Doug, "If Billy made these comments about me, he's gone. And if Chass wrote these comments out of context just to antagonize me, we're going to ban him from the clubhouse." Can you imagine banning *The New York Times* from your clubhouse? Newton told George I hadn't tried to discredit him, which was the truth. I had made those comments in spring training, and I had been teasing when I said it.

After the game Doug called to clue me into what was going on. I told him, "I said that thing four months ago. George knows better than to have that upset him." Doug told me Rosen wanted to meet with us. I told him I'd be there in ten minutes.

I walked into Rosen's office and said, "Al, where's George?" I wanted to talk to him about it, to straighten everything out. Rosen said, "George wants me to handle this. He doesn't want to talk to you." That was a large part of our problem. Even when there was a problem, George would never call me directly and talk about it. He'd go to Cedric or Gabe or Rosen to give me the information. I would have been glad to talk with him. In fact, this was the one thing I wanted more than anything else, to be able to deal with him directly rather than him getting something secondhand and getting it wrong, getting what I had said misconstrued. You tell someone something, and too often it comes out altogether different than what you meant to say. The only time he'd call me was after a game when we lost, and he'd act like a little baby. Maybe he was trying to impress the people sitting up there with him in his booth.

When Rosen told me George didn't want to talk with me, Doug and I heard footsteps behind his door. George's office is next to Rosen's, and I knew it was George listening behind the door. I asked him, "Why isn't George here?" Rosen said, "He wants me to handle it."

In a very condescending way Rosen ordered me to sit down. It was like he was the school principal and I was a naughty school kid. Rosen took the newspaper article with the "George's boys" quote in it and slid it over in front of me. "Billy, read this," he said. I took a brief look at it, and by this time my blood was really beginning to boil. I said, "Al, am I on trial here?" Rosen got all shook up. He stopped being headmaster of a prep school and he started acting like an adult. He said quietly, "No Billy, you're not on trial. I'd just like you to read this." I looked at it and shoved it back toward him. "What about it?" I said. He said, "What about it? I'll tell you what about it. Did you make these comments?" I said, "Yeah, I said something to that effect back in spring training." Rosen said, "George is very disturbed by these statements. If you made these statements, it's going to have to stop now."

I said, "Al, I told you I made these statements four months ago. Check with the writer, then come and talk with me. Why don't you get your facts straight before making such a big deal over nothing? Ask the guy who wrote it when I said it and what I meant by it at the time. Would you do that, Al?"

Al got a little flustered, and then he said, "Yes, Billy, but I'm here to give you a little lecture on . . ." I stood up and started to walk out the door. I said, "Listen, pal, if you or George want to fire me, just do it, get it over with, let's not go into any of this Mickey Mouse stuff." We were about to leave on a road trip that evening. I said, "I'm going to go down, get out of my uniform, shower, and change clothes now to get ready for this trip. If the man wants to fire me, let me know if I ought to take the bus or not." And with that, I walked out and slammed the door behind me. Doug stayed.

About fifteen minutes later I called Rosen on the phone from my office. I said, "Al, what's your decision? Am I going to take the team bus or not?" Rosen said, "Be on the bus, Billy. Be on the bus." Doug told me Rosen hung up and said, "I'm going to make this decision. I'm not going to fire him."

Things didn't get any better, however. If it wasn't one thing, it was another. A couple days later Rosen got a letter from Lee MacPhail reprimanding me for giving a fan the Italian salute. I very seldom yell back at somebody in the stands, but some guy in Cleveland was really on me bad, and finally I couldn't take it anymore and shot him the salute. Well, George's mother was in the stands, and somebody told George about it, and George must have told MacPhail, because they were talking about fining me for it. Here Reggie shouts those four-letter words to people in the stands all the time and people hear him and tell George, and George never says anything about that. I did it once, and George and the league come down on me.

The next thing that happened was we started losing. With Hunter, Gullett, Messersmith, and Tidrow all ailing, there was no way we could stay up with the Red Sox. Also Bucky Dent was out, and Willie Randolph was out, and then Mickey Rivers fractured his hand, and Thurman was playing on bad legs. Our only bright spot was Ron Guidry, who struck out 18 Angels in mid-June to run his record to 11 and 0. I was a little concerned, because every time Ronny got two strikes on a batter, the fans would start cheering for the strikeout, and I was concerned he'd try to throw a little too hard and it would take too much out of him. I didn't want to see the kid hurt his career going for the strikeouts. I called him in and told him he had to pace himself, and he said he would try. Guidry's a sharp person, a very good competitor, and he did try. Every fifth day I'd send him out there, and every fifth day he'd win. We were seven games out when we went into Boston in mid-May. If it hadn't been for Guidry, who knows how far back we would have been?

I started Kenny Clay in the opener against the Red Sox. Our staff was in such bad shape that I had to reach into the bullpen and take Clay out of there, and Kenny got hit hard. Actually, it didn't matter who we started, because the Red Sox were hot, they were hitting everything all over the park, and they would have killed us no matter what. We couldn't even slow them down.

That night I was told George called Clay on the phone to tell him he hadn't tried hard enough. Then two days later Jim Beattie started, and he got bombed and I took him out, and when the game was over I learned that George had sent him to the minors. He didn't even tell me, let me talk to the kid. I felt really bad. You don't do that to a young pitcher. It's the greatest way in the world to break a guy's morale. My job with pitchers is to build their confidence, just like I did with Guidry. Pitchers get to a certain point, and you have to go with them to get them over that hump. But if you break them down and keep breaking them down, they're never going to get their confidence. Pitchers have a pitcher's ego like a hitter has a hitter's ego. Pitcher's pitch to a hitter's ego. Hitters hit to a pitcher's ego. A pitcher has to have confidence, and a manager is trying to build the pitcher up to have that confidence in himself. The whole thing to managing is building up the ego, making a player feel he can do it. Showing him how to do it. Get him over the humps. And once you get him over the humps on the baseball field, that player will make it in any walk of life, because he'll have learned to be a competitor. But you have to have patience, especially with a young kid. I have patience, and when I get angry, I get angry, but I always try not to allow my anger to affect my thinking. You get mad at your mother, don't you? Does that mean you hate her? Of course not. Temper is not a bad thing, if you use it right. Jesus Christ had a temper. Didn't He take a whip to the money changers in the synagogue? We're the image of Him, aren't we? But if you let your temper rule your head, then you're hurting everyone. A pitcher does a bad job, George gets mad, gets rid of him, sends him down. When he comes back up, do you think he'll give you his loyalty, give you his best? It's not easy to do good all the time. You have to stick with them, even when they're going bad, especially when they're going bad. You can't keep fining players, blasting them in the papers, leaking quotes out in the papers on the players. It's no good. It disrupts the ball club. Disrupts everything. It causes chaos, and when you have chaos, you have players going different ways, no one's playing together as a team, and consequently, it makes winning that much tougher.

A couple days later there was an article in the papers from a "reliable source" that said the team was crumbling under its manager. What was actually happening was that because so many of our starters were hurt or on the disabled list, we weren't winning, and Rosen and George were beginning to panic. I kept telling them, "Wait till Dent and Randolph and Rivers and Munson and Hunter all get healthy," but they didn't want to hear it. What George wanted to do was fire our trainer, Gene Monahan. Monahan happens to be one of the finest trainers in all of baseball. I got George to back off. He fired one doctor because he didn't like the way he was handling things. George thinks he knows more than everyone, including the doctors.

George also tried to blame the injuries on my pitching coach, Art Fowler.

Rosen flew into Detroit, and he told me, "Billy, we're going to have to get rid of Art." I said, "No you're not. If you get rid of him, I want you to get rid of me at the same time." My coaches were loyal to me, every one of them, and loyalty has to be a two-way street. George doesn't understand that. He thinks it's a one-way street, with all the loyalty going back to him. And that isn't right. Loyalty is a two-way street, and the quicker he learns that, the quicker he'll grow up. If I had let Art go and hadn't stuck up for him, didn't take a stand, the other coaches would have said, "Why should we stick our necks out for Billy? Look how he defended one of his own." I wanted to defend Art to the hilt whether it cost me my job or not.

That kind of shocked Rosen. He said, "C'mon, Billy. We'll get Art a job in the minor leagues." I said, "No, it doesn't work that way, Al." Because I knew it wasn't Al making these decisions. It was George sending Al to do his dirty work. I guess Al went back to George and told him he'd better back off, because they never did fire Art.

Meanwhile I called all my coaches in and told them what they were trying to do. I said, "They're trying to fire Art today, but I'm not going to let them. If they do, I'm going with Art. I want you to be aware of this as a possibility." Art told me not to do what I was doing. "I'll go," he said. I told him, "No, Art, it doesn't work that way."

On the bus from the ball park to our hotel, Art cried like a baby. It was a terrible thing to watch a man Art's age cry like that. It was unfair, really unfair to a human being to do a thing like that to him. All the years he's been in baseball, they do that to him. Here's a guy who wouldn't hurt a fly.

When we got back to New York, Doug and I had a meeting with George to let him know face to face where I stood. He asked me if I'd let Clyde King come up and become a second pitching coach. Clyde was letting George think he was working with the kid pitchers in the minors, really helping them, and George didn't know any better. He didn't even know a lot of the pitchers didn't like Clyde at all. But George felt Clyde had helped Jim Beattie and a couple other kids, and he thought, "Boy, Clyde is really the one." Like this year George is going with Stan Williams as pitching coach, because Gene Michael is telling him how great Stan is. I'm not saying he isn't great, but he certainly didn't show it with Boston. Art showed it to me every place we've been. He showed it to me in Minnesota, in Detroit, in Texas, in New York. Since George is always talking about statistics, why didn't he check Art's record? Check how many 20-game winners he's had. George is so cuckoo for statistics, he'd find out Art's record is sensational. He's had more 20-game winners than Johnny Sain, who everyone raves about.

But Art couldn't stop the injuries. Injuries happen. Art had prepared the pitchers properly in the spring, ran them right, pitched them properly to loosen up their arms, didn't overthrow them. He did everything humanly possible to protect them, and they still got hurt. And when that happens, you can't blame the pitching coach. The staff was so crumbled by injuries that in one game I had to send Jim Spencer to the bullpen to warm up. Hunter, Clay, and Messersmith were all on the disabled list, and we called up this kid McCall, and he got a blister before I could even pitch him and I had to send him back down. I had to call for volunteers. Dick Tidrow went in the game in the fifth inning, and if he couldn't go the rest of the way, I didn't have another pitcher. Fortunately Dick made it through.

By mid-July George was putting more and more pressure on me. He leaked a story out to the newspapers that he had offered me a chance to quit because of my health, that he had offered me a consultant's job so I could spend my time setting up a boy's camp I wanted to start. He told the writer that he was doing it to save my health. He's never been concerned about my health or my welfare, not ever. If he had been so concerned about me, you'd have thought all the time I was in my New Jersey apartment all by myself he would have just once called me up and invited me out to dinner. Not once did he call me. In all the years I worked for him. If he had been concerned about me, he would have been my friend, and I never saw that in him. If he was interested in my health he would have quit second-guessing me, quit telling me how to manage.

Another reason we were falling farther and farther behind Boston was that Reggie Jackson had stopped hitting. First I moved him down in the order, and when the slump continued, I sat him down against certain left-handed pitchers such as Jon Matlack of Texas, Ken Kravec of Chicago, and Bill Travers of Milwaukee. The whole time Reggie was super about the whole situation. I don't know what he told the writers, but I felt he and I had a great rapport. He'd come into my office, we'd talk, and he'd lay a little poem on my desk for me to read. He was just super, didn't give me any trouble.

It was July seventeenth, we were playing Kansas City at the stadium. Reggie came out to the park and greeted me. "Hi, Skip." He was real happy, and I called him over and told him that George wanted to see him.

He went up, and after he returned he walked by me and scowled like he was madder'n heck, which was a shock to me. Whatever George said to Reggie when he was up there made him hot, and mad. He came down, walked over to his locker, and he told Dick Howser, my third-base coach, "Tell Martin I don't want to talk to him anymore, and tell him I don't want him giving me any more signs." Ordinarily the third-base coach gives the steal sign, but Reggie and I had had special signs. I was the one who gave him the steal sign. He'd watch me, and he was very good at stealing a base when we needed it.

Howser came over and told me what Reggie had said. I said, "Okay, we'll get to the bottom of it. There's something wrong. Something haywire someplace. I'll find out what's wrong." But I never did. I'd certainly like to know what it was that George told him that made him so mad at me, because until that time he had been perfect with me. Later I asked George what he had told Reggie, and George said, "Oh, nothing really. Somebody said that Jeff Burroughs's wife said that you had said something about Reggie, and it got back to Reggie." I had no idea what he was talking about. George twists things around so much, he twists things, distorts them. I can't imagine what he could have told Reggie.

We were tied with the Royals in the tenth, and we had Thurman on first, and their third baseman, Brett, and their first baseman were playing back, and I felt that this would be a perfect time for Reggie to bunt. I knew what Reggie had said about his not wanting me to give him signs, but when it comes to winning a ball game, if I think a guy should bunt, he's going to bunt. If I think he should hit, he'll hit, no matter how mad a player gets at me. I put the bunt sign on. They weren't looking for it, but Reggie fouled the ball back for a strike. The infielders moved in, so I gave Howser the sign to have Reggie swing away. Reggie looked at him, saw the sign, and when the pitch came in, he bunted anyway. Strike two. Howser called time and went down the line to tell Reggie that the bunt sign was off and that he was to hit away. Howser told him, "You're not to bunt." Reggie bunted anyway. He fouled the ball off for strike three, made an out. We didn't score that inning, and we ended up losing the game.

I was so mad, it was unreal. I was sitting there on the bench saying to myself, "Whatever you do, don't touch him, don't punch him, don't do it." I was so hot I was talking to myself. He came back into the dugout, walked right toward me and took his glasses off like he expected me to punch him. Maybe he even wanted me to punch him. I don't know. When he took his glasses off, I said to myself, "I wish I wasn't the manager." Because I wanted to haul off and punch him so badly I could taste it. I didn't make a move. Reggie sat down on the other end of the bench.

After the game I went into the clubhouse, went into my office, and I took my clock radio and threw it against the wall. It broke into pieces. Yogi came in and tried to calm me down. "Don't hit him. Don't do nothing to him. Don't do it," Yogi kept saying. He said, "I went through it, too. I went through it with Cleon Jones the same way. Don't do anything." I told Yogi, "I'm not going to touch him. I won't do anything," and I got on the phone and called Al Rosen and told him that if he didn't fine and suspend Reggie, I was quitting. I said, "He defied me, and there's no way he can get away with that. If he does, the game's crooked, and I don't want any part of it. Let him get away with that, and you might as well forget the ball club. Might as well make Reggie the manager."

I told Rosen I wanted him suspended for the rest of the year. I felt we could have won it with him or without him. We didn't need Reggie Jackson to win the pennant. Al said he wanted to suspend him for only five days. I went along with the short suspension.

Earlier in that same game there was another incident, one that the press blew all out of proportion. Sparky Lyle was having contractual problems, he wanted a new contract from

George, and he and George were fighting every day, and he was very upset. George would talk contract with these guys and make them mad, and then they'd come to play, and they'd be so damn grumpy I could hardly get them to play. Every time George talked damn dollars with a player he made it tough for me.

Another problem Sparky had was that I was pitching him in long relief, and he didn't like that. The way I saw it, Goose Gossage was pitching very well, and the only way I could keep Sparky sharp was to pitch him in the middle innings. I tried to make him understand that, but he was very upset about it. He just doesn't like to pitch long relief. In this game our starting pitcher got roughed up, and I sent Sparky in to pitch the fourth inning. He pitched the fourth, pitched the fifth, and when he walked into the dugout, he said, "I've had enough. I'm going home." All season long Sparky had been telling me when he had had enough. He said, "I'm not a long relief pitcher," and he left. I didn't mind. I understood what he was going through. The inning had ended, and he was giving me enough time to warm up another pitcher. I had time to get somebody up while we were at bat. If I hadn't had time, that would be a different story, I'd have had to take a different stand, but I had plenty of time to get Goose ready, and it was no problem.

Then in the newspaper I read where I was accused of being a bigot because I wanted Reggie, who's black, suspended, and I forgave Sparky, who's white. There was a big headline in the *Amsterdam News* saying that. Well, the *Amsterdam News* didn't know what it was talking about. If Reggie was green he was going to be suspended. His color doesn't make any difference to me. I've had more success with black and Latin players than I have with white ones. Color had nothing to do with it.

During the five games Reggie was suspended we made up five games on the Red Sox, who were starting to have injury problems of their own. While Reggie was out, we played the same way we had in 1976. We hustled, played hard-nosed, aggressive ball, and for the first time all season we really looked like a team. Paul Blair said it best. "If Reggie's here, fine. If he's not, fine." I think most of the players felt that way at the time. With Reggie gone, it seemed that my job was so much easier. First of all, I didn't have George calling me up and telling me where he should hit and where he should play. Secondly, during his suspension, it was like normal again in the clubhouse. There was no controversy. The writers concentrated on the games and left the controversy in the background. The sideshow, carnival atmosphere was missing.

The day Reggie returned the carnival atmosphere returned. Before the game George had called me up on the phone. He told me, "You play that boy. He's been working out." When he arrived I had Dick Howser ask him whether he had kept in shape. Reggie told him he hadn't touched a ball or bat. I didn't put him in the lineup. It would have been unfair to the other guys who were trying to win a pennant. Also, I wasn't going to put Reggie out there and make him look bad. I wasn't going to hurt one guy and hurt the club at the same time. I don't do things like that. He had already been fined, already been punished, that was enough. I wasn't going to do any more to him.

George had also told me that he had told Reggie to zip up his mouth, but it didn't quite work out that way. I was in the clubhouse before the game, and I turned around and there was a whole crowd of reporters standing around Reggie, and I could hear him tell all the reporters that he couldn't understand why I had suspended him. He was telling them that he thought he was doing the right thing by bunting; it was a lot of baloney. The first words out of his mouth were "I don't know why he suspended me." I was angry enough just seeing the crowd of reporters back in the clubhouse, and then to hear him say he hadn't done anything wrong, well, it was too much. We had a smooth-running ship, and we didn't need Reggie and his mouth coming along and breaking it up. I didn't want to hear another word from him. By Reggie saying he hadn't done anything wrong, he did two things. He gave the writers something controversial, allowed them to fan the flames. He was making my actions look absurd, because if he hadn't done anything wrong, he was saying that I was wrong in fining him, which was so far off base it was ridiculous.

We were playing the White Sox in Chicago, and we won again without Reggie, and after the game I went upstairs, and who did I run into but Bill Veeck, the owner of the White Sox and an old friend. We got to talking and Veeck said, "Did you know that we almost got you to manage the White Sox?" I said, "What do you mean?" Veeck said, "About a month ago Steinbrenner called to propose trading you to the White Sox for our manager, Bob Lemon." I said, "You're not kidding me, are you, Bill?" He said, "No, Billy. George wanted to trade you for Lemon."

I left him. We were on our way to the airport to fly to Kansas City, and the more I thought about what Veeck had told me, the angrier I got. To think I had busted my tail to bring the Yankees to their former glory and fame, and here the owner behind my back was trying to make a trade to get rid of me! I was in shock that he could have thought to do something like that. And here he was going around telling people how he's always looking out for Billy Martin! How could he tell everybody in the papers how he was looking out for my health when the truth was he was secretly trying to get rid of me?

When we got to the airport, I was very upset. Reggie had made a statement to reporters that I hadn't talked to him in a year and a half. How could he have said that? Why did he say that? He knew that wasn't true. I was walking down the corridor to the plane with Murray Chass of the *Times* and Henry Hecht of the *Post*. I was thinking to myself about Reggie's statement that I hadn't talked to him, and I was also filled with the idea that Steinbrenner had tried to trade me behind my back for Lemon. Chass, Hecht, and I were talking, and I made the comment: "The two of them deserve each other. One's a born liar, the other's convicted." I was madder than hell, and the line reflected how upset I was. I told them, "It's on the record. Did you get it?" That's how burned up I was. I wanted people to know how I was feeling. I used poor judgment. The comment got me in trouble.

When the big headlines came out in the papers the next day and I saw how upset everyone was, I said to myself, "They're talking about firing me. First they were going to embarrass me by trading managers, and now they want to fire me. I'm not going to give that to them. I'm going to quit. I've had it with this guy. He's deliberately trying to hurt me, and I've had it." I decided to leave the ball club, even if it meant giving up my salary.

I didn't sleep a wink. I called Doug Newton around two in the morning to tell him what I was going to do. I told him, "Doug, I don't want to continue. It's not good for the team. There's too much dissension. I'm certainly part of the problem, and in the best interst of the Yankees, I'd better step down. That's what George wants, and I've had it. I'm a nervous wreck. The man is constantly second-guessing me, and it's begun to affect my managing." I knew that even though George was upset with me, he didn't have the guts to call me directly. He never did. I figured he would call Doug. I told Doug, "Tell George and Rosen they can find themselves a new manager." Doug and I agreed to talk again in the morning.

In the morning I talked with Newton, and George had called him just like I thought he would. Doug told George that I was quitting. George's reaction was that what I said publicly when I resigned would be very important. George told Newton, "I'm under no obligation to pay him if he resigns. But if Billy says that he's quitting to take care of his health and to get himself back together physically and mentally, I'll pay him. If he says he's resigning because of my interference, I won't."

I told Doug, "I won't lie and say I'm about to have a nervous breakdown or am about to go into the hospital. I won't lie and say I'm undergoing a physical hardship. That isn't true."

I told Doug what I was going to say: that I want to step down, and I don't want to talk about it anymore. I want to stop all this media hype, stop all the dissension, I don't want to be in the headlines anymore. I want this team to have a good chance of winning the pennant, so I'm going to step down. That's all I want to say, I told him.

Doug said, "If you can say something about resigning because you owe it to your mental and physical well-being, you should, because it would be stupid for you to walk away from your salary."

I said, "I *am* resigning because of my mental health. I'll go crazy if I stay on. Steinbrenner is driving me crazy. I guess I could say something about my mental health." Doug then told me Rosen was coming out to talk with me. Doug said George didn't mention what Rosen was coming for or what he was going to say, but he suggested Rosen was probably coming out to fire me. I told Doug, "I don't care if they fire me or not, because I quit. And frankly, I don't think they have the balls to fire me. Because of the fans, and because they'd have to pay me. But it doesn't matter. I'm going to flat-out resign to keep them from putting me aside. I'm gonna do it myself, and I'm gonna do it as best as I can, and I'm not going to say a word about the real reasons for my resignation. All I'll say is it would hurt the Yankees' chances of winning if I stayed."

Around noon Mickey Moribito, the Yankees' public relations man, called to tell me Rosen was in the hotel and wanted to talk to me. I told Mickey, "I don't want to talk to him. Tell him I have nothing to say to him." To this day I don't know what he was there for, to fire me or reprimand me, or what, and personally I don't care, because I knew what I had to do. It was a hard thing to do, a very hard thing, because I felt that the team was coming on and the Red Sox were getting injured and were ready to be taken, but I felt that I could no longer tolerate being put down by a man who was younger than I was, a man who acts like a little teen-ager. I'd been in the game of baseball thirty-three years, and who was he to dictate to me what was right and what was wrong? Maybe that's the way he runs his shipyard, but he wasn't going to run this man that way.

I went down the elevator to the hotel lobby, walked right by Al Rosen, didn't say a word to him, and at my press conference I resigned. When I got to the end where it came time to thank the Yankee fans, I couldn't quite get it out. That's when I broke down. I wanted to say, "I want to thank the fans because they've been so great," but I was sobbing so badly I could barely get the last few words out. I was with Phil Rizzuto and he put his arm around me, and we walked out of the hotel.

I met my friend Bob Brown outside, and we walked about ten blocks, just kept walking, didn't say a word, and we pulled into a tiny country-and-western bar where I could sit by myself without the press. We sat there for hours, listening to the country-and-western music. The next day I flew to Florida to be with Mickey Mantle.

o　o　o

I was in Florida exactly one day when I got a call from Doug Newton. He said that George had called him to say he didn't feel right not having me as manager. I told Doug, "He should have thought about that the last six months. If he'd have treated me right, I'd have still been the manager." Doug agreed, and he told me George said he would pay my salary for the remainder of my contract. "That's nice of him," I said. It *was* nice of him. Technically, he didn't have to do that.

Bob Lemon, meanwhile, had taken over as Yankee manager. The very next day Newton called me again. He told me that representatives from several teams had contacted him for me to manage them. I told him, "Doug, I don't want another job with another team right now. I want to just step back and stay out of the limelight altogether, not say anything about anybody, and hopefully the Yankees will come back and win." Doug also said that five different people had called him with deals to buy the Yankees from Steinbrenner so I could go back there and manage. We laughed. We knew that was out of the question.

The other thing Doug said was that George wanted me to meet him in New York to talk about the possibility of my coming back for the 1979 season. "He'll take care of Lemon and bring you back in the spring," he said. The day before when he'd said it wasn't right me not being the manager, I thought he was making a condolence call, just being nice. I couldn't believe it. Nevertheless, I told Doug, "I don't know if we should even talk with him. I just resigned." Doug told me he thought George was just crazy enough to be serious. I said, "I don't think the two of us can work together, but I appreciate his sentiment, and I guess it wouldn't hurt to meet with him."

I flew to New York and met with Doug and George on Wednesday, July twenty-sixth, only two days after I had resigned. We were to meet at twelve-thirty in the afternoon in his suite in the Carlyle Hotel in Manhattan. About an hour before, I met Doug at his office on the East Side. We started talking about how unreal it seemed my no longer being the Yankee manager, and I was glad I was wearing sunglasses, because I started to break down in his office. We hugged each other, and both of us were crying. I said, "Do you really think

George is sincere?" Doug said, "Yeah, I do." I said, "Well, let's go meet him."

We had a limo take us to the Carlyle, we got in the elevator, went up to George's suite, and knocked on the door. George was sitting talking on the telephone, and he waved us in. Quickly he hung up. George asked me how I was. I said, "Okay. How are you?" He said, "Oh, fine. Can I get you something to drink? Would you like an ice tea or a ginger ale?" I ordered tea, and George called down for it. When the guy who wheeled in the cart with the tea came in the room, he took one look at George and one look at me, and you should have seen his eyebrows go up.

He left, and George said, "Billy, as I told Doug a couple days ago, I woke up, and I felt in my gut that it wasn't right not having you as manager of the Yankees." I said, "George, I've had the same feeling." George said, "Would you consider coming back and managing the Yankees in 1979?" I said, "George, I would, but I wouldn't." He said, "What do you mean?" I said, "If things were very different, I would. If things stayed the same, I wouldn't." George said, "You know, Billy, both of us are very strong-minded people. We both have strengths and both have weaknesses. One of my weaknesses is that I like to have my nose into everything. One of your weaknesses, Billy, is that you're not as disciplined as I am in certain respects. You don't operate with numbers and memoranda and things of that type. If both of us could give a little, I don't think we'll have any problem at all."

I said, "You're right, George, because you're really not a bad guy." He said, "Actually, you're not, either."

I said, "One of the problems is that you and I didn't talk to each other." He said, "I know, and that's my fault to a great extent. And another problem that came from our not talking to each other was that I'd see certain things in the papers I didn't like, and they'd rub me the wrong way." I said, "Well, that happened to me a lot, too, with some of the things you said about me. And another thing, you talk to certain players behind my back, and that's not good."

George said, "If you promise to do a couple of things and if I promise to do a couple of things, I don't think we have a problem." I said, "If we both keep our word, we won't have a problem."

George said, "One of the things I want you to promise is you'll cut down on your drinking." I said, "George, I don't have a drinking problem. You got guys in your organization who have drinking problems. Sure I take a drink and I'll get hot at times, but I'm not an alcoholic." George said, "Okay, but I'll tell you what. I've been drinking quite a lot myself, and it's not good for you. Let's make a little bet. Let's make a bet that the first one who takes a drink has got to give a thousand dollars to the other guy's favorite charity." We made the bet.

We then started discussing the problems we had with what we were saying about each other in the papers. I said, "George, it's not easy. Because I'm the manager I get put on the spot a lot, and sometimes I say things that don't come out the way I said them. You can't muzzle the press, but maybe if you assigned someone such as the traveling secretary or Mickey Moribito who could be with me at all times so that he knows exactly what I'm saying, and then if you have a question about it, you can ask not only me but you can ask him, too." George said, "That's a great idea. I'll assign Mickey Moribito to do that."

After about a half an hour of talking back and forth, I said, "One of your problems, George, is that you think you know how to run a baseball team, who should play which position, when you should bunt and steal. Really, you don't know that much, and you should stay out of it. I don't tell you how to run your shipbuilding company or how to run the financial end of the ball team, and you shouldn't tell me who to play and when." He said, "You're absolutely right." I told George there could be no restrictive clauses in my contract, and he agreed to that, too. I really enjoyed talking with George. I felt we had a real rapport, something we should have had all along.

George asked, "Billy, would you be prepared to give me reports on the different players, and would you be prepared to instruct me on why you do certain things on the field?" I said, "Sure, I'd be happy to tell you my thinking, my philosophy, my strategy. That's the way you learn." I asked, "Would you teach me more about the business side of the Yankees, tell me more about what the general manager does?" He said, "Sure I will."

We agreed to form a pact to communicate with each other and to level with each other. I said, "Look, George. If you got a problem with me, call me. You tell me about it. Don't send Cedric Tallis or Al Rosen." He said, "I will do that, but I want you to feel free to work with Al and Cedric as well." I said, "That's fine, but whenever there's a problem, whenever you're upset with something, I want you to call me directly." George said, "Similarly, I want you to feel free to work with me and to call me anytime." I said fine. It sounded so terrific.

George said, "It's Old Timers' Day Saturday, and I'd like to make the announcement that you're coming back in seventy-nine then. The fans will go wild, and it'll be tremendous." I was really touched when he said that. I felt that finally maybe I was getting the respect from George I felt I deserved. "I've got something I have to do first," he said. "I've got to tell Lemon and Rosen what I'm going to do. The way I operate, once I make up my mind to do something, I get it done, but I first have to check and see what kind of commitment Rosen made to Lem. But we're ninety-five percent there." George said, "Now, whatever you do, Billy, don't say anything to anybody about this conversation."

I said, "George, you have my word on it." I gave George my private home phone number, and he gave me his, and we left. I told Doug to be sure not to tell anyone, and I rode back to the Hasbrouck Heights Sheraton, where I was staying. I arrived, and I went upstairs and Art Fowler, my pitching coach, was upstairs. He was very upset that I was no longer manager of the Yankees. He said, "Billy, what should I do? Should I quit?" I told him, "You stay here and keep your job, and if they release you at the end of the season, you go home and we'll see what happens." I said, "I don't know what's going to happen." I couldn't tell him that on Saturday I was going to be announced as Yankee manager for 1979.

On Friday I got a call from Newton. He said that George believed the story was leaked and that George had heard from somebody at the Sheraton that I had spilled it. I said, "Doug, I didn't talk to anyone about anything. Let's just forget the whole thing. First of all, George should have called me rather than call you like he said he was going to do yesterday. Second of all, I didn't leak it out. I didn't even tell Art about it."

Doug called George to tell him what I had said, and he called me back. Doug said, "Let's forget about this leaking-out thing and let's discuss your requirements for coming back as manager in seventy-nine." I was too upset to change the subject. I said, "Doug, what did George say about me leaking out the story? Did he say I leaked it out?" Doug said, "George says he didn't leak it out, and so the only ones who could have were you or me. I didn't, so he assumed you must have." I got mad. I said, "The hell with you, and don't you call me anymore. And tell George he can stick the job up his ass—again." And I hung up. Newton tried to call me back, but I wouldn't answer my phone. Oh, was I hot.

Later in the day I cooled down sufficiently to talk to Doug again. He said George told him there was a problem. Rosen said he had brought Lemon from his home on the West Coast to be manager, and he felt he owed him till the end of the year and one full year in addition. Rosen said he would resign if Lem wasn't given a fair chance to be manager.

Doug said that I would work within the Yankee organization for a year getting my full salary, that I would actively participate in spring training, and I'd scout during the season, and then I would be the manager again in 1980. I said, "Doug, I think Lem should get his full year in, let's do it that way." Doug said, "What if Lem has a tremendous year, and the Yankees win the pennant? Do you think George is going to renege?" I said, "The Yankees will win this year. I expect them to win. I also believe George is a man of his word. If he says he's going to bring me back in nineteen eighty he's going to do it. I believe him." I said, "Do you believe him, Doug?" He said, "Yeah, I believe him, too."

In the late afternoon Mickey Mantle called Doug to find out if I was going to be in New York for Old Timers' Day. Doug said, "Mick, I really have no idea." Newton found out I hadn't even told Mickey, who's my best friend, about it. If I didn't tell him, I wasn't going to tell anybody else, was I?

Saturday came. No one was to find out before the announcement, so I wore dark glasses and a hat, and when the limo pulled up, I ran into the side entrance before anyone could see me. When I got inside I was surrounded by security guards, who rushed me downstairs. Pat Kelly, who's the stadium manager, had a walkie-talkie, and he was saying, "We've got the package, the package has arrived, the package is now being moved downstairs." It was high drama, like a CIA maneuver. They took me to a little closet underneath the stadium, where I put on my uniform. I could hear the loudspeaker announcing the names of the old timers as I dressed. They then sneaked me into a boiler room near the dugout. We were playing the Twins, and I had the clubhouse boy send a note over to Rod Carew asking him to meet me. He came in, and we hugged. He asked, "What in the world are you doing here?" I told him that in two minutes I was going to be manager of the Yankees again.

When Bob Shepard announced it and I ran onto the field, there was so much noise I couldn't believe it was me they were cheering. I was very embarrassed standing out there, waving for what must have been ten minutes, but Mickey and Joe seemed so happy, and the fans were so great, that I lost my embarrassment. I was so elated, after being so down, nothing like this had happened to me in my whole life. It was a tremendous salute to a .250 hitter who got fortunate, who got a chance to manage, and for the fans to show that they cared that much, it was something I'll never forget the rest of my life. Every time I think about it, it chokes me up. The New York fans are the greatest, simply the greatest. And they know their baseball, too.

After the Old Timers' activities, George held a press conference. George announced in advance that no questions would be asked. I was to make a statement, and that would be all.

Before the press conference George called Newton aside. He said, "I want Billy to make a couple statements at the press conference. I want Billy to say that I had given him another chance, that I had really shown him something, that I'm really a wonderful man, that I took him with his physical problems, emotional problems, his drinking problems, and I've given him a second chance." George also wanted me to say that I was going to spend the rest of the year taking care of my health, getting back on my feet. George said, "Doug, he's to say he's getting off the booze, that he had been drinking too much, that he's going to reform. Doug, you tell him to say all those things at the press conference."

Doug said, "Billy's not going to say those things, because they're not true." George said, "Goddamnit, he's got to say something like that. He has to."

At the press conference I talked in my best Stengelese. I said that we had had our indifferences in the past, but that it would be different in the future, blah, blah, blah. The press conference ended, and Mickey Moribito came over and told Newton that George wanted to see him. George wanted him to add a few statements to the press release of my speech, stuff about my drinking and my bad health. Newton said, "I'm not Billy's ghost writer. Ask him to add statements if you want." But, of course, he didn't dare. He knew better than that.

During the winter of 1978 there was one question uppermost in the minds of baseball fans and the press: Was George serious about hiring Billy Martin in 1980, or was it just a brilliant public relations move on his part? For months it was a question I was to ask myself over and over and over again.

CHAPTER

When the Minnesota Twins released me as a player in 1962—I had played in the majors since 1950—I was sure I could hook up with another club. Twins owner Calvin Griffith had offered me a $10,000-a-year job as a scout, but my heart was still set on playing, and I accepted eagerly when Kansas City manager Hank Bauer, who had been my teammate on the Yankees, called to ask if I would be a utility player for the A's. But two days later Hank called back to say that A's owner Charley Finley had changed his mind and he was sorry, and at that time it dawned on me that my playing days were in fact over.

I knew the Twins were making a mistake letting me go as a player. Bernie Allen had come along, he would be the Twins' second baseman, but I felt that I could have helped as a utility player, which later proved to be the case when the team was hit by injuries. I could not, however, convince Calvin and his baseball people of this, so I decided to accept their offer to become a scout. All of a sudden I was no longer playing baseball, which I loved so much. My whole childhood, baseball was all I did. Girls weren't the name of the game. Baseball was. So when the day came that I had to turn in my uniform, I was devastated. For days and days I couldn't get over it. I went down to the Twins camp in Melbourne, Florida, to scout the minor leaguers, and the whole time I felt terrible. I felt like the whole world had come to an end. I was depressed, despondent. I walked across a bridge, and people were standing on it fishing, and I sat down on the edge with my feet dangling out over the water, and for a couple hours I just sat there and stared down at the water. I couldn't believe my baseball career had come to an end. All I had wanted to be all my life was a baseball player, and here it was the end. No other club had contacted me, and I certainly wouldn't call them. I wouldn't beg for water if my heart was on fire.

Sherry Robertson, who is Calvin Griffith's stepbrother, ran the camp, and he was so supportive, so great, I'll be grateful to him forever. He saw I was really down, and he tried to cheer me up, and he told me how glad he and Mr. Griffith were to have me on his staff, and it just made me feel good.

After camp broke, I went back to Minneapolis, and I received a wire from one of the Japanese baseball teams offering me $100,000 to play baseball in Japan for three years.

In addition to my scouting job, I also had a job doing public relations for the Grain Belt Brewery, and with the two jobs I was making a decent living, but still, a hundred thousand dollars was a lot of money, and so I went to see Calvin. I showed him the wire, and he said, "Billy, I don't blame you if you take the job." I asked him what he thought about the offer. He said, "To be honest, I'd really like to have you in our organization. I'd like you to stay here." I said, "Calvin. I really appreciate that," and I tore up the wire right in front of him. "If you want me," I said, "I'll stay."

For three years, 1962, '63, and '64, I scouted for the Twins. I went to all the Twins home games and sat in the stands and evaluated the opposition, and when it came time to talk trades I'd sit with the rest of the team officials and give my opinion, whether we should acquire a player or not. Calvin would run the meetings, and each of the scouts would talk, and most of the time we pretty much agreed on what to do.

I'd also go scout high-school prospects every once in a while. One time Calvin sent me to scout Jim Palmer and Wally Bunker. I came back and told Calvin I didn't like Bunker. He'd pitch a great ball game one day, but if he was playing against a team that wasn't very good, he'd ease up and start toying with them, laughing at the batters until he again felt like throwing hard, at which time he'd strike everybody out again. I just didn't like his makeup. He wasn't aggressive enough, and I said so. Palmer, on the other hand, him I told Calvin to sign immediately. He wanted between fifty and sixty thousand dollars for signing. I said, "Give him whatever he asks for. He's worth it." And of course that's the way it turned out, except that Calvin wouldn't spend the money. He told me he didn't want to spend that much for a pitcher because pitchers get sore arms too easily, and if that happened he'd lose his investment. It's impossible to say how many more pennants the Twins would have won had Calvin listened.

In 1965 Calvin and Sherry asked me to be the Twins third-base coach, and I agreed, and the day camp opened the rumors started that I was after manager Sam Mele's job, which I just couldn't believe. Sam and I worked very well together. He appreciated my ability to teach, and he let me coach at third the way I felt was right. In spring training, I told the players that I was going to make them more daring base runners, that I was going to get them thrown out at home deliberately just so they'd be more aggressive. The spring training games began, and I did just what I said I'd do, and I got three or four of our runners thrown out at home during exhibition games. Billy Robertson, Sherry's and Calvin Griffith's brother, didn't like what I was doing out there. Billy didn't understand what I was trying to do, and he went to Mele and tried to get me replaced as third-base coach.

At the end of the season we won the pennant, largely because the players had been more aggressive, and Calvin went to Sam and asked him who had taught the guys how to steal and to run the bases. Sam told him the truth. He said, "Billy taught them."

That year we had seven regulars who drove in more than 60 runs—Don Mincher, Tony Oliva, Jimmy Hall, Bob Allison, Earl Battey, Harmon Killebrew, and Zoilo Versalles, and Versalles, our shortstop, was so tremendous that he won the Most

Valuable Player Award. Zoilo was the type of guy who would pout and get real down on himself, but the other players and I did everything we could to keep his head straight. I'd get Oliva and Sandy Valdespino, and later Cesar Tovar, to go over to him and keep up his spirits.

One time in spring training Zoilo and Sam Mele got into an argument, and Zoilo took his clothes and dressed in the shower room. I grabbed him and said, "You get your ass out here and change in my locker with me. I don't want you going around pouting like a little wet boy. You sit right here and change with me." All during the year we talked to him, and he would do anything I told him, and he had one of the greatest years I've ever seen from a player. He did it all and was just tremendous.

Only two things marred that year for me. The first was a fight I had with Calvin's right-hand man Howard Fox. The second was friction I had with two of the other coaches, guys who *were* trying to get Mele's job.

The problem I had with Howard began on a charter flight we were sharing with the Yankees. The Yankees' commercial airline was on strike, so the Yankees were sharing the plane with us, and a couple of the Yankee players were drinking rather heavily, and one pitcher, who had been drinking too much, began making some sexual remarks.

Now, the Twins used to make the mistake of allowing the players and other officials to take their wives along with them on trips, which is bad. Not because you don't want wives to go on trips, but because sometimes guys say things, and a player will say, "Don't talk that way in front of my wife," and it leads to trouble. Happens all the time. If the wives went on a separate plane, it would make life so much easier. On the Twins, so many guys and their wives would come along with us that the players would joke about the Twins' "freeloading plane." Friends of friends of friends of friends would come. If the car dealer gave a player a car, or the butcher gave him steaks, he'd get to go with the team.

The Twins were on one side of the plane, and the Yankees on the other, and this Yankee pitcher was swearing up a storm, and Howard Fox says to me, "Why don't you go over there and tell that guy he's swearing too loud, that it's embarrassing to the women around here." I said, "Howard, I'm not the manager of this club, Sam Mele's the manager. Tell Ralph Houk, the Yankee manager. He's the one to talk to." So that made him mad. He was upset that I had refused to do what he asked.

Later Mele said to me, "Howard's really hot at you." I said, "Yeah, I know. I can tell." And in Italian I said, "Fuck him."

The plane landed, and we arrived at our hotel in Washington, D.C., where we were playing the Senators, and it was Howard's job to give out the room keys. Ordinarily the manager and the coaches get theirs first, and then the players. Howard gave Mele his key, and the other coaches got their keys, and I didn't get mine. All the players except Allison and Killebrew, who had wanted bigger rooms, got their keys and left, and so I was standing there with Howard, Allison, and Killebrew. Howard looked at me, took my key out of the box, and he threw it at me, and it hit me right in the mouth, split my lip. I was about to put the slug on him, and I said to myself, "No. I better not." I started walking away. I stopped, faced him and I said, "Howard, one of these days I'm going to knock you right on your ass." And I started walking again. Howard shouted, "How 'bout now?" and when he said that I went after him, and I knocked him from one end of the corridor to the other. Allison had to restrain me to make me stop. There is only so much a man can take. I was standing over him thinking, "How in hell did I get in this fight? The guy throws a key at me, splits my lip. What would anybody do? Walk away? Should I have said, 'Excuse me, sir, but you struck my lip?' " Meanwhile Howard started screaming at me, "I'm going to get you fired if it's the last thing I do. You're going to go, ya hear me?" Calvin fined me two hundred dollars for fighting with Howard, because Howard threatened to quit if he didn't at least fine me.

The two coaches who were undermining Mele were pitching coach Johnny Sain and bullpen coach Hal Naragon. It looked to me all that year that behind Sam's back Sain was pushing Naragon to be manager. These two would hardly speak to me at all, and if I so much as went out to watch the starting pitcher warm up, it would make them mad. John and I had played together on the Yankees, but we disagreed as to the role of the pitching coach. To John, the pitchers' doing good came first, and winning was second. Also John treated the pitchers as though they were special players. A pitcher would go out and do a bad job and lose, and Sain would come up to him after the game and say, "Don't worry about it. You did a good job." To my mind that isn't right. If a guy does a bad job, he does a bad job. And Naragon, who Sam hired himself, would be following Sain around like a little puppy dog, and the two of them were trying to get close to Sam while at the same time they were undermining him. I kept telling Sam, "Before it's over, you're going to find out who your real friends are."

Despite all this we did win the pennant, and against the Dodgers we won the first two games of the World Series. We flew out to Los Angeles, and our coaching staff held a meeting to discuss the pitching rotation for the rest of the Series, and apparently Sain and Naragon didn't want me to come, because I wasn't invited. It was my opinion that Jim Merritt should have started the third game. He threw the hardest of all our pitchers, and he had a good move to first, and he could have kept Maury Wills and the other Dodger runners from running wild on the base paths. Instead they decided to go with Camilo Pascual, who had a big, high kick in his leg. Camilo went out and got beat, and we ended up losing the Series in seven games. They cost us the World Series, which we really should have won. The next year, 1966, it got even worse. Sain and Naragon were undermining Sam more than ever before, and there was a lot of talk about Sam getting fired, but by the end of the season Sam apparently finally got wind of what was going on because at the end of the year he fired them both.

On the last day of the season we beat Baltimore, assuring us of a second-place finish, and after the game I went up to Sam and hugged him, and he said, "What are you so happy about? We didn't win the pennant." I said, "We finished second, Sam, and now they can't fire you." It saved his job. However, the next year we started off playing .500 ball, and I came into the clubhouse, and Sam was sitting at his desk, and I greeted him. He said, "Haven't you heard?" I said, "No, what?" He said, "I've been fired." I couldn't believe it. We had a team I thought was going to win the pennant, and they fired him. I cried, because I really liked Sam. He was such a good man to work for, and he was such a fine person.

That spring training I had told him I had found us a second baseman. Sam asked me his name. I told him it was Rod Carew. He said, "You really think he'll make it?" I said, "I guarantee it." Sam said, "That'll be great if he can make it at second." I said, "He's it." So there was a meeting, and we were discussing Carew, and one of the scouts, Del Wilber, said, "He's a troublemaker," and another guy said, "I managed him for a year and didn't like him." After the meeting I told Sam, "Don't pay any attention to those guys, Sam. I'm telling you right now that the kid will make it, and make it right now." So Sam listened to me and went along with me, and that year Rod hit almost .300, and he almost led us to a pennant. We lost to the Red Sox that year by one game. We should have won it all, but at the end of the season we lost two straight games to Boston we never should have lost. In the final game Jim Kaat was beating the Red Sox easy, and in the fifth or sixth inning he hurt his arm, came out, and we ended up losing the game. We should have won. We were right in it until the last game.

When Sam was fired, he was replaced by Cal Ermer, a real knowledgeable baseball man who always did a good job managing in the Twins farm system. He was very astute, very loyal, and a real good guy. I was third-base coach for Cal, and he gave me the leeway to run things out there the way I wanted. I had special signs for guys to steal third base, special signs for them to steal home, and I had a sign for a double steal. I taught Rod Carew how to steal home, and he stole home nine times in ten tries, and he was safe the tenth time, but the ump blew the call.

I started the 1968 season as third-base coach, but early in the year Sherry Robertson asked me whether I'd go to Denver to manage the Twins' Triple-A farm club. When he asked me to go, my initial reaction was that Howard Fox, or someone else in the Twins organization, was trying to exile me off, hoping I'd never come back. I went to talk to Calvin Griffith about my going to Denver. I asked him, "What kind of team do you have in Denver?" He said, "Not too good." I said, "Got any pitching?" He said, "No." "Any hitting?" "No." "Any fielding?" He said, "No." I said, "Well why do you want me to go down there?" He said, "Jim Burris, the Denver general manager, asked for you, but if you don't want to go, you don't have to." I asked Calvin, whom I trusted, if it would help him if I went. He said, "I think it would help the attendance. It would help our organization, and I think the players would benefit, too." Then he said, "I'll tell you what. If you go down there, you can always have your old job back here. You don't have to worry about that." But that's exactly what I was worrying about. I consulted with everyone I thought was in my corner as to whether I should go. I asked Cal Ermer how he could afford to lose me as third-base coach. His reply was, "Cal Griffith thinks you should go down and manage." I asked Sherry Robertson, and he recommended I go. I still didn't think I should go, because deep in my heart I felt somebody was trying to get rid of me and this was the easiest way for him or them to do it. I told Sherry, "I don't think I'm going." He said, "You're crazy if you don't."

I went home that evening, and I couldn't remember when I was as disturbed as I was that night. I told Gretchen, "They're trying to move me out of here, and I'm not going. I don't know who's behind the movement, but there *is* a movement to get me out of here." Gretchen said, "Billy, why don't you trust Calvin? Go to Denver and show them you can manage. You're frustrated right now anyway. You'll be better off going down there and managing." I said, "I'm not going."

That night I slept maybe one hour at the most. I was so afraid they were pushing me because of the incident with Howard Fox and the room key that I threw up in the middle of the night. In the morning, I got out of bed and before I left for the ball park, I said to Gretchen, "I'm going to take the job." She said, "You are?" She was kind of shocked. I said, "Yeah. Don't ask me how I made up my mind, because I really don't know, but it dawned on me that I should go. If they don't want me here, why should I stick around?" And when I went to the ball park, I surprised Calvin when I told him I'd take the Denver job.

When I arrived in Denver, the first day I was there the players started telling me how general manager Jim Burris liked to come in the clubhouse and jump on the manager and interfere and how he would make the manager play tape recordings of his speeches. Later that afternoon I went to see him in his office. The ball park had just been remodeled, and he had a beautiful, large office overlooking the field, and he said to me, "This is my domain. This is where I watch and do all the second-guessing." He was very honest about it. I said, "It's beautiful. Where is my office?" He pointed down the right-field line to a door leading to an office no bigger than a postage stamp. I barely had enough room to dress in there. I said, "Seeing that we're going to work together, can I tell you something?" He said, "Sure." I said, "I don't want you coming into my clubhouse. You come to my office only when you're invited, and I'll come to your office only when I'm invited." He said, "Is that the way you want it?" I said, "That's the way it's going to be." And Jim was super. He never once interfered, and he and I would take rides together out into the country and talk about the West or talk about baseball, and of all the men I've worked with, only three guys, Jim, Jim Campbell of Detroit, and Gabe Paul had the great knowledge about baseball that made talking to them enjoyable.

The other fellow who helped me at Denver was Art Fowler. Art was a combination pitcher and coach, and the night I arrived I sat at the bar with Art and we went over the team, and I found out that even though the team had a 7 and 22 record, we basically had a good ball club. Pat Kelly, Bob Oliver, Ron Theobald, and Graig Nettles all made it to the majors later on. During the first week I didn't hardly say a word. I just observed and watched and waited, and I saw what was going on, who could play, who couldn't, who wanted to play, who didn't, and then I began putting in my methods and ways. It was my first opportunity to manage, but I had played under Charley Dressen at Oakland and under Casey Stengel, and I had seen how they handled their players, and I had played under other managers who did things I didn't like, and I learned from them things not to do, like not to yell at the players, not to show up your players in the papers, not to have a doghouse.

I taught them how to be aggressive, and I got them to do the things I thought it took to win. I taught them to knock down the fielder making the double play, taught everyone how to bunt, how to suicide-squeeze, how to steal bases. I had one guy who stole home twice in a game, a kid by the name of Mooring. I think we stole home 18 times that year. Even Nettles stole home once. I showed them the timing it takes to steal home, the lead, the pitcher's movements, to study how much time it takes for the pitcher to deliver the ball home. I showed them how to watch the third baseman in order to get a big enough lead, how when the pitcher starts to move his hands, you break for the plate, and how the pitcher, being a creature of habit, will go right through his windup so that by the time the ball reaches home, you're already there. And it doesn't matter how slow a runner you are, anyone can steal home.

We had guys who were just floundering, and I took steps to motivate them. One day the ball was hit to the left of our second baseman, and he broke to his right. Another ball was popped up in the infield, and he broke back to the outfield. I called time, walked out to second, put my arms around him, and asked him, "What's the matter, pal? You having matrimonial problems or something?" He said, "How did you know?" I said, "Your mind is not on the game." He said, "You're right, Big Guy." He called me Big Guy. I said, "You walk off the field with me. I don't want you out here with this mental problem," and I told him I wasn't mad at him. I told him to go home, relax for the night, and come back the next day. "If you're still feeling bad tomorrow," I told him, "stay home." He said, "Thanks, Big Guy," and the next day he came out and was fine.

I caught one pitcher coming to the ball park with liquor on his breath, and I made him go home. He was half snockered. I made him go home right from the ball park with his uniform on. I wouldn't let him change. When he came to the park the next day he figured I was going to suspend him, which I could have done, but when he got there I told him I was letting it go this time, but if I caught him coming to the park drunk again, he would be suspended without pay. He had been having trouble pitching, but after that he turned around and started winning for me, had a great year.

Our first baseman was struggling at the plate, and I forced him to be a more aggressive hitter. I pushed him, challenged him, and he responded and became a good hitter, and I did that with everybody. Most ballplayers aren't pushed to the extent of their ability. It takes a manager to do that. Whether they realize it or not. And some of them won't realize it until after they've quit the game. Then they'll look back and see what the manager made them do, because while they're playing, too often all they're thinking about is their own ego. I had one outfielder who was just kidding himself. An easy fly ball was hit his way, and he should have caught it with no trouble, but he didn't, and when he got back to the bench he started alibiing, making excuses like "the wind took the ball" or "the sun was in my eyes," something like that, and I pulled him right out of the game. He sat down on the bench and bawled.

After the game I took him alone and told him, "When you make a mistake, admit it. Say, 'It was my fault.' Don't alibi. Don't lie about it. If you make a mistake and are honest about it, I'll be the first one to back you. If you lie to yourself, you're not going to play." And I put him back in there the next day.

He was just a hardheaded kid who insisted on doing things his way. And it wasn't going to be that way so long as I was manager.

In another game we had bases loaded, and the same kid was up, and they brought in a left-hander, and he was having trouble hitting them. I wanted a suicide squeeze, so I walked from third base, from where I was coaching, all the way to home and I said, "Now lookit, Joe, they're bringing in a lefty. On the first pitch we'll try a suicide, and if it doesn't work, hit away." He said, "Skip, you got it." I went back to third base, and I told the runner, "There's no sense me giving you signs, the suicide is on the first pitch."

The first pitch came in, and the kid hit it nine miles for a home run. As he ran around the bases, I yelled at him, "What about the suicide?" He hollered back, "I forgot, Skip, I forgot." I said, "Sure you did." The kid never did make it to the majors.

One day I benched five of my most intelligent men, all college graduates, and Nettles was one of them. He asked me,

"What are we sitting here for?" I said, "You guys are the most brilliant guys on the club. A couple of you even have masters degrees. But you're playing so stupid out there, and I want you smart and brilliant guys sitting next to this dummy so you can learn something about baseball." I was talking to the whole gang, and I was agitating them, and Nettles knew what I was doing, and he finally turned to me and said, "Hey, Skip, I'd rather get out in the field and take a beating than have to sit here and listen to you anymore. Would you let me go out there?" And I did. But I was getting a point across. I wanted them to think baseball more, wanted them to live baseball, wanted them to be smarter and more aggressive. When you're on the field, you're at work. When you're off the field, it's a different story. I told them that off the field I didn't care what they did just so long as they behaved. I said, "I don't care what you do, and I mean that." Casey Stengel felt the same way. He'd say, "All I ask is that you bust your heiny on that field."

From the point I began managing, we won 58 games and lost 28, and though we finished fourth because of the bad start, if we had had one more week, we would have won the pennant. We should have done even better, but we had a couple of bad breaks and lost a few games in a row. Before the game that ended our losing streak I wrote the name of each of our starting players on a piece of paper and put the names in a hat, and I had the players pick the batting order for me. Our number-four hitter was batting eighth, and our ninth hitter was batting fourth, and this game proved to me that when players complain that they can't hit in this spot or can't hit in that spot, it's a bunch of nonsense. The problem is that sometimes players are so set in their ways, they have trouble mentally when they have to adjust to something new. But I learned that if they want to do it, they can. In this particular game it didn't make any difference where the guys batted, everybody hit like crazy, and we started winning steadily again.

Our two workhorses were Jerry Crider and Danny Morris. They and Art did most of the pitching, and all during the year Jerry and Dan had been trying to give me a hotfoot. They were bragging about how they were going to do this, and Art told them, "You ain't going to pull nothing on the skipper. He's gonna catch you before you do it." Well, it was the last game of the season, and I was sitting on the bench, and I looked down for a second, and under the bench was a rolled-up mat, and from out of one end of the mat I saw a hand slip out, and this hand was fixing a match to my spike. I didn't say anything, I just watched, and I saw the hand scratch the match to the floor and light it, and just as the hand was bringing the match toward my shoe, I started kicking that mat with both feet. Crider, who was inside, started screaming and yelling, and everyone on the bench, who was watching to see if he could do it, was laughing like crazy. Later Art said, "I told you."

At the end of the year Charlie Metro, who was in charge of player personnel for the Kansas City A's, came to talk to me about manging the A's. He said, "I like the way you manage. Your way is good. Just keep doing it that way." And I appreciated what he did, and it stuck with me. A week later Charlie called me again to say he was going to take the manager's job himself. However, not too long afterwards I got a call from Calvin Griffith. He asked me if I was interested in managing the Twins.

I took the job, and hired Art Fowler to be my pitching coach, and won the division, and got fired all in one year. When I opened training camp in Orlando, I saw I had a team that liked to run and do the things I liked to do, and that we had exceptionally good base runners in Tony Oliva, Cesar Tovar, Teddy Uhlander, and Rod Carew. Rich Reese, our first baseman, wasn't fast, but he was a good hitter. Reese wanted to do well all the time. He took extra batting practice and pushed himself, and he was a very big part of our team. Carew, of course, was just fantastic at second and Harmon Killebrew did a heck of a job for me. Usually he played first and the outfield, but I felt that if he played third, it would give us another bat in the lineup, and Harmon, who was willing to do anything for the team, agreed to give it a try. He ended up winning the Most Valuable Player of the league. Leo Cardenas played short, and he hit great and did everything a manager could want in the field. He was the kind of guy who if you left him alone, he'd do his job.

Tony Oliva, who hit over .300, was an exceptionally good base runner for such a big guy, and maybe he wasn't the best outfielder in the world, but he had a good arm, and he loved to play, and he did the job for me. Tovar was my little leader. He was the guy who got everyone going. When I wanted him to push Leo a little bit or if Rod was getting down and I needed someone to give him a boost, I'd get Cesar to do it. Teddy Uhlander was a Texan who didn't have all the ability in the world, but he was very aggressive and hustled all the time. He gave his all all the time.

Our catcher, Johnny Roseboro, was at the twilight of his career, but he was still better than average. He was good natured, but the one problem I had with him was he thought our pitching staff was the same staff he had with the Dodgers. He liked to challenge the hitters too much, and we didn't have the overwhelming arms of pitchers like Koufax and Drysdale, and I had to keep talking to him to change his thinking.

Graig Nettles was with us that year, and though he didn't play much because Killebrew had a great year, it was definitely in my plans to switch Harmon back to first the next year and play Graig at third. I would have traded Reese, because I felt Graig was eventually going to be the better hitter. That year Alvin Dark of Cleveland tried to make a trade with us for Nettles, and I told Calvin Griffith that under no circumstances should he ever get rid of Graig. No sooner was I gone at the end of '69 than he traded Graig, which looking back was a big mistake for the Twins.

I also had Bob Allison play left field for me. I played Bob mostly against left-handed pitchers, and though he didn't get up a hell of a lot, he had an important role as my liaison man. He was my leader behind the leader on the bench, a beautiful buffer for me. I'd say to him, "Bob, tell so-and-so about such-and-such when you get a chance," and coming from Bob they wouldn't resent it nearly as much as if it came from me. If he wasn't in business now, he'd have made somebody an excellent coach. My backup catcher was George Mitterwald, just a rookie. George asked Calvin if he could get married during the season, and Calvin forbade him from doing so, which was ridiculous. If two people want to get married, let them get married.

George married secretly, and I was there and very happy to be there, and George and his family come and see me whenever they can, and this year I hired George to be one of my coaches at Oakland.

If our team had a weak spot, I felt, it was the pitching staff. The Twins had finished seventh in 1968, and Dean Chance (16-16), Jim Merritt (12-16), Jim Kaat (14-12), and Dave Boswell (10-13) didn't have years that indicated we had a shot at the pennant.

Our two most consistent pitchers in '69 were Jim Perry and Boswell. Perry was the kind of guy who had a tendency to pitch around the good hitters, and he'd be fidgety and nervous out on the mound, and I would have to go out and push him and make him mad, to force him to challenge the hitters, 'cause when I got him mad, he'd throw that ball a little harder instead of just aiming it and trying to pitch on the corners. Boswell, on the other hand, was overaggressive, and I'd have to go out to the mound to slow him down. He wanted to blow the ball past everybody, which wasn't always a good idea, and other times he'd try to get too cute with his curve. Jim Kaat was another good competitor. His arm wasn't as strong as it once had been, and that year he had a tendency to throw too many breaking pitches, which would screw up our defense in the infield, but he was such a good competitor and he fielded his position so well that he was a plus for us. In the bullpen we had Ron Perranoski, who had ice water in his veins, and Bob Miller was my most consistent pitcher toward the end of the year during our stretch drive.

That, basically, was our ball club. We were a running club, a very aggressive club. We just took it to the other clubs, and Boswell and Perry each won 20 games, and we won the pennant.

What made the season particularly enjoyable for me was that Calvin Griffith, who's an old baseball man, never tried to interefere with what I was doing. He was the owner and the general manager, and if I wanted a player, Calvin would listen, and he had the good sense to let his manager do his job.

The problems I had on the Twins were with everyone else. For instance, one day I went up to Calvin and said, "Lookit, we have this kid pitcher Charley Walters who we're sending to the minors. I think he just needs one pitch to be a winner, and we ought to send him to Denver, and he'll be real close, and we can bring him back quickly. Can I tell the kid we're sending him to Denver, Cal?" Cal said, "Sounds good to me, Billy. Okay." Well, no sooner had I left Cal than George Brophy, the assistant farm director, went to Calvin and told him he was sending Walters to some dinky town in Georgia. I had already told the kid he was going to Denver, and they send him to Georgia, and how does that make me look? So I went to Brophy, and we got into a shouting match. The farm director, Sherry Robertson, was away scouting, and when he came back he took our argument as a personal affront against him, which it wasn't.

And then there was Howard Fox. Some people say Calvin must have killed somebody, and Fox hid the skeleton as a form of blackmail. I could always sit and talk with Calvin, but as soon as I'd leave somebody else would talk to him and that would cause a problem.

One night Leo Cardenas and Cesar Tovar were rooming together, and it was two in the morning and I get a phone call from Cesar that I better get up there or he and Cardenas were going to get into it. One of them had slept in the other's bed, or something like that, and they had started arguing, and I called the desk and arranged another room for Tovar because he refused to stay with Leo.

The next day Fox, the traveling secretary, got madder'n hell that I had gotten another room for Cesar. Sure it was Howard's job, but if I hadn't done it, I would have had a fight on my hands, so I felt I was doing the right thing. But it upset Howard terribly.

The players would constantly tell me that Howard was going up to them and saying, "Why do you listen to that guy? How can you listen to him? What does he know?" Here I was trying to manage a club, and my star players were telling me that a team official was maligning me behind my back! Finally I called Calvin. I said, "Do me a favor. I'm tired of listening to his guff. I know he doesn't like me, and that's his prerogative, but by his telling the players not to play for the manager, is he looking out for your best interests? Calvin, will you please get him off my back?"

Another incident that didn't set well with Fox was my fight with pitcher Dave Boswell. Davey was a funny kid. I don't know why, but Davey didn't think he was as good a pitcher as I thought he should be. I was very close to the kid, like a father to him, and I used to take him frog hunting or fishing or whatever it was I was doing. Whenever I'd see he was headed for trouble or doing something he shouldn't, I'd talk to him about it, and I'd have Allison help me with him, talk to him. Some nights he'd stay out after hours, and I'd call him into my office and instead of fining him I'd give him an ear beating, and he'd tell me, "Okay, I won't do it again," and then I'd catch him again, and we'd start all over again. But Bozzy could pitch, and he was a great competitor, so that other stuff didn't bother me that much. Part of his problem was that he was pitching in a lot of pain. He had bone chips, and his elbow just kept getting bigger and bigger as the season went on, and sometimes the pain got so bad that he was taking pills for it. I don't like to see any player take pills. I would check the lockers to make sure they didn't do it, but one way or another they'll get them if they want them bad enough, and how I'll never know, so it's really a waste of time to try and stop them. So Davey was taking these pain pills, and sometimes he'd drink, too, and the combination was very bad, and that was what he had in him the day of the fight.

We were playing the Tigers in Detroit, and I was sitting at a local bar after the game with Bob Allison when Art Fowler came strolling in. I said, "Art, how did the running go today?" I had brought Art with me from Denver to be one of my pitching coaches (Early Wynn was the other). Art said, "Boswell wouldn't run. He defied me." To me, that's a no-no. I require my starting pitchers to run twenty laps every day. I said, "Okay, Art, you go on back to the hotel and I'll handle Boswell tomorrow at the ball park," because I never reprimand my players in public. I like to talk to them head to head in private. Boswell had been sitting on the other side of the room, and when he saw Art leave, he came over and said, "Art Fowler told you about my not running, didn't he?" I said,

"That's his job. He's a good pitching coach. It's his job." He said, "Well, I'm going back to the hotel to kick his butt." I said, "Bozzy, you're not going to do anything like that. Number one, Art only has one eye, and number two, you're not going to kick his butt." He said, "Yes, I am," and he started out the door.

Allison, who was listening to this, ran out to stop him. Allison told me later that he yelled for Boswell to come back and talk, but Boswell repeated what he told me, that he was going to the hotel to hit Art. Allison, who stood about six foot three and weighed two hundred pounds, said to Dave, "If you're going to hit somebody, why don't you hit me?" Bob said he was standing with his hands in his pockets, and Boswell sucker-punched him, hit him so hard that Allison's hands came out of his pockets, ripping them wide open. Allison fell to the ground out cold, and someone came running into the bar screaming that Boswell was kicking Allison in the face, so I ran out and when Boswell saw me he ripped open his shirt, with the buttons flying every which way like you see in the movies. He shouted, "And you, too, Skipper," and he hit me three times to the head, three good shots, and he really had me groggy. He was wearing a great big chain around his neck, and I had learned as a kid fighting in the streets that when you're fighting a bigger guy, it's best to get close in rather than stand away, so I grabbed hold of the chain, got in real close, and I started punching him in the stomach as hard and as fast as I could. I just kept pounding him in the stomach with my right hand, must have hit him forty times until I heard him grunt, and I thought I had him. Right then I backed off, and I punched him three or four times to the face, and he bounced off the wall, and when he hit the ground he was out. I had been fighting for survival, I didn't want to hurt him, but when you're fighting a bigger man the most important thing is to make sure he doesn't hurt you. When he fell to the ground I was about to pull him up and let him have it again, when Jimmy Butsikaris, the owner of the bar we were in, grabbed hold of me and said, "Billy, he's out."

I looked at Boswell, and I felt sick. His face was bleeding badly, and I felt terrible because I really liked the kid, he was like a son to me, and here this happened. I was saying to myself, "How in the world did this happen? Nobody's going to believe it. How the hell do I get myself in these situations?"

I had Bozzy taken to the hospital, and when he came back to the hotel, he went back to his room, and I went to see him. I felt real bad about it, and he did, too. I told him, "Bozzy, don't let the other players see your face the way it is. Get out of here early in the morning, go back home to Baltimore, we'll be there in a few days, and by that time the swelling will have gone down." So he went home, and I thought I had managed to keep the story out of the papers, but when his father saw him, he called the papers, and so it got out.

When I got back to Minnesota, Calvin Griffith and Howard Fox were waiting. They said they had heard that three guys held Boswell while I beat him up. I mean, they even had Boswell believing that for a while! Normally if a player hit the manager, he'd be suspended for life. In this case, because I won the fight, they were talking about suspending me!

Calvin said, "Why did you hit him so many times?"

I said, "I don't know if you've ever been hit by a guy who's six three, two hundred pounds, but when it looks like he's going to hurt you real bad, you're frightened for your life, and all I was doing was keeping him from hitting me again." I told him, "I had no intentions of hurting him as bad as I did. I just kept punching until he quit punching me."

Fox wanted to fine and suspend me. I told him, "Maybe you would have preferred if I had lost the fight? Would that have made you happy?" It probably would have.

Later in the year I got into it with Calvin when I wouldn't let then-Vice President Hubert Humphrey into my clubhouse after a tough loss. The game had ended, and we had lost when we shouldn't have, and I got a call that Mr. Humphrey was going to come in the clubhouse and shake all the players' hands. I said, "No, he isn't. If Mr. Humphrey wishes, he can come into my office, and if there are any players he wants to talk to, I'll bring the players in to see him." Mr. Humphrey understood completely. I told him, "Mr. Vice President, I'm trying to teach these guys that losing is a hard thing to take, and I just don't want you to go around shaking hands and having them smile, because they're taking the loss hard, and that's the way it should be." He told me he understood completely. Calvin, though, got mad.

"How can you keep the Vice President of the United States out of the clubhouse?" he said. I said, "Calvin, when we lose a ball game, nobody comes in there. I'm trying to teach them that there's a difference between winning and losing. Mr. Humphrey understood." But apparently Calvin didn't.

We won the division by eight games, and against Baltimore in the play-offs we lost the first game in eleven innings and the second one in thirteen, and they beat the heck out of us in the third game in Minnesota. I was duck hunting when over the radio I heard that I had been fired. Howard Fox read the press release, and when he read it he sounded real happy about it. The Twins public relations man, Tom Mead, tried to talk Howard out of announcing my firing that way, but Fox wouldn't listen to him. He had been feeding Calvin untruths about me, and apparently he had never forgiven me for hitting him when he threw the room key at me, and when he got his chance to help get me fired, he took full advantage. I never disliked Howard. After the incident with the room key, it was over as far as I was concerned, but apparently in Howard's mind it wasn't, and he carried it with him all those years. And the shame of it was that by pushing Calvin to fire me, he cost Calvin perhaps five million dollars. We had a sound, aggressive ball club, and I was convinced we could have won the pennant five years in a row. We needed maybe a couple more pitchers, maybe another outfielder, but not much else. The kids we had were so good, and they were molded right, and we would have won for five more years.

I loved it in Minnesota. The people there were just fantastic to me. They were great supporters, great fans, and they were really enthusiastic because we had a winner. I lived in the community, knew the area well; Calvin had no idea how many banquets and luncheons I went to for free during the year, plus I was working in sales promotions for Grain Belt Brewery, and in every bar I went I'd be talking up the Twins, cultivating new fans. And Calvin just didn't realize what was going to happen until he fired me.

I must say this about Calvin: Even though he fired me as manager, he had been the one who hired me as a major league scout when I got released as a player, and it was Calvin who helped me as a coach, and it was Calvin who gave me my opportunity to manage in the majors, so even though these other things happened, I have nothing but praise for the man because he was so good to me. I know he's not too popular in Minnesota right now, but that's because he listens to the wrong people. If he had listened to the right ones, things would have been so much different. He'd have had a few more pennants and been a lot richer.

Calvin hired Bill Rigney to replace me. Rigney had managed in Minneapolis when it was a minor league city, and Calvin figured he'd be popular. In 1970 the team won the pennant, and Rigney said, "That was Billy Martin's team that won. Next year it's going to be my team. I'm going to do it my way."

That year the Twins finished fifth, and they haven't won since.

I was out of baseball in 1970. Vic Armstrong, president of the Valjohn Corporation, hired me to be his assistant, and he was teaching me the radio business. I was the coordinator for a sports show, and my job was to go around to the different stations he owned around the country and talk with their officials. I was reading a lot of books about the radio business, and Vic was going to send me to Dartmouth for a month to take a course, but I never went because I got a call from my close friend Bob Short that Charley Finley of Oakland wanted to hire me as manager. I told Short I had reservations about working for Finley, but Short advised that I fly out to Chicago to talk with him. I told Vic Armstrong about my reservations, and he too suggested I at least talk with Finley. I told Vic that I wouldn't make any decisions until I came back and talked with him.

I went to Chicago, and Finley and I must have talked for five hours in his office. It was a Sunday, and he said, "Monday's a day off. Will you take over the team Tuesday in Washington?"

I told Finley, "I'll take the job under one condition." John McNamara, who was a friend of mine, then was the manager. "If you keep McNamara as my third-base coach, I'll do it." We agreed to contract terms and I really thought we had a deal.

The next morning I was going to call Vic and tell him about it when I got a call from Finley. "I've been talking to my wife," he said, "and she says I've been firing so many people lately that maybe it would be better if you took over a little later in the season. Would that be okay, Billy?"

He said, "During the season you can go to the various cities and watch the team play, and I'll send you the statistics, and you can study them, and then you'll take over." I said, "Well, okay, send me the statistics." He said, "You can always get ahold of me, just call my private secretary. She knows where I'm at all the time. You'll have no trouble getting me." I said okay.

So on Tuesday the Oakland A's won, and on Wednesday the Oakland A's won, and on Friday they won. They won about five in a row. I called the secretary to get ahold of Finley, and I couldn't reach him. I got no answer. In the meantime I got a call from Jim Campbell of Detroit. Could I fly there and talk to him about managing in 1971? I flew to Detroit, and we agreed to a two-year contract with a nice raise. I wrote Finley a letter. I said, "If you can't answer my phone calls, I can't work for you."

Before I opened Detroit's spring training camp in 1971 I wrote letters to the players and made it a point to visit most of them to tell them what my first year with them was going to be like. Jim Campbell had told me that there were cliques on the club and that I had to be tough on them. He told me to do what I thought I had to do to turn the club around and he'd back me. The team had finished fourth in '71, and being a team of older veterans they were set in their ways. They had won a pennant in 1968, and they were still thinking they were World Champions, and they refused to admit to themselves that '68 had come and gone. There was no speed on the club, and they didn't want to bunt or hit-and-run. All they wanted to do was go up there and swing the bat, the way they had played under Mayo Smith when he managed them to the pennant in '68.

We had Norm Cash at first, Dick McAuliffe at second, Eddie Brinkman at shortstop, Aurileo Rodriguez at third, with Al Kaline, Mickey Stanley, and Willie Horton in the outfield. Bill Freehan was my catcher. Campbell had stolen Brinkman and Rodriguez from the Washington Senators, and they were just fantastic for me, but the rest of them had been in Detroit awhile, and I had to push these guys very hard, because they were bickering or complaining or alibiing like a bunch of babies.

In addition I had Jim Northrup, who thought he was the most valuable player in the league. Northrup thought he could do it all. He was a left-handed hitter with a short right-field fence, and on a 2 and 0 count, 3 and 1, all the time he would hit to left field instead of driving the ball over the the roof in right. And he had the power to hit it over the roof. I'd scream and yell at Northrup, and he just hated my guts, but I didn't care because I wanted him to do what was right, and he was pigheaded and wouldn't. Northrup and Freehan hung out a lot together, and I also used to get Freehan mad, but he was such a good, hard battler that he'd take it and run through a wall for me if he had to. I had problems with Willie Horton. He would show up when he felt like it, and one time he didn't run a ball out, and I pulled him right out of the ball game. Benched him in the middle of the game the same way I did it to Reggie Jackson when he was loafing in the field. I had made a rule that if anyone didn't hustle, I was going to yank him, and that's just what I did. But Willie was man enough to accept it. He went up the runway madder'n heck at me, and he tore up every light in the runway. But after that I didn't have any more trouble from him.

Our pitching staff wasn't the best, but Mickey Lolich and Joe Coleman each won 20 games, and Fred Scherman did a nice job for me. Lolich had never won 20 games before in his life, but again I hired Art Fowler, and Mickey loved Art, and he ended up winning 25 games to lead the league. Coleman was a super kid. He hated my guts, just hated everything about me, because I used to get him so mad. He wanted to throw his horseshit forkball, and I'd make him throw his fastball. I'd go out to the mound deliberately to make him mad at me. One day he and I almost got into a fight coming off the mound in Texas. Texas had just gotten three or four hits and a couple runs off him, and it was the last game before the All Star break, and he became furious when I came to take him out. He just refused to leave the mound. "What am I doing wrong?" he was hollering at me while we stood out there. Since we were getting three days off, I had the luxury of being able to use all my pitchers if I wanted to, to win the game. Also, he wasn't pitching so hot. Besides, I was the manager, and it was my prerogative to take him out whenever I felt like it. Boy, was he hot.

We had a pitcher named Les Cain who kept telling me his arm was all right, when we all knew he had a bad arm, and he never did pitch his best for me. Campbell kept telling me how good he was going to be, but I never did see it. Joe Niekro was on the staff, and at the time he didn't have his knuckleball. He only had two pitches, and the hitters would pick them up and just rack him good. Dean Chance was in the twilight of his career. Fred Scherman was great. He had a fantastic arm, won 11 games that year, and was one of those happy-go-lucky guys you love to have on a ball club. Our other starter was Mike Kilkenny, who should have been a 20-game winner every year he pitched, but he never challenged the hitters like he should. He went out and pitched to spots, and though he should have been great was just mediocre.

Our reliever, Tommy Timmerman, was just the opposite. He didn't have that good of an arm, didn't have much velocity, but he had the guts of a lion who'd give you everything. He was all competitor, always gave me a hundred percent.

When Kilkenny and Timmerman pitched, I was very rough on them, and when that happened some of the regulars would get mad at me because they felt I was being too rough. Northrup was always mad at me, and so was Freehan. But if these guys hadn't been so stubborn, hadn't been so let's-wait-for-things-to-happen in their attitude, I wouldn't have had to be so hard on them. I don't get players mad at me because I enjoy it. I do it because I think it will help the team.

We came in second that year, losing to Baltimore, which had

four 20-game winners. Over the winter I kept telling Campbell that we had to get rid of some of the veterans and some of the guys I didn't feel were going to help us win a pennant. I was pushing Campbell to trade Cain and Niekro and Kilkenny, and McAuliffe had had a bad year and I felt we should trade him. Also, I felt we could get a top starter if we could trade Northrup. But Campbell for many years had been the farm director for the Tigers, and these were all the kids who had won the pennant for the team in '68, and though some of them might have been going downhill, he wouldn't listen to me because they were his babies, and he didn't feel he could get rid of them.

By the second year the guys knew my system a little better, and they began bunting, using the hit-and-run, and suicide-squeezing, and we beat Boston out for the division by a half game. We had a slow ball club, but everyone had a good year at the same time, and they played together. Everyone contributed. Cash was really the only guy who had any power, and he ended up leading the team with 61 RBI's. Freehan was our leading batter with a .262 average, and Al Kaline had a fantastic year. He was tremendous for me, did everything I asked of him, and was just a super individual.

I had played with Al in 1958, and when I came to that club I didn't like him. I even had my locker moved away from his. Nobody on that '58 team seemed to give a damn whether the team won or lost, and that made me mad. Our manager was Bill Norman, who died only a few years afterward, and I felt everyone was being unfair to him with their lackadaisical attitude. Winning just wasn't important to them, and when I saw this I got mad and demanded I have a locker off by myself. I didn't even want to be associated with them.

However, when I took over this ball club, I realized that Al Kaline wasn't one of those guys I had seen on that '58 club. He was a truly great ball player, and it was a pleasure to manage him.

Primarily we won with pitching and great defense. Brinkman didn't hit much that year but he made plays at short you wouldn't have believed. He ate everything up. Between him and Rodriguez, nobody could get anything through the left side of the infield, and on the right side McAuliffe turned around and had an excellent year. Tony Taylor filled in wherever I needed him, and though he was in the twilight of his career, he was amazing. He knows his baseball, he's keen, and he could be a coach for me anytime, anywhere. Lolich won 22, Coleman 19, and after we got Woody Fryman from Philadelphia, he was 10 and 3 with a 2.00 earned run average, and he really did a job for us. Even the games he didn't win he was in the ball game. He was a country boy, a tobacco grower, and his arm hurt him badly, but he'd say, "Just give me the ball, and I'll do the job for you," and he did just that.

I didn't have much trouble that year, except with Northrup, who was acting up, making comments against me all the time. I didn't pay much attention to it, because I always said I'd play my worst enemy, so I just kept playing him even though I knew he hated my guts. During spring training he told me that he'd lead the league in homers if I played him regularly. In '72 he played almost every day. At the end of the year he had exactly eight home runs.

What was also funny that year was that some of the pitchers were very jealous of Mickey Lolich. Every once in a while Mickey would call and say he had to take his wife someplace and that he'd be a little late, and I'd tell Art, and if he walked in five minutes late Coleman and Kilkenny acted like little babies. Lolich was our stopper, but even so, if any of the others would have asked, we would have allowed them to do the same thing. But Coleman and Kilkenny felt we were giving Lolich special treatment, and they'd get upset.

The play-offs against Oakland went five games, and we got beat by a call by an umpire in the final game. We also should have won the first game, and that would have won it for us, but with the score tied and men on first and third with one out, I gave Northrup the sign for the suicide-squeeze, but he swung and hit into a double play and cost us the game. He said he didn't see the sign, and to this day I don't know whether he did or didn't. Blue Moon Odom shut us out in the second game on a three-hitter, but we got a big break when Campy Campaneris got mad at our pitcher Lerrin Legrow and fired his bat at him. I don't know why Legrow didn't go after him, but I came racing out of the dugout, ran across the field, and I tried to get Campaneris. He was suspended for the rest of the play-offs, and it almost won us the pennant.

Coleman shut out Holtzman, striking out fourteen to win the third game, and though we were behind 3 to 1 in the bottom of the tenth in the fourth game, we rallied for three runs, the winning run hit by Northrup, to win 4 to 3.

The final game we lost 2 to 1, but it never should have ended that way. It was 1 to 1 in the fourth, and with George Hendricks on first and two outs, Reggie Jackson hit a ground ball. The infielder threw it over to first, and Jackson was out by three feet, but the umpire ruled that Cash had pulled his foot off the base too soon, and Jackson was safe. I hadn't seen that play called in twenty years in the major leagues. I couldn't believe it. And when I studied the movies later, it was clear he didn't come off at all. Gene Tenace, the next batter, singled to Duke Sims, who I had just put in left because he had a strong arm. Hendricks rounded third and headed home, and Sims picked up the ball and made a perfect one-hop throw to Freehan. The runner was out by five feet, but Freehan tried to make the tag before he had the ball, he dropped it, and that was the run that beat us. Woody pitched a super four-hitter. We were about to get to Odom, but Dick Williams brought in Vida Blue, he pitched great, and it was all over for us. After the game Jim Campbell second-guessed me for putting Sims in left.

I spent 1973 arguing with Campbell. I felt we had caught lightning in a bottle in '72, that some of our regulars were getting old, that we had to make some trades 'cause these guys were going backwards, and fast. But Campbell just kept holding on to them, and he kept telling me that the kids in the farm system were going to come up and make the jump to the majors. Well, I had looked at our prospects, and it was my opinion that none of them would make it. I knew their shortcomings, and I told Campbell he was wrong. I said, "These guys are not going to make it, and you're strapping me into a position where our club is getting so old we're just going to be out of it. We can't depend on these young guys. They're not that good." But he insisted guys like Marvin Lane and Ike

Blessit would be stars, and of course not one of that group ever did make it.

The biggest battle we had was over signing Deron Johnson. Rather, not signing him. We needed a right-handed power hitter desperately, and Woody Fryman, who had come over from the Phillies, told me Deron would be perfect, because he could play first base and pinch-hit and he was still swinging the bat good, and I told Campbell to go get him. The Phillies didn't want him anymore, and he would have come cheap and been great for us, but Jim said that one of his scouts had said Johnson could no longer hit, and he wasn't interested.

I even had Woody call Deron, and his car was packed, he was ready to come to Detroit, wanted to play for me bad, but we didn't go after him, and Deron went to Oakland and drove in 81 runs and hit 19 home runs for Dick Williams. If we had signed him we would have won the pennant instead of them.

Oh, did I yell and scream! I told Campbell, "How the hell can you pay a scout ten thousand dollars and pay me seventy-five thousand and take his word over mine?" I said, "I do my homework too. I scouted before." He said, "You have to listen to your scouts. I'm running an organization, and you have to listen to the people you hire." I said, "Fine, listen to them, but when they're wrong, correct their mistake. You don't have to go by them all the time. They're human. They make mistakes." I was almost pleading with him to sign Johnson. What would it have hurt to try? We needed a guy like him so badly, and he wouldn't sign him. Maybe he was being considerate of the kids in the farm system, that it might hurt their morale if we signed someone from another club. I can understand that. But I'm looking to win the pennant, not win popularity contests. The hell with the kids on the farm. What about the guys on the Tigers?

Campbell ended up signing Frank Howard, and Frank did a good job for us, but he didn't drive in any 81 RBI's. We had Duke Sims to back up Freehan, who was having trouble throwing, and what saved us from sinking deeper than third, where we ended up, was the pitching of John Hiller, who was simply fantastic. Coleman won 23 games, but Lolich and Fryman were struggling, and John ended the year with a 10-5 record, a 1.44 ERA, and 38 saves.

It was all I could do to get Campbell to let Hiller play that year. He had suffered a heart attack the year before, and in spring training he was pitching batting practice, and I saw that he could pitch. I went to Campbell and said, "This guy can really throw the ball. Let's put him back on our roster." He said, "Oh, no, Billy, he's had it. The doctors say he isn't able to play anymore." I said, "Let's talk to some more doctors. Let's get some more advice on this. The way he can throw he'd be great for us now." Jim was concerned he'd have another heart attack, which I understood, but Jim did agree to have other doctors check John out, and they said it would be just as healthy for him to be pitching as doing anything else, so we signed him, and it was the best move we made because he was simply unhittable that year. John was a gutty guy who gave you his all, and he was a big asset to our ball club.

Another player I convinced Campbell to sign was Ron Le-Flore, who I first met in Jackson State Prison. I have a friend named Jimmy Busakeris, the owner of the Lindell A.C., and he has a friend who had been in prison with LeFlore. Jimmy's friend knew a lot about baseball, and he was telling Jimmy about this inmate who could really play ball, and he asked Jimmy if I would go up to the prison and see him. Jimmy was pushing me and pushing me to see the kid, and finally I agreed, and on one of my off days I went. The prison team was supposed to play that day but it was raining, and they couldn't play, but I walked around and talked to the inmates and talked to the kid, and I discovered that he was really a nice kid. He told me he was in for armed robbery, told me all about it, and how sorry he was about what happened, and after talking to him I became convinced that he was really a good person. Before I left I told him I would get him a tryout with the Tigers, and I got permission from the warden. The kid came to the stadium, and I had Kaline and Freehan and some of the other players who had been around watch him. I told them, "You guys judge him like I'm going to judge him." He batted and hit some balls into the upper deck, and in the field he was like a reindeer out there, catching everything hit his way, and he had a good arm. Kaline came over, and he was really enthusiastic about him. Freehan was, too, and so was I. Everybody was. I went up to Campbell and I said, "If you saw him on the sandlots, you'd give him a hundred thousand right now." Jim said, "He's a jailbird." I said, "I know that, Jim. But where did you get Gates Brown, out of Sunday school?" Gates had been in jail, too. When I left, I didn't think he'd sign LeFlore, and shortly after our meeting I was fired, and it was in the papers that I read that the Tigers had signed him, which made me very happy. They got Ron an early release from prison and sent him to the minors, and he soon became one of the top players in the major leagues.

I had signed a two year contract with the Tigers in '71, and it had run out, and I was pushing Campbell for a three-year contract. He told me he didn't believe in long-term contracts, and in the middle of our fighting about this, we were arguing all the time about the players, and I kept telling him they were too old and too slow, and what happened was that he finally got tired of putting up with me. I guess he felt I had become like a broken record, repeating the same arguments over and over, and he just didn't want to hear what I was telling him. Even though we had to make changes to keep winning, he didn't want to give up the guys he really liked, and when he had to choose between them and me, he chose them. With nineteen games left in the season he called me in and told me I was fired. I knew he had been talking to Ralph Houk, who was unhappy managing under George Steinbrenner in New York, and after he fired me, he signed Ralph. The next year the Tigers finished dead last, and the next year they finished dead last, and the next year they finished fifth, and when you think about what I had been telling Campbell, who do you think was right about the Tigers being too old and too slow? And later I got a real shock when Campbell, who kept telling me he doesn't sign managers to long-term contracts, turned around and signed Sparky Anderson to a five-year contract!

The night I was fired by the Tigers, I got a call from Bob Short, who, as you remember, I had known for a long time. I had been a close friend of Jim Pollard when Jim was playing basketball for the Minneapolis Lakers. Jim and I used to play semipro baseball against each other when I was growing up in Oakland, and he had introduced me to Bob, who was the owner of the Lakers. Later, when Bob ran for governor, I flew with him from town to town campaigning. Short was running against the Democratic party's candidate in the primary, and Bob beat him, but the asshole, after he got beat, refused to back Bob, and the Republican candidate beat him. There was no party loyalty there, which I thought was terrible. It had been Short who recommended I go down to Denver to manage, and that turned out well, and here he was calling, the day Detroit fired me, to manage the Texas Rangers, the team he had bought and moved from Washington. However, I was so hurt and down from getting fired at Detroit, at first I told him I didn't want the job.

Short said, "Don't do anything. I know you don't want to talk now. I'll talk to you tomorrow. You'll give me a call, won't you?" and I told him I would, but I didn't. I was feeling like a wounded lion, and I packed my bags and flew to Kansas City to get away. However, when I got to Kansas City, Bob had tracked me down, and he asked me to meet him at the Kansas City airport to talk to him. We talked for about three hours, and I kept telling him I didn't want to go, but he was persistent, and he wouldn't take no for an answer, and he finally was able to convince me that he needed me to turn the Rangers around. He told me he felt that if I would take over during the final couple weeks of the season I could evaluate the talent and help him make trades over the winter. Bob had agreed that I had the say as to which players came up and which went down, and I was very encouraged by this because I didn't want a repeat of the battling I had had with Jim Campbell over which players should be on the team.

Another reason I took the job was that Bob was losing his shirt with the Rangers. I was concerned he was going to lose something like ten million dollars if the situation didn't get turned around, and I felt I owed it to him to help out. In fact, I told him I'd agree to a $35,000 pay cut if the team didn't draw a million fans in '74. In '73 it only drew around six hundred thousand. This shows you what kind of businessman I am. A smart businessman would have said, "If we draw a million, you give me an extra $35,000." Not me. I told him, "If we don't, I'll give you back $35,000."

When I took over, the Rangers had a 48-91 record, worst in the league, but after I was there just a few weeks, I could see that the team had potential. The guys were doing their own thing, just putting in the time. They weren't executing, and they didn't know how to play together, weren't hitting the cut-off man, weren't playing aggressively, weren't doing anything right. But I saw that these were players who were eager to win. They didn't give up. Their problem was that they didn't know how to win. On the last day of the season I predicted that the Rangers, who finished the year 57 and 105, would be a contender in '74. I felt that when spring training rolled around, I would be able to teach them and show them how to win.

We had a nucleus of solid players. Up the middle we had Davey Nelson at second, who would have been an outstanding player had he not hurt his leg, and at short Toby Harrah was just super. He did everything I ever asked him to do, including shift to second when Davey was hurt. Jim Fregosi was at the end of his career, but he was a valuable infield sub, and he did a lot of buffer work for me on the bench. He was a leader who made a real contribution. Jeff Burroughs had a great year. He also helped me a lot with the bench guys, the guys who were moaning that they weren't playing, and on the field he batted .301, hit 25 home runs, and drove in 118 runs to win the Most Valuable Player Award, and his stats would have been even better had he not been playing in a park where the wind was always blowing in from left field. He was one of the big reasons we finished second in '74. Joe Lovitto was an outfielder with great potential, he could have been a great player, but he was also hurt for me all the time. Injuries plagued him, and it was a shame. I asked Short to get Cesar Tovar from the Twins, and Cesar, as always, did a great job for me. I figured when I went to spring training the next year we could use a third baseman, another hitter, a catcher, and a couple of starting pitchers.

Of the pitchers we did have, Jim Bibby was a great big strong pitcher who could really throw, and we figured he had the potential to be a 20-game winner, which he nearly proved when he won nineteen games the next year. We tried so hard to get him his twentieth win, too, but he ended up losing his last six decisions in a row. Jackie Brown started and relieved, and I liked him very much because he was a gutty guy. He had such a good curveball, and he was always trying to throw his fastball by the hitters, and I was always getting him mad and forcing him to throw that breaking ball. Steve Hargan was a fine pitcher, but he developed a sore arm during the season and never was as strong as he once was, and Steve Foucault was my primary reliever, and he did a great job.

During the winter I had gone to the Rangers' instructional league, and I saw two kids from the low minors I liked very much, Jim Sundberg, a catcher, and Mike Hargrove, a first baseman. I told Dan O'Brien, who was the general manager, that I was going to play Sundberg. We had another good, young catcher by the name of Bill Fahey, and O'Brien said, "He can't catch as good as Fahey. Sundberg was in Class D last year." But Short had given me the say, and I said, "Sundberg is my catcher." And he became one of the best catchers in baseball. I told O'Brien I was going to bring up Hargrove. He said, "Hargrove can't hit." I said, "He's going to play first base for me," and he hit .323 and was a hard-battling guy. Another player I wanted was Ferguson Jenkins. He had had a mediocre year in '73 for the Cubs, but I felt he could help us, and we traded Bill Madlock for him, and in '74 Fergy won 25 games for us. He was just like Catfish Hunter, a player who doesn't bother anybody, just goes out and does his job, a real good competitor.

Because of Short I was able to bring up Sundberg and Hargrove and get Jenkins, and I was able to promote Lenny Randle from the minors, and Lenny just did everything for me. He played wherever I needed him to play, including catcher one day, and he was aggressive, and he had so many tools to help in so many ways.

It's so much easier not to have to fight with other members of an organization to get the players I want. If I hadn't had the say-so at Texas, no way I would have gotten Sundberg and Hargrove. The farm director or the general manager would have complained. They'd be yelling at me, "Are you trying to tell us how to do our job?" Typical red tape crap, instead of just giving me who I want and helping me and the team. I had scouted. I know about player personnel—as much as anyone else in the world. I consider myself a professor in evaluating players. I'm not just guessing or playing a hunch. I know when a player has talent, and I know when he doesn't. I've gone from player to scout to third-base coach to minor league manager to major league manager, and along the way I've picked up many years of knowledge and experience. But when I sit and talk to personnel directors, they fight me. "Are you trying to tell me who to bring up?" they say. It's ridiculous. You'd think we were from different organizations.

I would have stayed with Short for the rest of my life, but when I signed with him it looked to me that he was having financial difficulties with the team, and that it would be only a matter of time before he had to sell. We had a pitcher, Sonny Siebert, who I liked very much, but Bob needed money and he sold him. We had this kid, Jim Mason, a shortstop, who had good tools. He should have been a better hitter, but he wasn't aggressive enough. Short sold him to the Yankees for $100,000. Another player Short sold to the Yankees was Elliott Maddox. I had been the manager at Detroit when he was traded to Texas, and at the time Jim Campbell made that trade I didn't know whether Maddox, who accused me of trading him because he was black, was white, black, green, plaid, or what. I had absolutely nothing to do with that trade, which sent him and Denny McLain to Washington for Brinkman and Rodriguez, which was a great trade for Detroit. Then I went to Texas, where the Washington Senators had moved to, and I really hadn't seen Elliott play much there, either. If I made a mistake in personnel it was in trading Maddox from Texas. We needed a center fielder, and it wasn't until I saw him play with the Yankees that I realized that it had been a shame we didn't keep him, because he was a great center fielder. He wasn't a good hitter, didn't drive in enough runs and didn't have much power, but with the Rangers he would have helped us. However, when Short asked me if we could sell him because he needed the money, I hadn't played Maddox much, so I agreed that Bob could sell him.

When Elliott got to the Yankees he started badmouthing me real bad, and in one of our games against the Yankees one of the Ranger front-office officials told Jim Bibby that if he beaned Maddox, he'd give him some money. Right away I got the blame, of course, but I asked Bibby, and he told me about what the official had offered him, and I jumped all over Bibby's ass about it. It didn't sit right with me, and I told him he better not do something like that ever again.

When I took over as Yankee manager, Elliott was hurt all the time, and when he didn't play, he would be complaining all the time. Another thing I didn't like was that Henry Hecht of the *New York Post* would be going over to Elliott every other day, and he was getting more ink than the guys who were playing. After a while I didn't feel he was good for the ball club anymore, and this time I did get rid of him. Took me a long time, but he was hurt so long I just didn't feel like waiting any longer for him to recuperate. I certainly don't dislike Elliott. Never did. I was simply doing what was best for the ball club, which is always my primary consideration.

Another player Short sold to the Yankees was Alex Johnson. This guy had the greatest natural ability of any one man I've ever seen, but he was one of those strange kind of guys who nobody could reach. He didn't want to come out and take batting practice, and he was moody all the time. He was great with little kids, loved the little kids who came into the clubhouse, but when he put that uniform on he became another person. I never could reach him, never could figure him out. No manager ever did, and it was too bad because he had great ability to do many things. One day he'd play hard, and the next day he wouldn't. I wanted to get rid of him, and Short needed the money, so we did.

Despite his financial problems, by midseason the Rangers were challenging the A's for the Western Division lead, and if we had had just one more consistent pitcher, we would have won it. We were suicide-squeezing and making delayed steals, executing the hit-and-run, stealing home, and playing exciting baseball. During spring training I had shown them how we could beat the other clubs, and when the bell rang the guys went out and proved to themselves I knew what I was talking about. On defense we were hitting the cutoff man, backing each other up, playing tough, and we were having fun and laughing our way through the league.

Also by midseason it became apparent that the club was in serious trouble financially, and in 1974 Short sold the Rangers to Brad Corbett, who had made millions of dollars in the pipe business. Short told me about the sale, but what I didn't know was that he hadn't told Corbett that I had the right to say who comes up and who goes down to the minors. I discovered this when I called Corbett and told him I wanted to send down young David Clyde, a teen-age phenom who threw the ball well but was much too raw to be playing in the major leagues. Short had kept him up because he was a Texas boy and very popular, and every time he pitched he drew twenty thousand fans more than we normally drew, but since Corbett had bought the club and had plenty of money, we no longer needed the extra money the kid was bringing in, and for the team's sake and the kid's sake I felt it was to everyone's advantage to send the kid down for seasoning. Art Fowler and I loved the kid, but he was starting to develop bad habits. He was getting too big for his breeches, staying out late, drinking like he'd been in the majors for twenty years. I felt he was way over his head, and I wanted to get him away from there before he hurt himself too badly.

We had about five weeks in the schedule where all right-handed-hitting teams were coming in, so I suggested to team president Bobby Brown, who had played with me on the Yankees and who had been hired by Corbett, that we send David to the minors for the five weeks. He was a left-handed pitcher, and I had no intentions of using him during that period, and by sending him down he would have had the opportunity to get some work and regain his confidence, and then we'd have brought him back. Brown told me, "Billy, we can't send the kid down. It'll hurt his feelings." When he said that, I saw red, and we really got into it. It was the beginning of the end for me in Texas. Clyde ended up sitting on the bench, not getting a chance, and he's never become the pitcher he could have and should have become.

By 1975 I was arguing with Corbett and Brown all the time over players, and Corbett got into the running of the club strong, and he started doing some things I had never seen an owner do before, and before the season was over I found myself in a totally impossible situation. Corbett thought it would be a good idea to get involved personally with his players, and he'd have players coming over to his house for dinner, and they started making contract deals with him personally, and before long the players were going behind my back when they had a gripe, and if they weren't having a good year, they'd be blaming the manager, and the togetherness we had had the year before quickly disappeared. To give a player an avenue to the front office or to the owner is the most destructive thing that can be done to a ball club. In the first place, player happiness is not the goal of a major league manager. Winning the pennant is the goal. On a team of twenty-five, it's rare when more than fifteen of the guys are happy, the eight starters, the DH, and perhaps four starting pitchers and the short-relief pitcher. Everyone else is sitting, and they want to play. And even some of the starting players may be unhappy with the manager, because maybe they aren't playing the way the manager wants them to, and then the manager is jumping all over them to do it his way, and he's mad, too. This is what it's like on a baseball team, especially if the manager is pushing his players to do their best and be successful. A manager isn't trying to win a popularity contest. So when the owner or the general manager opens his office to the players and sits and listens to their complaints, what do you think that does to the manager's authority? It cuts the balls right off the manager. And I tried to tell Corbett and Brown that, and here Bobby hadn't been in the game for over twenty years, and he was trying to tell me how to handle these kids, and I just didn't agree with him at all. The players were going behind my back, and they had created a monster. I even had one of my coaches, Frank Luchese, going up to the front office every day, and I resented that, too, and so did the rest of my coaches.

Corbett and Brown also were discussing salaries with the

players during the season, and I felt this was also wrong. Contracts should be negotiated before the season or after the season, not during the season when a guy will end up more concerned with what he's going to be making than how he's playing out on the field. He won't give his best, because his mind won't be on what he's doing, and it isn't fair to the fans who come to the park, and it isn't fair to the manager. We were having enough problems with our pitching and defensive play during the '75 season, but with these other disruptive influences brought on by the team owner, we were barely a .500 team.

There was, too, an incident on one of our plane flights that didn't help my standing with management. Texas' traveling secretary was a man named Burt Hawkins, and he had never done anything like this before and never did anything like it after, but this one time he had had too much to drink, and in the middle of the flight, from out of nowhere, he told me his wife was going to start a club for the players' wives. She was going to be president, and the wives were going to travel together so they could be with their husbands. I said, "Burt, I won't have that. I don't allow it, and I don't want the wives together."

It's not that I have anything against them personally. I just don't want the wives bothering the players on the road and giving them a bad time when they have a job to do, especially if it's a crucial series. Players have enough on their minds, worried about the ball game, and they shouldn't have to concern themselves with socializing with their wives and taking them out. For instance, if a guy's a starting pitcher, the wife wants to go here and wants to go there, and the pitcher has got to go with her, and by the time he gets out to the ball park he's tired. This has happened to me more than once.

Anyway I told Burt, "No way." There was no argument about this. This was the way it was going to be.

Burt, who was about 60 or so, of course didn't like it one bit, and he started popping off at me, and I told him, "Burt, shut up, you've had too much to drink," and he said, "I'm not afraid of you. Maybe these players are, but I'm not." I told him again to be quiet. He stood up, and now I was beginning to lose face with my players, so I stood up and with my open palm I slapped him hard, gave him a good crack. And after that he sat down and kept quiet. I didn't hold it against him. The man just had too much to drink, that's all. Of course, when the story came out in the paper they made it sound like I had punched out an old man, which just wasn't true.

The showdown between Corbett and me came over personnel. Corbett wanted to buy Willie Davis, and I didn't want him. I had been told by other people in baseball that Willie wasn't somebody I wanted on my club, that he was a bad influence on the other players and that he was over the hill. Corbett said to me, "Billy, please go along with me on this one," and I told him, "Make the deal if you want to, but I don't want to have anything to do with it." And it was a bad deal for us in many ways. Willie turned out just as my sources predicted: He was a veteran player who thought he was still a star with the Dodgers, and he was set in his ways, and wasn't a team player, and he was going downhill and didn't know it. We never should have gotten him.

The last straw came in July. We needed a backup catcher real bad, I felt, and L.A. had just released a guy by the name of Tom Egan, who could have helped us. I called Dan O'Brien and told him about Egan, that he had just been released and that he was out in L.A. doing nothing, and that we could get him cheap. O'Brien told me no, we wouldn't get him, which was a shock to me. Then O'Brien convinced Corbett and Bobby Brown we didn't need him. Boy, did I chew O'Brien out. I said, "What the hell do you know about what I need? You're the same guy who told me Sundberg couldn't make it." I felt that he didn't know the needs of our club as well as I did.

When I went to Corbett, again I was told I couldn't have him. I told Corbett, who ran a pipe company, "You know as much about baseball as I know about pipe." Two days later he fired me.

The Rangers held an Old Timers' Day the day after our argument, and I was still so mad about the Egan thing that I refused to participate in the game. I wouldn't come out of the clubhouse I was so disgusted. I had taken over the job the year before, and we had improved dramatically, and here I was in the middle of the same old bullshit again. Upstairs interference. Players going behind my back when they weren't supposed to. Short had sold the ball club, and I was left all alone. Everything had gone haywire, just haywire. Here I was having trouble with the front office over a utility player, which was ridiculous. It was apparent that Corbett wanted to take over and do everything, he wanted to run the club his way, and I didn't agree with him, so the handwriting was on the wall. The rumors were swirling around the ball park that soon I would be fired.

That afternoon I called Corbett on the telephone to ask him about the rumors. "Are they true?" I asked. He said, "There's some truth to it." I said, "You've got to be kidding." He said, "No. No." I said, "Is it because I don't come up to the front office every day like Frank Luchese?" He said, "That might be the reason." I said, "If that's the reason, you go right ahead and do it if you think it's right."

I called a meeting with the coaches during the evening. I was really down, depressed, because the year before we had had such a happy ball club, everybody was hustling and jelling, and the players were just learning that winning is fun and that if someone believes in them long enough and they work hard enough, they can win it all, and they almost did. I was also depressed because when you're fired, you take the coaches with you, and it's hard for them and their families.

I told the coaches that I was probably going to be fired, and that when I was let go, they probably would be, too. I told Luchese, "You're crazy if you take this job, Frank." He said, "I haven't talked to anybody about taking the job, Billy," which I didn't believe for a minute.

After the meeting I told Art, "I bet you Luchese is named manager tomorrow." Art said, "I know he will be."

I was fired the next day, and Luchese was named to replace me. In 1976 the Rangers finished tied for fourth. I swore at the time, I'd never get myself into another situation like that, and it was at this time, while I was fishing in Colorado, that I got the call from George Steinbrenner and Gabe Paul to manage the Yankees.

CHAPTER 7

It took George only a few days after our patch-up-our-differences meeting at the Carlyle Hotel for him to prove to me that he wasn't about to change. Mickey Moribito, the Yankees' public relations man, asked me if I would have lunch with the New York reporters at a little Italian restaurant near Yankee Stadium. He said I could talk about what I was going to be doing for the Yankees during the year and a half Lemon was managing. Mickey said the writers had been upset that George hadn't allowed any questions at the press conference on Old Timers' Day. This would be a good chance to sit and talk with the press, he said, and I agreed. Because Mickey had set it up I assumed that he was doing it with George's permission, or at least with his knowledge. After all, Mickey was director of publicity for the Yankees. Who would have assumed otherwise?

We ate lunch, and afterwards the reporters asked questions. One of the questions was, "How did it happen you got your job back?" I told them the truth, that George had called Doug to set it up. I found out later that George had been telling the press that I had called him to apologize after I had resigned, which was not true.

Another question they asked me was, "How's your health, Billy?" because George had been telling them that I was staying out for the good of my physical well-being, which was another lie. I told the reporters the truth, that the reports of a serious liver ailment were greatly exaggerated, that it simply wasn't true that I was waiting a year and a half to manage in 1980 because I needed that much time to recover my health.

I was also asked whether one of the reasons I had quit was because of Reggie Jackson. I told them it was, that the attention of the press was a distraction that was interfering with my ability to run the team, that I had made the quote about Reggie and George because I was angry more with George even than Reggie, angry that George was taking Reggie's side, angry that his interference had made it so tough for me.

We tried our best to keep the discussion focused on my future duties on the Yankees, not on the past, but it seemed that the writers were not at all interested in the summer camp I was going to open or in the Western-wear shop I was planning or in my duties with the Yankees. They wanted to know about George and Reggie, and since I figured that the press conference was with George's approval and since I hadn't been told of things I shouldn't say, like George often did, I felt free to speak my mind.

That evening Mickey Moribito called. He was very upset. George had heard about the press conference, and he was so upset he was talking about firing him. If my comments came out in the papers the next day, George told Mickey, he was gone. Mickey was heartbroken, and I tried to console him. The following day Mickey called to say he wasn't going to be fired. That night the New York papers had gone on strike.

Nevertheless this wasn't the new, understanding George that he had promised he would become. It was the same old George. He had not, apparently, changed very much at all from the person I had worked for in the past.

Things got worse. At our meeting at the Carlyle, George had said that he would put our agreement into writing within the next two weeks, that when I came back there would be no restrictive clauses in my contract, and that he would let me manage the way I wanted, without interference and notes and phone calls in the middle of the game. The Carlyle meeting was in July, but by the end of the fall I hadn't gotten the contract from George. In fact, I hadn't heard a single word from George.

Meanwhile George's friend Bill Fugazy was calling me, asking me to make appearances for him. He asked me to attend a golf tournament, so I went. I figured George would have wanted me to go. Fugazy called Doug Newton and asked if I would attend a dinner at the New York Athletic Club. My presence would be in the "best interests of the Yankees," Fugazy said. I went, and it turned out to be a dinner honoring Bill Fugazy.

At the dinner Newton managed to corner George and ask him about his promise to reduce our agreement to writing. He told Doug, "Oh, yes, yes. We must indeed get that all wrapped up. I'll be in touch with you in two weeks. I'll call you when I get back in town." He didn't, however, call. I was beginning to get the feeling that George had no intention of putting our agreement in writing, that maybe the announcement on Old Timers' Day was just a publicity stunt, that maybe he was looking for the first excuse not to hire me back or perhaps was looking for a way to get better terms when we did sign.

That excuse came on November 28, 1978. A fellow by the name of Bill Musselman called me and asked if I would fly to Reno, Nevada, and make a personal appearance during half time of the Reno Big Horns basketball game. Musselman, who had coached at the University of Minnesota when I was living in Minneapolis, was the Big Horns' coach, and he thought my appearance would bring customers into the arena. Bill was an old friend, so I didn't even ask for a fee. I made just one request: no press interviews. I would show up at halftime, wave to the crowd, and after the game I'd stay and sign autographs for the kids. Musselman agreed, and he assured me that my request for no press interviews would be taken care of.

At half time I walked out onto the floor, the announcer introduced me, and I waved. The Big Horns were in the Western Basketball Association, sort of a minor league to the NBA, and they drew a nice crowd compared to usual, and I was glad to have been able to help them out. After I was introduced, I went into a cocktail lounge adjacent to the court with another close friend, Howard Wong. Howard owns a restaurant in Minneapolis, and he had accompanied me on the trip. Howard and I ordered a drink, and I didn't get to take a sip when this kid wearing a Yankee T-shirt came up to me. He didn't introduce himself as a member of the press. He didn't seem to be carrying a pen or paper. I figured he was a fan who wanted to talk baseball. Standing with us was the media coordinator of the Big Horns. He was the guy with the responsibility of keeping the press away. He knew of my request for no interviews, and here he was standing with this kid and me listening to our discussion. At first the kid's questions were general, and he was very friendly. He was asking me questions about the designated hitter and what I thought about it, and we were talking about the height of the pitcher's mound and whether it should be raised, things like that, and then all of a sudden he began asking me about personalities. He started by quoting something Dick Young had written, asking me to comment on it. I said, "Dick Young doesn't always quote people properly, so I don't want to hear any of that stuff. Don't tell me what Dick Young says. Ask me your questions, and I'll answer them. Don't ask me about Dick Young." The kid then said, "You had said that Reggie Jackson was not a true Yankee." I was starting to get upset. I said, "Did you hear me say that? Did you ever hear me say that, or are you quoting what you heard someone else say? If you didn't hear me say it, don't quote me as saying it." As I was talking, the kid whipped out a pen and a notebook from a back pocket, and he started taking notes. I said, "Wait a minute. Who are you?" He said, "I'm Ray Hagar from the Reno Something-or-other." I said, "Look, I told these people I didn't want to do any interviews. I thought you were just a fan, that we were just rapping, and I'm not going to have something put into the paper I didn't say. I want to stop right now. Now I know it's an interview, I don't want to do interviews, and I want you to stop it, and I want you to give me the notes back." The kid said, "I can't give you the notes back. I work for a newspaper, and these notes are part of my story." Howard told the kid, "Give Billy the notes." By this time the kid had put the notes in his back pocket, and Howard went to grab them, and the kid shoved Howard, which really made me angry. Howard's about seventy years old, and who was this kid to shove Howard like that? The kid said to me, "If you want the notes, you're going to have to fight me for them." I said, "I don't want to fight you. Little kids fight. Men don't fight." The kid said, "Look, I don't want to fight you, but I will." I said, "No, I just want the notes." At this point Hagar took his glasses off, and he made a move like he was about to go after me, and at that point I pulled the trigger and I hit him with a left hand, gave him two good pops. He called the police, and the police took him to the hospital. I gave him a black eye and a cut lip, and I felt bad about the incident, but I felt he had started it, and I had been provoked into fighting him. And this whole time the media coordinator, the guy whose job it was to keep the press away, was standing there watching. Did he do anything to keep the kid away from me? No. When he saw us starting to argue, did he do anything to get us apart? No. In fact he didn't do anything to keep his part of the bargain. He could have avoided the whole thing, but because he didn't, I found myself in another fight I didn't want to be in.

After it was over, however, I didn't think any more about it. It was no big deal. After the game I hung around and signed hundreds of autographs for the kids as I had promised, talked baseball with them, and had a great time. I didn't think there would be a problem until I saw the newspapers the next day. There were big headlines about how I had slugged a newspaper reporter. No one called to find out my side of the story. No one wrote about my only request—no interviews—or how he had tried to trick me or how he had taken his glasses off and had come after me. All anyone wrote was: Martin Slugs Reporter.

Even after the Reno incident I didn't hear from George. He never sent the contract, and Doug and I were more and more concerned that George really had no intention of keeping his promise and bringing me back to manage the Yankees. We thought that maybe he was, on the one hand, keeping another team from hiring me, and, on the other, preventing me from talking about his interference and all the things he did which drove me crazy. George was having his cake and eating it, too.

A couple weeks before the start of spring training Doug received in the mail a copy of *W* magazine, a weekly published about south Florida. One of the articles was titled: "George Steinbrenner's Farm Team." In the article he said that the reason I was coming back in 1980 was that my doctors and agents felt it would take that long for me to be in shape to come back. He also said I wouldn't return unless I lived up to the clauses in my contract. When I saw that, I couldn't believe it. The restrictions were supposed to be on *him*. He was going to control himself and stop sending me notes and stop leaking things to the press about me. *He* was the one who was supposed to control himself! Not me. And as for those doctors and agents, I don't know who he was talking about. Maybe it was a horse doctor in Ocala, where he has his farm.

When spring training opened in early February I was reluctant to show up without being invited, because I didn't want to draw any media attention away from Bob Lemon and the job he had to do with the team. On the other hand, George had promised I would be a part of spring training. He had said he wanted me there, and I wanted to be there to fulfill whatever duties the Yankees had for me. I was puzzled. I didn't know what to do, whether to stay in New Jersey or to go to Fort Lauderdale. I finally decided it would be a good idea to let the Yankees know I was around, so I went.

Doug Newton, meanwhile, had written George a letter asking for the contract he had promised. Then he sent George a telegram. There was no answer to either.

At Fort Lauderdale I spent enough time in the clubhouse to say hi to Lem, grab a few towels from Pete Sheehy, and to talk with Jack Butterfield about my assignments. Apparently Jack had sent my assignments to my home in Texas. I hadn't been living there for more than a year, so I didn't get them. Jack and I had a nice conversation. He asked me to go to Arizona to scout the West Coast teams. I said fine. After our meeting I ran into a couple of reporters and told them where I was going and little else, except that I thought George had been avoiding me, which he was.

The next day George went crazy in the papers. The quotes were attributed to Al Rosen, but it was a smear campaign that was purely George. I don't think Al would have deliberately hurt me in any way. I personally liked Al very much, and in fact, when I first took the Yankee job in '75, Rosen had called me and warned me about George's ruthlessness. Al and George were both from Cleveland, and Al knew him from there.

In the papers Al talked about a "series of fights" I'd had besides the Reno fight. He said I had been drunk at a country club. He quoted an article in *Time* magazine that said I had gotten in a fight in a Florida bar. He said my actions weren't in the best interests of the Yankees, and he said that if I wasn't cleared of the Reno charges completely, I wouldn't be rehired. He said, "This is not the time to be talking about next year. Billy has to get by Reno first."

I called Al on the phone. He said, "Billy, please believe me. I didn't want to say those things. I was told to say them. George made me say them." I said, "What the hell did I do wrong to make the guy so mad all of a sudden?" He said, "I don't know, Billy, that's just the way he is."

When I read what they said about me in the papers I was in a state of shock. The party at the country club they were talking about was a charity dinner in honor of Gene Michael. Mickey Mantle and I were the special guests, and I had had a drink or two, but I certainly wasn't drunk. In fact, I had such a nice time, I can't remember anything close to even an argument with anyone. Why did George say I was drunk? Why would he have done a thing like that?

The so-called Florida bar fight they were talking about also never happened. It was the grand opening of Bachelor's III, and I went with judges Lou Trent and Eddie Sapir and was with them the whole time. The place was packed, people standing in there like sardines, and when we arrived around eight-thirty that evening, I had some pictures taken with Joe Namath, who owns the place, and I had some pictures taken with little kids and their dads. I ate dinner, and it couldn't have been later than ten-thirty when Judge Sapir from New Orleans drove me home. I didn't get into a fight. Again, there wasn't even an argument. But George made the statement he was investigating the "incident" and so Judge Sapir did his own investigation, took affidavits from people there, to prove to George if need be that the story was a vicious lie. When Judge Sapir compiled all his evidence, he called George to ask him if he was interested in seeing it, and he wasn't. Later I found out that George had been the one who had floated the story to make me look like a bad guy fighting in a bar. Why was he doing this to me? What had I done to him for him to treat me like this?

Despite all this I still wanted my job managing the Yankees back. The attraction of the Yankee uniform was stronger than everything else, I suppose. I knew in my heart that George wasn't going to change, that when I took over in 1980 nothing would change, but I still wanted to come back. I belonged in that uniform. I had started as a Yankee, and that's how I wanted to finish.

When Judge Sapir read that the only way I'd get my job back was if I was cleared completely both criminally and civilly in the Reno matter, he called me on the phone. I hadn't realized it, but Judge Sapir said that George had set up a monumental task. He said that the way George laid it out, even if I settled the case, I couldn't come back. Settling a case is done every day without any admission of guilt. The two parties don't even have to go to court, they agree how much one party pays the other, and it's resolved, with no one having to admit guilt. But to George that wasn't good enough. If I had to pay Ray Hagar two cents, to George that meant the fight was my fault, and he wouldn't hire me back. George was playing lawmaker, judge, and jury, and I was getting the feeling that he was out to hang me.

When Judge Sapir told me how hard a task I had to get off scot-free and without liability, I got very upset. I asked him, "Judge, can it be won? And will you handle it?" I had known Eddie Sapir for several years. I knew how loyal he'd been to me. I knew that he had a brilliant legal mind. I wanted him on my side. Judge Sapir said, "Billy, you can count on me. Don't worry about it. I'll look into the law and come up with a strategy. We can lick it."

Several days later Judge Sapir asked to meet me in Fort Lauderdale. He said, "You realize that the lawsuit doesn't only read Ray Hagar versus Billy Martin, but also includes the Western Basketball Association, the Centennial Coliseum, and the Reno Big Horns as defendants." I hadn't. I had thought Hagar had sued only me. Judge Sapir said, "I read all the statements and admissions, and the Reno Big Horns have some serious exposure here." I asked him what he meant, and he recounted to me how the Big Horns' media coordinator had sat next to Hagar at the pre— —ble and had failed to tell Hagar of my request for n— ——— and how he had admitted standing nearby ——— ———— got into our argument. "He admitt—" ———— —— your request for no interviews — ——— ——— — — —nd that is an act of negligence. — ——— — —— — —— suit against the Big Horns." — —— "—— — —— — —— e you weren't protected by — — — ———— —— ——— earnings you lose, they are —— ——— — — — w what Ray Hagar is looking for, —— — —— — — — get Bill Musselman to see what the Big — — — —e doing about this."

— —apir, Bill Musselman, and I met in New Orleans a —it time later. The judge said to Musselman, "We have to get Billy out of this without suing the Big Horns," and the judge explained to Bill how the media coordinator had screwed up, how the Big Horns potentially could be open to a lawsuit from me. Musselman understood. He said that the owner of the Big Horns, Bill Myers, was a nice guy and quite unhappy over what had happened. He would give him a call immediately, Musselman promised.

"When Myers wakes up to what this is all about," Judge Sapir told me, "he'll be more than happy to help." What he meant was, Bill Myers was a land developer, a developer of shopping malls, a guy who had to borrow millions of dollars to get his malls built. When he found out I was in a position to sue him for a lot of money because of the negligence of his media coordinator, he would want to do something to help me and help himself.

Soon after Bill Musselman called Bill Myers, Myers's attorney was on the phone with Ray Hagar's lawyer, Tim Dixon. Hagar told Myers's attorney that he didn't want to see me hurt, that he wished the whole thing had never happened, that he didn't want to be the cause of my losing my job, which I appreciated. Judge Sapir told Bill Myers's attorney, "If you settle with Hagar, Billy will be out of it, and what we'll do for you, we'll give you a release that Billy wouldn't sue him for negligence." They agreed. They called Hagar's attorney and agreed to pay Hagar $5,000 for his doctor's bills. Judge Sapir called Hagar's attorney and said, "If you agree, the Big Horns are willing to settle with you, and Billy will be let out of it. And what we'll do for you, Billy won't countersue against Ray or his newspaper. We'll give you full releases, and of course, you have to drop the criminal charge." Hagar agreed. The Big Horns paid the five thousand, Hagar dropped the criminal charge against me, the civil suit against me was dismissed, and thanks to Judge Sapir, I was away scot-free, as George Steinbrenner had required. As Judge Sapir said, "It fell together A, B, C."

Judge Sapir and I decided it would be a nice gesture on my part if I flew back to Reno to shake hands with Ray Hagar, to tell him how glad I was that the thing was over, to show him that I really wasn't such a bad guy, to tell him I didn't hold a grudge and that I hoped he'd have a very successful career as a sportswriter. We could have resolved the thing on the phone, I didn't have to go out there, but I wanted to. I also wanted Hagar to understand that more than anything else, I wanted the affair behind me so I could go back to the Yankees, that I wasn't interested in a fast buck from a lawsuit, which I felt I could have won if I had wanted to sue.

Hagar's attorney withdrew his complaint against me, then Judge Sapir and I flew out to Reno to meet with Ray and his attorney.

Everything would have been fine, but the media had to get into the middle of it, like it usually does. The night before we were to meet, Ray Hagar told the writers, "Billy Martin is coming out here to apologize to me." But that wasn't why I was coming back to Reno. They had agreed to drop the civil suit. There was nothing for me to apologize for. And when the reporters asked if I was meeting with him to apologize, I told the truth. I told them I had no intention of apologizing. The next morning the headlines in the papers read: Martin Won't Apologize. At which point Ray Hagar must have told his lawyer something like: Martin has got to say he's sorry. I can't eat all this crow.

The next morning Judge Sapir and I went to the meeting. On the way the reporters caught up with us. Judge Sapir did all the talking. He didn't want me blowing the whole deal. He said, "Both men mutually agreed they wish it hadn't happened. You guys keep saying 'apologize, apologize, apologize.' Why don't you get off that word? Get off the words 'I'm sorry.' " The reporters were thinking too much of *Love Story*—love means never having to say you're sorry. I didn't have to say I was sorry to be in love with Ray. Anyway, we went into the meeting, and all the parties exchanged releases, and the matter was settled. I talked with Ray, told him I hoped he got to know me better in the future, wished him success, told him I recognized that what happened probably happened because he was new at reporting, that certainly he would have handled it differently had he had more experience. I told him, "If somewhere along the line our paths cross, I want to be your friend, and I want you to be my friend." He was very appreciative, and I'm sure that he was as sorry as I was that the incident had happened at all.

After the meeting Judge Sapir and I were deluged with telephone calls from reporters. The judge explained that I had been exonerated fully, explained that the Big Horns had settled with Hagar and not me, but the press still managed to get the story wrong. *Sports Illustrated* wrote that I had made a civil settlement. Judge Sapir explained the whole thing to Dick Young, and Dick Young also wrote that I had made a civil settlement.

When I saw their stories, I asked Judge Sapir how they could have written that, when I had nothing to do with the settlement between Hagar and the Big Horns. He said, "Billy, don't worry about it. If these guys want to say you made a civil settlement, I have the documents to show otherwise. The only person we have to account to is George Steinbrenner. We'll offer to meet with him personally or to provide him with the documents showing that the criminal charge was dropped and the civil matter dismissed, and that you have completely satisfied his criteria. He will now take you back as manager."

While I was in Reno, I got a call from Jack Butterfield, the Yankee farm director. He told me that George wanted me to scout, and I asked the judge whether I should do it. Judge Sapir told me, "Billy, be very gracious, because you're a winner. You've won it all." He was right. I decided that I would do anything George asked me to do. He wouldn't stop me from becoming manager again now.

The amazing thing is that George still doesn't know what happened in Reno, except what he may have read in the papers. He never met with Judge Sapir or me to discuss it, and he never asked for the documents. As far as I knew, he wasn't even interested in finding out the facts.

I went to see George to find out what he wanted me to do. I said, "Lookit, I'm not doing anything. Do you want me to advance-scout, look at some clubs in case you want to make trades? I'll be glad to do anything." He said, "Yeah, go ahead." I said, "Can I make my own schedule?" He said yeah. I said, "Okay, how about if I fly out to California to pick up the Angels and then go on to Oakland to scout the A's and at the same time visit my mother? Then I can scout Seattle." George said, "Yeah, that sounds fine." I said, "I'll leave tomorrow." He said fine.

I flew out to Anaheim, and that afternoon I got a call from Jack Butterfield. He said, "Billy, George is going crazy." I said, "What's the matter?" He said, "What are you doing in California?" I said, "I'm scouting the Angels and the White Sox." I said, "I spoke to George about it yesterday and he said it was all right." Jack said, "He wants you in Boston, and he wants you there right now. He's screaming at us, Billy. Do me a favor, please go to Boston." I said, "How many games is Boston playing?" He said, "One game." And they sent me all the way across the country to scout Boston for one game. Then they tell me to fly to Toronto. I went to Toronto. Butterfield called. "They want you in Cleveland right away." I flew to Cleveland. By now it's early June. I got a call from Doug Newton. "Cedric Tallis called to say that George wants to meet you in Columbus to see if you'd be interested in taking over the Yankees from Lemon," he said. I said, "That's very nice for me; it's not very nice for Lem." I thought a few seconds. I said, "I don't think I ought to do it. I don't think I should come back and manage this year. It's not my team, it's been significantly changed from the one I left, and this team is now in trouble. I don't think I should take it now."

When I met George in Columbus, he picked me up at the airport, and boy, when we met, he was happy to see me and bubbling, just as great as I've ever seen him. We drove out to the home of a doctor friend of his, and as we sat around the swimming pool, George said, "Billy, Lemon is doing a terrible job, just terrible. He has no control over the players, he's not doing anything, the poor guy can't do it." I wanted to remind George that Lemon had just lost his son in a car accident, and that it isn't easy to get over something like that so quickly, but I kept quiet. I let George keep talking. He said, "I want you to take over the club." He said, "You don't have to take it over now if you don't want to. You can wait till eighty. I could put Gene Michael or somebody else in there if you don't want to take it now." I asked George about the clauses in my contract and about George's interference, and he promised me there would be no clauses and that he wouldn't send any more notes during the game, wouldn't call me on the phone to make suggestions. I was so happy with our discussion that even though I had gone out there with the intention not to take the job now, I felt that maybe I should take over the team to find out who would help us for the 1980 season. I said, "What do you think I should do, George?" He said, "It's up to you." I said, "Okay, I'll take it."

Why did George decide to take me back after months of refusing to offer me a contract, after his smear campaign during spring training, after his demand that I be cleared of all charges in Reno? I can't say for sure, but I have a pretty good idea Judge Sapir may have had something to do with it.

After Reno was settled, Judge Sapir thought it might be a good idea to ask the American League office whether I was free to sign with another team. I had been scheduled to attend an Old Timers' game in San Diego towards the end of June, and

Judge Sapir knew that Ballard Smith, Ray Kroc's son-in-law who was running the Padres, was interested in my taking over as manager. Judge Sapir asked Lee MacPhail, the American League president, "Is Billy Martin free to sign with San Diego? Does he belong to the Yankees?" Judge Sapir said, "Lee, people are calling me all the time. They want to talk with Billy, but they can't. They're afraid to, because they don't know where he stands with George, and they don't want to be accused of tampering. George hasn't offered Billy a contract, and we don't want to be out in left field when the season begins."

Judge Sapir told Lee that he thought I could get a fantastic contract with the Padres but that he wouldn't talk to the Padres until he got a ruling from him. Judge Sapir figured Lee's first phone call would be to George to find out where I stood with the Yankees, and that George would want to know why Lee was asking. And apparently that's exactly what happened, because a week didn't go by before George called and asked if I was interested in taking over the Yankees again.

The day before I was to fly out to San Diego, he called me and told me I couldn't go to the Old Timers' game in San Diego. He wanted to meet with me in Columbus, which is where he offered me my Yankee job back.

George said, "Billy, what will it take to get you to manage the Yankees for the next two years?" I said, "I want to make at least what Earl Weaver makes." George said, "You got it," and that's what I got, $125,000 a year for three years. George said, "I don't think you have a chance to win this year." The Yankees were eight games behind Baltimore and were playing poorly. I said, "George, you said the same thing last year, and I told you we were going to win, and we did."

But when I went back to the team, I could see we weren't going to win. Things had changed on the team. The aggressiveness was gone. They were lackadaisical. They were playing with the attitude: We know we can do it, it'll come automatically. And nothing comes automatically. You have to work for it.

During spring training George had been making statements that it had been one of the best-run spring trainings he had ever seen. But when I took over the team the players were complaining to me that the coaches hadn't done anything with them. The pitchers hadn't practiced their pick-off plays. They hadn't practiced the defense against the bunt. They were telling me they hadn't done anything in spring training except take batting practice. Their pitching coach, Tom Morgan, hadn't even had them practicing covering first on the bunt.

There were other problems. Reggie was hurt and missed a couple weeks. Ron Guidry, who last year won 25 games, injured his back and this year was 6 and 7. Goose Gossage had missed the first three months of the season after getting into a shoving match with Cliff Johnson. With Goose out they used Tidrow in short relief, pitched him too much, and when he went bad, George got rid of him, which I thought disgraceful. How can you get rid of a Dick Tidrow? When he's used right, he's a very valuable man to have on a team. I asked George, "Why did you get rid of him?" He said, "Rosen made the deal with his buddy on the Cubs, Bob Kennedy." Now, I know Rosen couldn't trade anybody unless George wanted him to. George must have told Rosen something like "Get rid of him. I don't want to see his face around here anymore," and Al had no choice. Then when the deal went bad, he blamed Rosen. You never hear George say he made a mistake. Oh, no, George is too big a man to be making mistakes.

Afterwards I was with Tidrow and his wife. They said, "Billy, if you were there just a month earlier, we wouldn't have been gone," and they were right. I wouldn't have been involved in the trade, but I could have put up a strong voice to stop it.

One of the first things I did when I came back to the Yankees was to try and make my peace with the New York writers. After I had left the Yankees, Henry Hecht, in particular, did a real hatchet job on me, ripped me real bad, but I wanted to show him I was a bigger man than he was, and when I came back I went out of my way to be nice to him. The first week I came back I told Mickey Moribito, "Let's take the writers and coaches out to dinner." He said, "Do you want Henry to come?" I said, "Sure." Mickey invited them, and I think Henry may have been a little hesitant at first, but he came, and we were sitting talking baseball, and by the end of the evening we were toasting each other.

Everything was great with George, too. Instead of calling down in the middle of the game and being real mad, he would have somebody call down after the game and ask me to come up and talk with him. I'd go up, he'd ask if I'd like a beer or a drink, and we'd go over the personnel together. He'd ask me about what went on in the game, and I'd explain what I was doing, try to make him more knowledgeable. I was amazed, because he was so pleasant to get along with. I couldn't believe it. And it was that way all during the season. He was just great. It was the closest I'd ever been to him, and I felt happy about the whole thing. I would tease him, and he'd take it from me pretty good. I'd tease him about how he was always losing secretaries. I'd say, "Jesus, George, this is a record, you got the same secretary for three months." I'd agitate him. He'd laugh. Everything was great.

During the game I could see George in his box, and I could see him jumping up and down when something went wrong. I'd tell him, "George, I can tell when you get mad. I can see the way you carry on. The TV can see it, too. You told me you'd try to control yourself, and here you're doing it again." He'd say, "Billy, I'll try to control myself better."

Or sometimes he'd be suggesting lineups to me. I wasn't there a week when he told me, "Billy, Thurman isn't producing like he should be. I want you to bat him eighth." Munson was having trouble with his legs. I said, "There isn't any way I'm going to do that. No way in the world I'd do that to Thurman." And then when I wouldn't do it, he'd get mad. I said, "George you promised me when I came back you wouldn't interfere with my managing, that you'd let me do my own thing." He said, "I admit I've been interfering too much. You're the manager. I'll leave you alone." But of course he couldn't.

Sometimes he'd make suggestions, ask me to try some things, and I'd do them, just to pacify him, to keep him happy. The club wasn't going anywhere, and I thought I'd let him call a few shots to get him off my back, because I knew that the next year I was going to go back to my old way and win a pennant. I didn't want him mad at me all winter and spring, so a couple times he suggested a lineup, and I used it, though not for very long because I didn't like it. He was crazy about a young outfielder by the name of Bobby Brown. George thought he was the greatest all-time player, and he wanted me to play him regularly. Brown's problem was he couldn't hit an offspeed breaking ball. At Columbus he was hitting the cover off the ball, but they don't throw the slow curve at Columbus the way the pitchers do in the majors. Brown had been released by two other major league teams because he couldn't cut it. I told George, "He's got all the tools, but unless he learns how to hit the breaking ball, the kid is never going to make it in the big leagues." George said, "Billy, if you don't play him, you're going to hurt his confidence." He hadn't made it with those other teams, but I was the one who was going to hurt his confidence? I was worried about the ball club and winning games. George still wanted him to play.

After Thurman was killed, George wanted me to try our young catchers, wanted me to play a kid named Robinson, and I did, and we took a look at the other kids, too, and George was telling everyone how easygoing I had become, how I had changed. I hadn't changed. I was just pacifying him, like you pacify a little kid. If I had come in at the beginning of the season, there's no way I would have been doing it any other way but my own.

Meanwhile, Reggie had returned, and he played terrifically for me. I couldn't have asked for more. He played hurt, and the few times when I benched him, he didn't complain, and he and I got along great. Reggie's a good person. He did everything I asked him to do. We really got to know each other, and we became friends.

During this time I was meeting with George, and one time he told me, "Billy, Reggie hates you. He called you a lousy dago bastard." I said, "But George, Reggie's been sensational." George said, "Just watch what I say. I'm telling you right now he's no good. He hates you, Billy. Now don't you go thinking he likes you. He really hates you. That boy is sick."

George was also telling me that Jim Campbell, the Detroit general manager, hated me. He said, "When you go to Detroit, don't sit with Campbell." I said, "Why? Jim Campbell's a good friend of mine." Even though he fired me at Detroit, he's still a friend, and he'll always be a friend. George said, "He hates you, he doesn't like you. You're crazy to sit with that man."

In July Al Rosen quit. I'm sure Al was upset that his friend Bob Lemon had been fired. Also, sometimes George would yell at Al, just like he yelled at everyone else. At some point I guess Al decided he didn't want the job anymore.

And apparently Reggie was a lot closer to Al than anyone thought, because in the papers the next day Reggie accused George of treating Al poorly. Reggie said, "George thinks he can buy everybody. Some guys have pride. You can't buy them."

Blasting George in the papers is the worst thing you can do. George, I really believe, leaked it out in the papers that Reggie was going broke, that he had loaned Reggie $250,000 at five percent and that Reggie was having problems repaying the loan. George also called Cedric Tallis and Mickey Moribito and told them to tell me to blast Reggie in the papers for him. George didn't like it that Reggie and I were friends. It bothered him, and by asking me to blast Reggie he was doing two things: He was getting back at Reggie for what Reggie had said about him, and he was maybe trying to get Reggie and me a little bit apart. George wanted me to tell the papers that he wasn't a true Yankee, that he wasn't playing hard, and that he had made obscene comments near the stands which wasn't in the Yankee tradition. Tallis had called Doug Newton and told him to have me say this. George was going for the jugular, what he does when he gets mad at someone, but I wouldn't go along. Reggie was having a good year for me, and he had been perfect with me. I had nothing bad to say about Reggie.

I called Reggie into my office. I told him, "Reg, don't say anything more about George in the papers. Just let it go, calm it down. You're not going to get anywhere by it, and, knowing George, if you keep it up, he may try to kill your deal with the candy bar company, and he'll come up with ways to hurt you." I said, "You don't know this man. He lays awake nights thinking up ways to hurt people. If you get him mad, it's not enough for him to just hurt you bad. He wants to destroy you. When you get a chance, call George and patch it up." And Reggie did.

Meanwhile, to pacify George, I made one statement to the papers. I said, "No player on this team gets special treatment. Everyone's going to be treated the same way." I talked in generalities. "I'm getting tired of hearing people talk about the owner . . ." and I didn't mention Reggie's name, talked like it was for everyone. George felt better when I said that, but it wasn't enough. George was madder than hell when I wouldn't really blast Reggie. I wouldn't nail him like he wanted me to, and George saw that as an act of defiance, an act of disloyalty to him.

At that time George was negotiating contracts with Bucky Dent and Graig Nettles. Both of them would have been free agents if they hadn't signed by the end of the year, and he was trying to get me to bench Bucky to make him worth less, and he wanted me to say things publicly about Graig, which I wouldn't do, things to injure the negotiating position of Bucky and Graig. I wouldn't do that, either, and George was also unhappy about that. George was making remarks about Nettles in the papers, putting him down, and Nettles was madder than hell. I mean really mad. But Nettles wouldn't back down on his demands. Graig told me, "I'm not backing down one inch." George was going to let him go, but I convinced him to sign him. I told George the Yankees had to have him, and I finally talked him into it.

In August a couple of writers who didn't cover the Yankees wrote stories which were out-and-out lies, but which got George all upset. We were playing in Chicago, and after our first game we got on the bus, and before we drove to the hotel, this cute blonde walked near the bus, pulled her pants down, and mooned us, showed us her behind. The next night after the game she did it again. The third night I asked Mickey Moribito to find a photographer to take her picture. I didn't know if she'd be there again, but if she was, I wanted a picture of it. It was no big deal. I couldn't believe this girl was doing this, and I wanted a souvenir. After the third game I was with my son Billy Joe, and what I was told was that before I left my office, the girl had walked on the bus, pulled her pants down, and a few of the players signed their autographs to her bottom. Bill Kane, the traveling secretary, threw her off when he saw what was going on. When I walked onto the bus, she was back outside. I got on, she mooned us again, and all the players cheered like crazy. They were like little kids. It was funny. I don't think any group of guys, whether a college team or pro team or pickup team, would have reacted any differently. But because it was the New York Yankees it became a big deal. What happened was, two weeks later a woman who had been standing in front of the bus with her son wrote a letter to Mike Royko of the *Chicago Tribune*. I guess she was mad that the players wouldn't give her son an autograph, but when this cute blonde came along, she got invited into the bus. She told Royko that I was standing out front of the bus taking a picture of the girl while she was mooning, which wasn't true. It was no big deal. The five New York writers were on the bus when it happened, and nobody wrote it at the time. They thought it was funny. If they had thought it was a story, they'd have written it. But you can't write everything you see traveling with a ball club. You can't do it. It's not right. That day the writers laughed along with everyone else. Then this guy Royko writes it, screws up the story, and George was mad as hell. He was furious. He was going to fine me, and then when he found out the story wasn't true, he was going to sue Royko for libel.

George came into the clubhouse huffing and puffing about it. I said, "George, it was no big deal. Ask the players." He did, and finally he calmed down. But after the story came out, the players still had to explain to their wives what had happened, why they were signing her bottom and all.

On the heels of that wrong story came another wrong story by a writer who wasn't covering the team regularly. He was a writer for *The New York Times*, Gay Talese, who showed up with a pen and pad of paper one day and decided that he instantly was an expert on the Yankees. He wrote a story on the front page of the *Times* that I had paid two of my young pitchers a hundred dollars to throw at Cliff Johnson.

When I first met Talese, he had a big smile on his face, and he seemed nice enough, but there was something about him I didn't like. I told Art Fowler, "Watch this guy. There's something phony about him. This guy's going to be vindictive." I asked Moribito about him. Mickey said, "Aw, he's just doing a story on players and the music they listen to, their tapes they bring along with them on the road."

Then one day in Toronto one of the veteran writers couldn't come down to the clubhouse after the game. He was writing his story, and he couldn't come down, and Talese told me he was standing in for the other writer. Talese came down to my office and started asking a bunch of really stupid questions in front of the other writers, and I looked at him and gave him dumb answers to his dumb questions. He was writing everything down, and all the other writers were laughing at him. When the veteran writer—and I just can't remember which one it was—came down, I asked him about Talese. He said, "I didn't send him down to take my place at all." Then I really knew this guy was going to be vindictive, and he was. He wrote that stupid story with no truth to it whatsoever quoting people on the bench, quoting the bat boy, the announcers.

We were playing the Cleveland Indians, and I had started a young kid by the name of Bob Kammayer, and he got creamed. Cliff Johnson and the other Indians were swinging from their asses, falling down laughing when they swung and missed. They were really teeing off on the guy. One time Johnson swung and missed and stood up there grinning, and I got mad. Johnson had hit a home run off Kammayer the time before, and I yelled out from the dugout, "Don't let him laugh at you like that. Knock him on his ass."

So Kammayer hit him on the arm. At the end of the inning he came in and I said, "When I yelled for you to knock him on his ass, I didn't say you had to hit him. I just wanted you to get his respect because he was laughing at you." He said, "I wanted to hit him, Billy. I did it on my own." I said, "Well that's your prerogative as a pitcher."

Later in the game I put in another kid, Paul Mirabella, and Cleveland must have been hot that day, because Paul got shelled, too. The two of them were sitting on the bench together, real down, depressed, and I saw that and felt sorry for them. Here these guys were struggling to get out of the minors, trying to make it, and the first time they get a shot they don't do good. They looked so down, and I said to myself, "Hell, I'll get my money," so I ran up to my office and got two hundred dollars and came down and gave them each a hundred dollars. I told them, "Don't worry about it. Go out and have a good time." I felt bad that they were feeling so bad, and it wasn't because Kammayer had hit Cliff in the arm that I was giving them money, as Talese wrote.

We were playing better, more aggressively, but Baltimore wasn't losing, and it was frustrating, and then when we lost Thurman in a plane crash, the whole bottom fell out of the team. It was difficult from then on. Wins didn't matter quite so much, and the losses became tougher. Thurman's death took a lot out of the ball club, took everything out of the club.

I flew with Thurman in his plane about three weeks before he crashed. It was the All Star break, and we were in Anaheim, and I asked Thurman if he would fly Howard Wong and I to Kansas City where we were going fishing. We were in the jet, which Thurman had just bought, and he landed in Albuquerque to gas up, and coming out of Albuquerque we hit an ice storm. I was looking out the windows, facing the engines, and I saw a flash of flame hit one engine. I didn't want to say anything because Thurman's wife, Diane, was sitting right across from me and I didn't want to scare her, but when we landed in Kansas City, I took Thurman aside. I said, "You better check your engines. Did you see flames coming out of that right one?" He said, "Maybe that was when I switched on the deicer." I said, "No way. I've never seen flames come out of an engine like that. You better check it out." My car came, and Howard and I got in, and two days later we opened in Chicago, and Thurman came over and said, "You know we had to take another plane out of Kansas City after we dropped you off. We had to stay overnight and take a commercial jet out." I said, "You're kidding me." He said, "The rotors of the right engine were all mashed in, bent. They must have put them in wrong when they built the plane."

That scared me. Here was a million-and-a-quarter-dollar plane, and the engines weren't working right. They had to put a brand-new engine on the plane.

I told Thurman I didn't like him flying. I said, "Why are you flying this thing? Does George know you're flying?" He said,

"Yeah, he gave me permission." I said, "You gotta be kidding me." But I understood why Thurman wanted a jet. His wife lived in Canton during the season. She didn't want to live in the New York City area, didn't like the fast pace. The jet gave Thurman a chance to fly home on off days to be with his wife and kids. I didn't like Thurman flying his plane, not because it was dangerous. I figured that Thurman, who was a bright guy, knew what he was doing. I didn't like it because here this guy could fly all over the country whenever he wanted, and I was yelling at the other players that they had to be on the bus on time. He was being treated differently than the other guys, and it wasn't right.

Two weeks before Thurman died, George called me into his office. He was madder'n hell at Thurman's flying. I said, "George, you're the one who gave him permission to do it." He said, "Billy, I'd appreciate it if you'd talk to Thurman about it."

I went down and talked to Thurman, and he told me that he and Diane were planning to take an apartment in New Jersey so he wouldn't have to fly anymore. I said, "I think that's a good idea. You'll be with your wife, you won't have to fly anymore, and it won't take so much out of you." He agreed with me on that.

I went back up and told George about our conversation, and that's when George got mad about Thurman's hitting. He showed me his stats, that his average was down, his RBI's down. I said, "Don't you understand, George, his legs are killing him. He can't push off his legs to hit. The guy shouldn't even be playing right now." He was playing in great pain, playing in hell. That's the kind of guy Thurman was. I said, "He shouldn't be playing, but we don't have anyone else." George said, "Why don't you bat him eighth, that'll show him." Bat him eighth? I wouldn't bat Thurman Munson eighth. I told George, "I won't."

We were in Chicago on a Wednesday, and in his last at bat he got hit by a pitch, and I had to take him out of the game. The next day was an off day, and we flew to New York to open a series with Baltimore. Thurman flew his plane to Canton. I learned he needed to accumulate hours so he could get his jet license, and he was practicing takeoffs and landings at the Canton airport when the plane crashed.

I was fishing that afternoon, and I had left a number where I could be reached. Mickey Moribito called me. He said, "Thurman got killed in a plane accident." I was standing there, holding the phone, and I started crying. For five minutes all I did was cry. I couldn't say a thing.

Thurman was such a big kid. During the game he was serious, but before he was always agitating me. He called me "Martian." I wear dark aviator glasses, and when I wore them he'd call me "the little Martian." "Here comes the little Martian," he'd shout. "Here comes our little Martian." He loved to tease me. How I loved that kid.

Around this time my wife, Gretchen, and I broke up for good. I had stayed in New Jersey during the winters, and then we started to talk about working things out, maybe getting together again, when I found out she was seeing another man. I filed for divorce. She had gone to Europe with a girl friend, she bought a BMW, toured Europe in it, and I had planned to have the papers served on her when she got back. However, her mother died, Mary Winkler, who I really loved, and I felt it was unfair to have her served then. In December I asked her to come in and see Roy True, who's my lawyer in Dallas. She came in and, thinking she'd surprise me, served papers on me. My lawyer showed her that we had filed papers four months earlier. She was the one in for a surprise.

September was an anticlimax. Nothing much happened. I did have a big argument with Goose Gossage. The team was in Boston, and I walked into a restaurant about three blocks from our hotel, and Art was sitting at the end of the bar, and he was almost crying, he looked so bad. I asked him what was the matter. He said that he was with Goose, Catfish, and one of the young rookie pitchers. Goose, I guess, had had too much to drink, and in front of Catfish and the other pitcher he started giving Art hell, telling him off, and he was talking about fighting Art. I said, "Oh, is that so," and I went back to the hotel, went up to Gossage's room, and really gave him hell. I spelled it out to him, read the riot act to him. I was really mad. I said,

"I'm going to tell you something. You're not the whole team. You're one of twenty-five guys. Everyone thinks your hurting your hand is what ruined our chances this year, but I don't think that's it. You're going around here like a big prima donna, and I'm not going to buy that bullshit. You're not going to talk to one of my coaches that way, and if you want to fight, get off that bed, come on and fight me."

Goose decided not to try it, and after I left his room I called George and told him what had happened. I said, "If Gossage mentions it to you, I want you to know about it ahead of time."

Art is such a fine coach. Under Lemon, Guidry had gone from 25 and 3 to something like 6 and 7, and then Art took over, and he won eleven in a row to finish 18 and 8. Guidry had been experimenting with a change-up. Art told him, "Cut out the change-up and just throw." Art straightened him right out.

As the season wound down, George and I were already planning for the next year. One of the things I wanted was for Mickey Mantle to come back to the Yankees as first-base coach. It would have been great for Mickey, because he would have been back on the pension plan, and it would have given him more exposure, and it would have been great for me because I'd have a close friend with me, someone I could pal around with instead of being alone all the time. As a manager you're always alone. The players go off in every direction, and very seldom are you even with your coaches. With Mickey there, I'd have had companionship. I told George, "It would be great. I could put Mickey out on the lines, just as long as he doesn't have to be there all the time so he can do his other promotional duties for the bank and insurance company in Dallas." George said, "How can I hire him? You and Mickey will be out partying all the time." I said, "Don't be silly. When I'm working, I'm working, and nothing gets in the way of that. Even when Mickey comes to visit me, he knows my job comes first. Now, don't you be silly about this." George never did give me an answer on Mickey's coming back.

At the same time Jeff Torborg had just been fired as Cleveland manager. I told George, "He just got fired. Why don't we carry him for the rest of the year? We can use him in the bullpen." Torborg lives in the New York area, and he's a good guy, and I thought it would be good for him. George thought that was a good idea, and he signed him, but he signed him to a two-year contract. I said, "George, what are you doing? We didn't talk about him signing for two years. He was just going to finish out the year, and I was going to pick my own coaches for 1980." He said, "I thought you wanted him, Billy."

On October tenth I, all the coaches, Cedric Tallis, Jack Butterfield, the scouts, and George met to discuss 1980. We knew we had some holes to fill. The kid catchers in our farm system weren't ready, and we knew we needed to acquire a catcher. We needed another right-handed power hitter. We needed a center fielder. Despite what George thought, Bobby Brown couldn't have hacked it, couldn't hit the slow curve. In '80 I intended to have Bobby bunt that slow curve more, because with his speed he could have beaten out bunts for a lot of base hits. Pitchers then would have gone back to throwing him fastballs, and those he can hit. But until Brown learned to do that, he wasn't the man. We needed to trade for an experienced center fielder. We also needed left-handed pitching in our bullpen. Gossage and Davis were a tremendous combination. Still, it never hurts to have a lefty available against the left-handed batters.

The meeting began at nine, and I thought it was a good meeting. George asked each of us about Bob Watson of the Red Sox and Dave Winfield of San Diego. Watson was a free agent. I liked him. He can swing the bat pretty good. Winfield is one of the best young players in baseball, but San Diego wanted an awful lot. They wanted Willie Randolph and Graig Nettles and a couple of pitchers and a ton of money, and it seemed like too much to give up. Who was going to replace Randolph and Nettles? No one in the farm system. Our Triple-A team had a bunch of older players, no one who was going to take their place. Our Double-A team had some good young prospects, but they weren't ready yet. Our outfielders were strong. It would have been wrong to have made that trade with the Padres.

We talked about acquiring Rudy May, who had been with me when I started with the Yankees. He's got the big curveball, and I felt he would help our bullpen. We also talked about Tom Underwood of Toronto. I felt he could help. I liked him as a left-handed reliever. George liked Bruce Kison of the Pirates and Dave Goltz. I wasn't too crazy about either of them, even though they are good pitchers.

There were three catchers I wanted. One was Rick Cerone of Toronto. I suggested him. I liked him. The two I wanted more were Mike Heath or Jeff Newman of Oakland. Newman could also play first, and Heath also played third. George had traded Heath to Texas in one of his deals, and though he's now with Oakland, I heard that he's on loan to Oakland from Texas and that George was to get him back, but being as the commissioner started sniffing around and discovered something was fishy, I think it kind of killed the deal for a while. You watch, eventually Heath will be a Yankee. George always has his way. For center field we all agreed on Ruppert Jones. He would give us a little more speed in the outfield, and I liked him even though he was another left-handed batter. He's a good center fielder.

George wasn't going to sign Jim Spencer, but I talked him into changing his mind. I said, "George, I want Spencer. We can't afford to lose him."

I felt the Yankees were going to win the pennant again in 1980. I knew that George would get the players he wanted, because he always has, and I've always admired him for that. I also knew that we had a kid by the name of Dave Righetti, who, if used right, would turn the whole team around. I felt he was going to be the big difference in the Yankees. He was a young Guidry, with a better breaking ball. His fastball isn't as good, but I knew when he came up with an offspeed pitch, he was going to be tough. I was going to work him in the same way I worked in Guidry, and when Righetti became ready, a staff of Guidry, Tommy John, Righetti, Ed Figueroa, and Luis Tiant would be the best in the league. The season was just over, and already I couldn't wait to get to spring training.

It was about three o'clock, and Art and I and Jerry Walker, who's a Yankee scout, were sitting around, and George came over. He said, "The meeting's over. We're just going to chew the fat a little bit. If any of you guys want to go early to catch a plane, go ahead." I said, "I have a plane to catch," and Art and Jerry said they did, too, and I went back to my room and packed, and Art and I met Jerry at the airport, and we flew home.

I got home that night, and I got a call from Cedric saying that George was hotter than hell that Art and I had left early. I said, "We didn't. George gave us permission to leave." Why George says things like that, I'll never know. He had told us, "Any of you guys want to leave, go ahead." So we left.

About three weeks later—it was the end of October—I went hunting with Howard Wong. I was in the Minneapolis area, and that afternoon I was going to fly to Dallas to be with Mickey Mantle, but we got back late and I missed the plane. Normally I stay in a hotel in Minneapolis that Bob Short owns, but it was late, so I asked Howard if there was a hotel convenient to the airport, so I could get an early start for my flight to Dallas. He said, "We'll stay at the Hotel de France. It's a nice hotel, and I have a room there."

We got to the hotel about nine at night. I asked Howard if he wanted to have a drink with me before we turned in, and he agreed, and so we walked to the corner of the bar, where we stood and ordered a drink. We weren't there three minutes when two men came over, and this one big guy, he must have weighed two hundred and thirty pounds, introduced himself. I introduced myself, and introduced him to Howard, but the guy didn't even acknowledge that Howard was there, ignored him completely, which made me upset. He didn't even say hello to Howard. He wanted to talk baseball with me, and in the middle of our conversation he said, "You know, you didn't deserve to be manager of the year, Earl Weaver or Dick Williams did." I asked him what he did for a living. He said, "I'm the Marshmallow King. I sell marshmallows." I said, "Well, maybe you're not the best marshmallow salesman." The conversation was joking, light, but I was getting bad vibes from the guy, like he was trying to pick a fight. Then the guy started telling me I didn't look so tough. He said, "You're the little guy who gets in all these fights, aren't you?" I said, "Yeah." He said, "I can lick you, I can lick you. I'll bet you I can lick you." I said, "You can't. And don't even talk about it. I don't want to keep talking about things like that." I wanted him to go away so Howard and I could enjoy our drink in peace. He wouldn't go, and he wouldn't quit talking about fighting me. He said, with a sort of a laugh, "You don't look like you're big enough to be a fighter." I said, "I'm not too big, but I don't think size is important. Big guys go down as easily as little guys." I said, "Pal, I don't want to listen to this anymore." I didn't want to leave the bar, which is what the guy was forcing me to do. I had as much right to be there as he did. And no one from the hotel was making a move to get the guy away from me. I wanted to come up with a way to make the guy go away. I said to him, "Here's three hundred dollars," and I took out three one-hundred-dollar bills and put them on the bar. I said, "You got a penny on you? If you're a betting man, I'll bet you three hundred dollars to your penny you can't whip me." If that didn't scare him off, nothing would. He and his friend walked out of the bar. Howard and I were alone again. I figured I had gotten rid of him.

After about five minutes the guy returned. He put his penny on the bar. He said, "I thought it over, and the odds are too good to pass up." He took his jacket off. He said, "Let's get it on." I said, "You're serious, aren't you?" He said, "Yeah, I'm serious." I really had no other choice, though I was still hoping there was a way to get out of this. I said, "Let's go outside. We don't want to cause any problems in here." He said, "I'm ready. Let's go," and I said to him, "Hey, pal, why don't we forget this? I'll just go home." He said, "No, I'm serious."

It wasn't like I was picking on the guy. This marshmallow guy must have weighed two hundred and thirty or forty pounds. He was huge. I didn't know whether he was an ex-football player, a wrestler, an ex-Marine, or what, but whatever he was, in his state there was no way I could have avoided this guy. I tried in every way, but it was no go. I couldn't shake him.

I walked out of the bar with the guy following behind. I decided that I would head across the lobby to the elevator and try to go up to my room, but as I began to pull ahead of him, he said something. I don't remember whether it was, "We're going to fight," or "Where are you going?" but almost as soon as he said it he closed ground, grabbed my right shoulder, spun me around, and threw a left at me. I slipped his left and hit him with a right hand. He went down like a sack of coal. He was out. I stood there looking down at him, and it was an old story: I was saying to myself, "How in the hell did I get into this?" There was no one else around, and as I stood over him thinking what I could do to help the guy, a security guard came over and said, "We'll take care of him." I'd have stayed with him, picked him up, helped him, but the security guard said he'd take care of it, so I walked back into the bar, and said good night to Howard, picked up my three hundred dollars and his penny. I didn't even tell Howard what happened.

The next morning Howard and I went to breakfast, and as we were sitting there the guy walked right past me and didn't even recognize me. I said to myself, "He must have been loaded. He didn't even recognize me or say a word when he walked by." Howard and I were talking about what had happened, and he said, "I talked to the security guard last night, and the guard said there'll be no problem. The guy said he fell down." I was puzzled by that. Why did he say that? I knew I should call George and tell him what happened in case something came out in the papers, but I didn't know what to say. Should I tell him the guy fell down? That I hit the guy? I had nothing to hide. The guy pushed me and pushed me. He started the fight. Don't blame me that I finished it.

I called Eddie Sapir in New Orleans, and I told him what had happened. I said, "For some reason, this guy doesn't want to say what happened. He said he slipped and fell down, and I can't understand why, and I don't know what to do." Judge Sapir said, "It could be one of several things. You're a hundred fifty pounds soaking wet, and he's two thirty, and you agreed to go outside, he started a fight, he swung at you, and you busted his ass. Maybe he was a golden glover or a wrestling champ or a pro football player, and he's embarrassed to get beat by you. Or he may be married with kids, and he might have a history of that kind of stuff, and he might not want the publicity. Or he could be on probation. There are a lot of reasons for it, Billy. Maybe he'd been drinking all night, and if his employer found out, he'd get shit-canned."

I asked him, "What should I do? I have an obligation to George to tell him what went on." He said, "Billy, you're right. This is what you ought to do. I don't think you have to come forward and nail the guy. It's obvious he doesn't want the truth to come out, and if you really don't want to hurt him, you can tell the Yankees that the guy said he slipped. However, you should also tell them what really happened. Let them use whatever story they want to."

I called the Yankees about noon and spoke with Mickey Moribito. He asked me if I had seen the *New York Post*, and I told him I hadn't, I was in Minnesota. Mickey said that George wanted a statement from him, and I did what Judge Sapir suggested. I said that the guy must have slipped and he fell and hit his lip. Mickey typed it up, read it back to me, I okayed it, and he ran it.

Realizing in all this confusion that I hadn't done everything that the judge told me to do, about five minutes later I called Mickey back. I wanted George to know the true story, and I told Mickey exactly what happened and told him to tell George so he'd know. If George wanted to talk with me, I gave Mickey my number. George never called. I found out later that when Mickey took my second conversation to George, his response was, "He's in trouble on that other one." It's a shame George saw it as two different statements.

By the next morning, which was Saturday, neither Judge Sapir or I had heard from George. Judge Sapir had been leaving messages all over the place, at his office, the Carlyle Hotel, in Cleveland, in Tampa, everywhere, and he didn't get a call. Finally, on Sunday afternoon, George called Judge Sapir. Judge Sapir said, "We've got to talk about Bloomington," which is the suburb the Hotel de France is in. George said, "We're not going to talk about Bloomington." The judge said, "What do you mean you don't want to talk about Bloomington?" George said, "I do not want to talk to Billy Martin about Bloomington." Judge Sapir asked him, "How will you be able to resolve in your mind what happened and make a fair, honest, astute, and educated decision without at least talking to Billy Martin?" George said, "Bowie Kuhn has this FBI guy, and he's looking into the matter." Judge Sapir said, "What did he find out? Did you get any statements from him?" George said, "I don't even know if he took statements. I know he made some phone calls. I don't have all the details." It was obvious George didn't care what really happened, except that I had been in a fight. He said, "It seems to me this pattern is never going to end." Then he told Judge Sapir that he had heard that the lobby of the Hotel de France was made of marble, and that the marshmallow guy could have hit his head on it and been killed. "I don't want a Yankee manager being involved in a guy being killed," George said, "no matter who started the fight." What if the guy had hit me and I had been killed? Would George have been concerned about that? And what was this pattern he was talking about? Reno was over with. What pattern? Pattern of what? It didn't make any sense.

George said, "Several of the players or their agents told me that if Billy came back, they wanted to be traded." He mentioned Bucky and Spencer and Gossage. "I can't put up with him anymore," George said. What a bunch of bull that was. I don't ask that a player like me, I only ask that he give a hundred percent. Bucky pouted sometimes, and I'd pinch-hit for him more than maybe he liked, but for him to say he wouldn't play for me, I don't believe it. When he talks about Spencer, who I had in both Texas and New York, not wanting to come back and play for me, that's crazy. George said, "Billy challenged Gossage to a fight, and he can't play under those conditions." George knew why I challenged Gossage to a fight. I'm not going to let any player abuse one of my coaches. Still, I don't believe Gossage would say that. I liked Gossage, and I'd be surprised to learn he didn't like me. Somebody ought to ask those guys.

Judge Sapir said, "George, you're a very intelligent guy, but if I were your attorney, I'd advise you to at least let Billy Martin come in and try to justify what happened, let him talk to you, fully explain, and then fire him if that's what you want to do. To fire the guy without having it investigated personally, to make a judgment on hearsay and a so-called investigation by Bowie's office is in my opinion a tremendous mistake. I don't think you ought to do it. If you're going to fire the guy, at least call him in, let him tell you everything, and then decide whether you believe him or not."

George said, "I'm not going to talk to Billy about it at all. Billy's fired. I'm going to replace him this afternoon. I've already called the representatives of the American League and the commissioner's office and told them what I'm going to do. If you'd find out how we can mutually work this thing out with the media, I'll call you back later this afternoon."

Judge Sapir said, "Okay, George, we'll talk later in the day," and they hung up. Judge Sapir called me and told me what was said and that it looked like nothing Judge Sapir could say would make George change his mind. He also told me that George would not talk with me. Apparently George was waiting for something to fire me over. He was looking for his first excuse. There had been certain things I'm sure he considered acts of defiance, my not blasting Reggie in the papers like he wanted me to, my wanting my own coaches, things like that. If I had sneezed wrong, he would have fired me. Why? This is something he's going to have to answer himself. You don't fire a man for getting into a fight. Do you fire a man because he gets into a car accident? Hell, I was away from my job. It was the winter, and this had nothing to do with my job. I'm a man first and a manager second. I've always said that to my players. "When you yell back at me, remember you're talking to a man first, not just a manager." And I tell them, "The man part I'm very proud of." I honestly believe George hired me back to fire me again. I couldn't believe I was fired for something as silly as that.

Judge Sapir asked me how I wanted to handle this thing with the media, and I told him I didn't care. I was really down. I told him, "When you and George decide what you want to do, let me know."

Judge Sapir called George. He decided to give it one more try to save my job. He said, "Look, George, you won't talk with Billy. You haven't investigated this matter, and you're talking about the commissioner's FBI guy doing an investigation. I don't know what he found out, but why not do something I think is prudent. Why not let this go to the commissioner's office. You say they have some information? Why not let them complete their investigation, and we'll be willing to go by what they find." Judge Sapir said, "You've already become the judge and jury in the matter. Billy's been convicted without trial, which has to be the most brutal thing in the world." He said, "Billy and I will roll the dice. Let it go to Bowie Kuhn's office, and we'll go along with whatever they do."

Judge Sapir said, "If they conclude that Billy Martin is not at fault, if they find that Billy was provoked into it, perhaps, George, you will reconsider and not fire Billy."

George said, "No, I'm not going to do that, because the commissioner's a tough guy, and he will ban Billy from baseball just like he did Willie Mays." Willie Mays had signed a contract with a gambling casino, and Bowie ruled that he couldn't be under contract with the Mets so long as he worked for a casino. Judge Sapir said, "George, I can't believe you're telling me that. One's apples and one's oranges. Why don't you do this for Billy. We're willing to roll the dice and abide by the commissioner's ruling." George said, "No, I'm not going to do that. Billy is fired, and I'm going to replace him this afternoon, and I'm going to make it public tonight." And that's what he did.

The next day was a Monday, and that evening on Monday night football, Howard Cosell interviewed Commissioner Kuhn to ask him about me, and Kuhn said he was investigating Bloomington. Cosell told Commissioner Kuhn, "The man has already been fired. Why are you looking into it?" Kuhn said he wanted to find out the facts to see what action he would take. He said, "I have several options. I could ban him from baseball. I could suspend him. I could put him on probation, or I could fine him." He also said, "It has come to my attention that Billy has financial problems and that he has problems when he drinks. We're going to check on this."

When I heard that, I said to myself, "The 'it came to my attention' came from George." George was the one who had told Kuhn I had financial and drinking problems in order to publicly discredit me. George fed that information to Bowie and Bowie said it over the air. It's not bad enough George fired me, he had to find a way to justify his firing me, so he tried to make me out to be a drunken bum. I felt so bad for Commissioner Kuhn. Here the commissioner of baseball was being deliberately fed false information to hurt me. George has never seen me drunk in his life. When I go out, sometimes I drink, but I can handle myself. In fact, when I drink I don't get mad, I get easygoing, maybe too easygoing. Sometimes when I should tell a guy to go take a hike, I let him stick around, and sometimes that's when I get in trouble. If I were a little more curt, I could cut things off a little quicker. And as for my finances, I own real estate, a couple of condominiums, my net worth is into seven figures. There was no basis whatsoever for anyone saying I had financial troubles. And my money is all mine. I didn't inherit it, like some owners I know. It took a lot of years but the money I made was all mine. When I heard what Commissioner Kuhn said on TV, I said to myself, this sounds just like George. George did the same thing the year before after he traded Sparky Lyle, and Lyle wrote his book, *The Bronx Zoo.* George came out and told the press about Sparky's so-called income-tax problems and he told everyone that Sparky was the dumbest ballplayer he ever knew. Sparky couldn't have been so dumb. He managed to get away from the Yankees and George.

As soon as Judge Sapir heard what Commissioner Kuhn said, he called me and suggested we arrange a meeting with him as soon as possible to straighten everything out. We wanted to talk to him about my finances, my so-called drinking problem, and what really happened in Bloomington. George had told Judge Sapir the reason he fired me was that if he didn't, Bowie Kuhn was going to ban me from baseball. Well, we knew that was not going to happen. We wanted an investigation, because I knew the true facts would come out if the commissioner looked into everything.

Judge Sapir arranged a November ninth meeting in the commissioner's office in New York. Judge Sapir flew up from New Orleans, and I met him, and we went to the commissioner's office with Doug Newton and my accountant, Mort Leventhal. When we got there, we were shocked to learn the commissioner wasn't even there! We had to talk with his attorney, Sandy Hadden, and his investigator, Art Fuss. I couldn't believe that nobody had called ahead of time to tell us the commissioner wouldn't be there. It was so unfair to make Judge Sapir fly all the way from New Orleans only to be told Bowie wasn't attending. We walked into the commissioner's office, and the first thing Sandy Hadden said was, "It's ten-fifteen, gentlemen. We have exactly fifty-two minutes." What could Hadden and Fuss have to do at minute fifty-three that would be more important than my career?

Judge Sapir told Sandy Hadden, "I want to start out by making it crystal clear that it was Billy who requested this meeting. We weren't called in. We requested it." Hadden acknowledged this. Judge Sapir said, "I understand that if anywhere along the way the commissioner's office should have in mind to take harsh action against Billy, we are entitled to a full hearing, as opposed to a meeting, so we can introduce evidence, documents, witnesses, and sworn testimony." We had hired our own private investigator, who spent hours of work, and we were ready for anything they might say. They weren't going to bum-rap me on this one. Hadden again told the judge that his understanding was correct.

I said, "What do you want cleared up? We intend to show you that wherever the commissioner got his information about me that he said on Monday night TV, he was wrong." Hadden said, "I want to make something clear. The commissioner was told that information by somebody." We asked him who. "That's not important," he said.

Judge Sapir said, "We're prepared to talk about drinking. We're ready to answer any questions. If somebody intends to prove Billy's got a drinking problem, we want them to personally come forward, and we'll resolve it."

He continued, "You won't tell us who told the commissioner. The commissioner just said that 'it came to his attention,' and we're entitled to show you it's not true. Billy does not have a drinking problem. How can we clear this up to satisfy you? Perhaps the commissioner would be interested in doing something to the person who gave him this false information. We'd like to know where it came from and get it all cleared up."

I then told Hadden and Fuss about my finances, including my home, my condominiums, and my Western-wear business, and my accountant showed them that my financial condition was anything but the way it had been represented.

"Now the other lie," I said, "the one about my drinking. We're prepared to take testimony of bar owners—friends of mine—to prove that I don't have problems when I drink. I'll bring in a liquor expert." I said, "I don't even drink in my home. You'll never see me take a drink in my home. Maybe I'll have a beer or two, but the booze I have is for other people." Then I told them how drinking calms me down. "I don't drink that much," I said. "I could stop drinking right now, if I had to, without a problem. It would be easy."

Judge Sapir then said, "We want the commissioner to thoroughly investigate Bloomington. Then we want to know the commissioner's findings and recommendations regarding Billy's actions in Bloomington." Judge Sapir then reminded them that he had already put his own investigator on it.

Instead of responding to what the judge was saying, Sandy Hadden's first words were about my "pattern of behavior." I looked at Judge Sapir. He looked at me. Here was George's word "pattern." I felt the long arm of George Steinbrenner reaching into our meeting.

Judge Sapir said, "Wait, Sandy, what are you talking about?" He mentioned the "incidents" at the Gene Michael dinner, at Bachelor's III, at Reno. They brought up a fight I had had in Baltimore about ten years earlier when I shoved a fan who was pushing me, the Brewer fight, the Boswell fight. I told them about each of those incidents, that I hadn't broken Brewer's jaw, someone else had, that I was only protecting Allison when I got into it with Boswell, that Boswell had hit me, not the other way around. As to Bachelor's III and Reno, the judge showed them his files of testimony and documents. He showed them there was no fight at Bachelor's III and that at Reno I wasn't at fault.

Judge Sapir said, "Billy didn't fight Reggie in the dugout in

Boston. Did that break the pattern?" He said, "I think that Billy's big problem is that he won each of these fights. What would you like him to do, go out and take a dive, get his tail kicked? Is the problem that he wins all these fights?" He said, "Billy doesn't want to be in these fights. They're unavoidable. If you or the commissioner can find me some way when he gets confronted with these situations, find me a magical solution to tell him what to do when some nut comes over and says, 'Mmmm, there's Billy Martin. I can make every newspaper in the country by getting my ass whipped,' " Judge Sapir said, "you tell us how to avoid it. We'd love to know. Maybe you have superior knowledge or intelligence we don't possess."

Neither Sandy Hadden nor Art Fuss said a word, because obviously there is no magical answer.

Judge Sapir said, "We ought to be talking about Blooming-ton. What bothers you about it?" They asked me about the bet I had made with the guy, and I told them why I had done it, in hopes of scaring him off. Now we had talked about everything, and when the meeting ended they seemed to be satisfied.

Before we left, Hadden said, "Billy, if you would like to, you can meet with the commissioner one on one." I said, "I'd love to, and the sooner, the better."

Two weeks later I met with the commissioner by myself at his home in Ridgewood, New Jersey, and I felt embarrassment for the commissioner because I have a lot of respect for him, and Fuss and Hadden had showed him that the information fed to him about my finances and my drinking had been wrong. Nevertheless he said he was considering putting me on proba-tion because of my fight with the marshmallow salesman. I said, "Mr. Commissioner, no, you can't put me on probation. It wasn't my fault, and if you do, that's like sticking a red flag out and saying, 'Hey, come on, somebody punch Billy Martin and he'll be out of baseball.' It's like having a sword hanging over your head, an impossible situation." George did that when he told the public that if I got into any more trouble, I'd be gone. He was telling the whole world, "Go ahead and start something with Billy Martin so I can get rid of him." I don't know, maybe that was his scheme right from the beginning. I told the commissioner, "If you put me on probation it's going to make it that much more difficult for me to live my life. I've already been punished. I've been fired, and nobody has even proven I did anything wrong. Nobody saw a punch thrown. It would have been his word against mine."

Commissioner Kuhn said, "What about these other fights?" I said, "Let's go down these fights one by one." We went over Baltimore, and then the Boswell thing. I told him, "It was between Boswell and Allison. Allison was trying to stop Boswell from punching my pitching coach." I told him about the Michael dinner and Bachelor's III. I couldn't understand why he was bringing up all these things. I think he was misled, and I'm sure it was George's doing, George trying to get him to do something harsh so George would have his justification for having fired me, which he didn't have and never will.

I told Commissioner Kuhn, "I've been in the major leagues for twenty-nine years. For twenty-nine years I've signed autographs for kids. I go out of my way to be nice and polite to the baseball fans in every park, and when I go to banquets I talk nothing but baseball. To hear someone say I hurt the game by my actions, that hurts me." I told him, "I'm in love with the game, and I wouldn't do anything to hurt it."

When we finished talking, Commissioner Kuhn asked me what I thought he should do. I said, "Mr. Commissioner, can't you just give me a warning?" He said, "That satisfies me. But in the future, Billy, you're going to have to try harder to stay out of these situations, even if you're not wrong."

I left the meeting feeling relieved and also impressed with his fairness. The next day Sandy Hadden called Judge Sapir to discuss the text of the letter Commissioner Kuhn was writing to me about what he would do. I had told Judge Sapir exactly what had gone on, and Judge Sapir was shocked when Sandy Hadden said he was going to put the word *probation* in the letter.

Judge Sapir said, "No way, Sandy. Billy and the commissioner had this crystal clear. The commissioner agreed he was not going to make Billy fair game, open season, a target, by putting him on probation." Hadden apparently didn't want to remember that *we* had called the first meeting to clear things up. The commissioner hadn't called *me* in, and Hadden was trying to put me on probation despite the fact that we never had a formal probation hearing and despite Commissioner Kuhn's statement that he would only issue me a warning and nothing stronger. Finally Sandy Hadden gave in (why he even brought up a probation in the first place I'll never know), and Judge Sapir and I felt we had reason to celebrate. I had proved that the public statements made by the commissioner about me were wrong, to a point that drinking or finances weren't even mentioned in the commissioner's letter to me, and we felt we had cleared my name with the public.

The press interviewed Judge Sapir, who told the writers he felt I had been vindicated, which I had. What the commissioner told me was, "If you brawl again, I will not hesitate taking harsh action against you." That was the full extent of his warning.

A few days later I spoke at the University of Rhode Island, and during my talk I took questions from the students, and I was asked about George. I said, "I feel sorry for George, he's sick, he doesn't know his friends from his enemies." I didn't say he was sick mentally. I said he was sick because he doesn't know his friends from his enemies, but Dick Young wrote it up like I had said that George was sick in the head. I wanted George to like me, not just as a manager, but as a friend, as a person, but maybe it's impossible. Now, that's a shame. But he was born rich, and if you're born rich like that, I guess, you never really understand how important a friend is. Another student asked me, if the Bloomington incident were to come up again, would I do the same thing. Judge Sapir and I had discussed what I should say if the question arose. I answered, "Since I didn't feel I did anything wrong the first time, the obvious answer is yes, I wouldn't do anything differently, because if I did it again, I still wouldn't have done anything wrong."

A few days later I got a letter from Sandy Hadden saying that the commissioner had been dismayed that Judge Sapir had characterized his actions as a vindication and that I had made the remarks I made at Rhode Island. At no time had the commissioner restricted me from speaking my mind. All he warned me against was getting into another fight. Hadden's letter said that I was now on probation because of what I had said. Judge Sapir called Hadden. "What has Billy done?" he asked. "The commissioner didn't say anything about Billy talking. Get the commissioner's letter. Read it. It doesn't contain one word saying that Billy can't speak his mind." Judge Sapir and I decided that Hadden couldn't have been doing that with the commissioner's knowledge. He had to have been doing it unilaterally. What did the guy have against me? Was he perhaps deliberately misleading the commissioner? Was George pushing him to do this? I respect the commissioner, and I remember George trying like heck to get him fired, and yet it seemed George and the office of the commissioner were ganging up on me. I couldn't believe this was happening to me. What else could they do to me?

I found out a few days later. George called Judge Sapir. When he fired me, George had promised the judge he would pay me the last two years of my contract. "I'll do that much," he had said. Now George was on the phone telling the judge, "On advice of counsel, I am stopping Billy's salary. You do whatever you have to do to protect Billy with Lee MacPhail's office. Tell Billy not to get alarmed. Tell him I will call later, and we will work something out."

At $125,000 a year for two years, it wasn't small change he was keeping from me. I had hit bottom. A guy picks on me, swings at me, I fight back, and because I beat him, I get fired, they try to put me on probation, and I lose my pay. It was like a bad dream. Why was this happening to me?

Judge Sapir knew what to do next. He called American League President Lee MacPhail and requested a hearing on my salary claim. George had no legal right to stop my salary, and I intended to fight him for it. Mr. MacPhail set March sixth as the hearing date.

George said he would call Judge Sapir back about my salary, and he did. After Commissioner Kuhn had told everyone on TV that I had financial troubles, we told the writers it wasn't true, and apparently George read what I said, because when he called Judge Sapir, he said, "I've been hearing how financially sound Billy is. Eddie, I'd like to make a couple of proposals." He said, "Number one, would Billy be interested in a first-class, four-year college program for his son, Billy Joe? I figure it would cost about ten thousand a year for four years, and I would set that money aside so that he would know his daddy had provided him with that first-class college education." In addition, George proposed: "Would Billy be interested in an annuity-type insurance plan where he could end up with a couple hundred thousand dollars when he's sixty-five?" The whole package would have cost George the $250,000 he owed me.

I appreciated George's offer, but I told Judge Sapir, "He owes me a hundred twenty-five thousand a year for two years, and I want my money with no strings attached. I don't want him to be in a position to tell people he's supporting me. I can take care of myself. Also, Billy Joe was already protected for college. I've already put money away for that." Judge Sapir called George and declined the offer.

The next time George called, he said to Judge Sapir, "Eddie, I'll tell you what. I think Billy still would really enjoy being part of the Yankees, and if so would Billy entertain doing the color commentary with Phil Rizzuto, Bill White, and Frank Messer on our television broadcasts? I'd pay him his full salary."

George said, "Billy can represent the Yankees, he can appear in golf tournaments, whatever would make Billy comfortable. Also, Eddie, I've been hearing a lot about his Western-wear stores. Billy could dress in his Western wear on TV, and at the same time he was promoting the Yankees, he could also be promoting his Western wear."

I was surprised by the offer and touched by it. It was an appealing offer, but after I thought about it, I told Judge Sapir I had to decline. I would have had to travel with the team, the same team I had just been fired from, and I felt it would have caused too many problems for the new manager, Dick Howser. Being with the players and with Howser on the road was just too much of a conflict. I just couldn't see doing it.

I said to Judge Sapir, "Why doesn't George make me his personal advisor? I could be his right-hand man, go around and talk up the Yankees, and this would also be good for George." Judge Sapir said, "Billy, when we get together in Tampa, throw it out to George and see what he says." I was going to do just that, but when the date of our meeting came, I had the flu and was bedridden, and I wasn't able to attend the meeting.

Before I got the chance to propose that to George, Charley Finley, the owner of the Oakland A's, called. He said, "Billy, I want you to come and manage my ball club." I told Charley to call my agent, Doug Newton, and talk to him about it. Newton called me. He said, "Billy, the first thing Charley started talking about was how you needed this job." Charley was trying to figure out a way to get me for bottom dollar. Newton told me that Charley said, "I understand Billy was making a hundred twenty-five thousand dollars with the Yankees. I'll pay Billy fifty thousand dollars a year, and the Yankees can pick up the rest." I felt George owed me $125,000 a year for two years. If I signed with another team for less, George would be obligated to pay the difference. George, of course, was saying he didn't have to pay me. Charley Finley didn't know that George and I were battling over whether he was going to pay me or not.

Doug told Charley, "Just because Billy was making a hundred twenty-five thousand a year with the Yankees, don't assume he'll come to you for the same money. Also, Billy is not interested in going anywhere for a contract less than three years. And three, Billy Martin must have control over the team without interference from anybody, including the owner."

Finley got hot, Doug said. Finley said, "I'm the goddamned owner, number one, and I'm the general manager, and I do anything I want with the team." Doug told Finley, "Find yourself another manager."

Later in the day Finley called Doug back. He said, "I'll give Billy a contract for three years. I'll pay fifty thousand dollars the first year, fifty thousand the second year, and one hundred twenty-five thousand the third year. The Yankees can kick in seventy-five thousand a year for the first two years."

Doug said, "We'd have a number of matters to consider even if the dollars were acceptable. You said yesterday you're the owner, and you run it your way. I'm telling you that once the game starts, Billy Martin has got to be in complete control. Billy Martin does not want to get a call from you in the middle of the game, suggesting or telling him what to do. Billy will talk to you before the game, but once that game starts, from inning one to the end, Billy is the general." Finley said, "We don't have any problem there." Doug and Charley then discussed that I wanted my own coaches, and they reached agreement on that.

Doug then asked Charley what he intended to do with the team. Every year there were reports of Charley selling the team, and I didn't want happening to me what had happened in Texas when I went to work for Bob Short and ended up getting fired by Brad Corbett. Charley told Doug what he did with the club was none of our business. Doug said, "It does concern us, Charley, because if we commit Billy to a long-term contract, his future is riding on what you do." Charley said, "Let me kick that around. Let me think about that, and I'll get back to you." Doug called me and told me what they had discussed, and I told Doug I was interested.

The next time Charley called, he made a conference call to Doug and Judge Sapir. Finley said he had found out about George's and my contract dispute. Charley said, "I can't afford to pay Billy a hundred twenty-five thousand dollars a year." He said, "I have an idea. You sign a contract with me today for fifty thousand dollars the first year and fifty thousand the second year, and a hundred and twenty-five thousand for the third year. If MacPhail rules in favor of Billy, he gets his seventy-five thousand dollars from George, and everyone's happy." Doug said, "Yeah, but what if MacPhail doesn't rule in favor of Billy? You're asking us to lock ourselves into a two-year contract at fifty thousand dollars a year, and we just cannot do that." Finley said that if we lost our case before MacPhail, he'd pay the full $125,000 for two years, and pay $125,000 for the third year. Judge Sapir had a quick answer for Charley. He said, "If we do that, Charley, no matter what, you're going to have to pay. If we don't show up for that March sixth meeting, if we don't challenge George in our salary dispute, we lose automatically, and you have to pay."

Finley digested that, and he said, "I don't want to give Billy a three-year deal, because if I sold the club I'd be strapping the new owner with a manager for three years, and that will make it tougher for me to sell the ball club." Judge Sapir told Finley he didn't buy that. "Charley," he said, "there's no way in the world you can make me believe that having Billy Martin will do anything but enhance your chances of selling the team." Charley huffed and puffed. "I only want to talk two years," he said, and he hung up.

Meanwhile Finley called George, and when he called Doug back, he was furious. Now for the first time I understood why George had cut off my salary. It wasn't so much to punish me. It was to give him an advantage in negotiating with someone like Charley Finley. Finley told Doug that George was interested in helping, that something could be worked out if he could get a good right-handed pitcher from Finley. Finley told George, "I don't want players to be in this deal." George told Finley, "I guess we have nothing to talk about." They hung up. I told Doug, "I don't want the careers of young players to hinge on my signing with Finley. It isn't right." Finley had forced the Pirates to give up a player, Manny Sanguillen, when they wanted to sign the A's manager, Chuck Tanner. Now George was turning the tables on Charley, and Charley was screaming bloody murder.

George, meanwhile, met with Judge Sapir in Fort Lauderdale. He asked the judge, "Eddie, does Billy want to manage the A's? Is this what Billy wants?" It was, and the judge told him so. George said, "If that's what Billy wants, we'll have to put our heads together and see how he can get the job without Finley getting him at my expense. I am not going to be put in a position where he uses Yankee money to hire Billy Martin." He said, "I told Finley that if I was going to put money in the pot, he would have to give me players." He said Finley was yelling and screaming at him. According to George, he told Charley, "Don't let that stop you. Billy's the best in the game. We've had our differences, but he's still the best. He's a great manager." George said, "Judge Sapir, believe me, Charley really wants Billy, and something will work out. I think you'll get your deal with Finley."

Doug and Judge Sapir then started talking about how they could get a deal with George without George helping Charley pay my salary. Judge Sapir called Lee MacPhail about it. MacPhail said that if we settled with George before we signed with

Charley, they would be separate deals. MacPhail said, "If you can settle this thing before the March sixth meeting, I owe you all a big steak. It'll take a lot off my mind."

Doug and Judge Sapir put their heads together. Doug told Judge Sapir that he would have to deal with George, because George was angry with him, and that he, Doug, would negotiate with Charley.

Judge Sapir called George. He said, "I think I have something you can live with. If we can get a hundred twenty-five thousand a year for two years from Finley, and if Billy gets not less than a hundred twenty-five thousand a third year, would you be willing to put X number of dollars into the pot?" That way Finley would have to pay the $125,000 a year himself. George said, "How could we do it? How do you know I'll be protected from Finley?" Judge Sapir said, "I already have that resolved. I spoke to Lee MacPhail, who said if we make a contingency settlement, then you won't be subsidizing Finley if we then make a deal with him. You can call MacPhail and put up the money with him." George said, "Eddie, I like that. I can live with that."

Judge Sapir said, "Please come up with a significant and substantial figure, something that will look attractive and will be appreciated." George said, "Eddie, I'd be willing to put a hundred and fifty thousand dollars in the pot as a settlement." Judge Sapir said, "George, that's very fair," and it was very fair. George didn't have to pay me that much. Apparently it was something he wanted to do for me.

Judge Sapir then told George, "Finley has been telling us that Billy's a hungry hog, that he needs the job." George said, "What do you suggest?" Judge Sapir then asked George about my earlier suggestion: "Would you entertain Billy coming back to the Yankees next year in an executive position, say personal advisor to George Steinbrenner at no reduction in salary?" George said, "I would, Eddie, absolutely. We'll have to define the job a little better. He can even have his own private secretary." Judge Sapir said, "Can you live with that title?" George said, "Yes I can, and I can live with Billy working at the same salary for two years." Judge Sapir asked George if he could tell the press about their discussion. George said, "I don't mind, if it will help Billy."

Judge Sapir then called some writers and told them that I now had another offer to return to major league baseball immediately. He didn't say who the offer was from or what it was, but it served the purpose of letting Charley Finley know I wasn't a hungry hog anymore, that my availability was a day-to-day thing, that if he wanted to sign me, he'd better do it quickly.

Doug Newton called Finley. He reminded Charley that he'd said he'd pay me $125,000 a year for two years if I lost my case with MacPhail. Doug said, "All along Billy has wanted a three-year contract. Charley, are there any circumstances under which you'd consider a three-year contract?" Charley said, "No, no, no. I want two years." Doug had thrown out the bait, and Charley had taken it. Doug said, "Billy and Steinbrenner have settled their differences, and Billy is now free to sign with anyone he wants. Charley, you can sign Billy for two years, only you have to come up with a hundred twenty-five thousand dollars a year." Charley said, "Do you mean to tell me George isn't going to pay any of his salary?" Doug said, "That's correct, Charley. That money will be Billy's financial security in place of the third year you don't want to give him. You didn't want three years. You wanted two years, and you can have your two years at one hundred twenty-five thousand dollars per."

Finley was furious. He accused us of working both sides against the middle, of taking money from him and money from George. Doug told him, "Billy's settlement with George is no concern of yours. Either you pay Billy the money, or you can find another manager. If you agree to it, Billy has an airplane ticket in his hand, and he can be in Oakland tomorrow for the press conference."

Bob Short called Finley. He told Charley, "You're not going to be able to get Martin for less than what George is paying him. If you pay him a hundred twenty-five thousand a year, George has agreed to pay Billy a hundred fifty thousand dollars as a settlement. You're not drawing flies, and the first time the A's come into Yankee Stadium, you'll get your hundred twenty-five thousand back. You want to fix George? Pay Billy, and make George pay the hundred fifty thousand."

Charley must have bought Short's argument. He decided to pay my price.

When I got to Scottsdale, where the A's are located during spring training, I called George. It was the first time I had spoken to him since he fired me. I thanked him, because I knew the great assistance he had been in getting me my new job, and George suggested that perhaps after I had finished my managerial career that I would go back to the Yankees as an executive and end my baseball career where I had started it, with the Yankees. In a press release I thanked George, the Yankees, and the Yankee fans, and that was my final connection with the Yankees. Everything in the future would concern the Oakland A's, a young team with great potential. I wanted to manage Oakland because I was from the Oakland area, and I wanted to try to bring the fans back. My strength is in teaching, and here was a young team ready to be taught.

Charley Finley called me a few days after I opened spring training camp. He said, "Billy, I'll be happy if we finish third this year."

I said, "Charley, don't be talking that way. I don't look to finish third. I'm looking to finish number one."